SUEZ:

THE SEVEN DAY WAR

A. J. BARKER

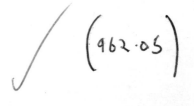

FABER AND FABER LTD

24 Russell Square

London

First published in mcmlxiv
by Faber and Faber Limited
24 Russell Square London W.C.1
Printed in Great Britain by
Latimer Trend & Co Ltd Plymouth

Contents

Suez: The Seven Day War

by the same author

*

THE MARCH ON DELHI

Illustrations

9

ILLUSTRATIONS

MAPS AND DIAGRAMS

10

ILLUSTRATIONS

Foreword

The so-called 'Suez War' was a unique event; unique not only because outside pressures caused it to be called off in the middle when another forty-eight hours ought to have seen the occupation of the Canal Zone, but because it also revealed a state of military unpreparedness that had never been appreciated until the need arose to mount an operation like 'Musketeer'. In the following year the provisions of the Defence White Paper were intended to take care of the military lessons; in it a radical overhaul of British defence policy was announced; underlying this new policy was an acceptance of the fact that Britain could never undertake a limited warfare operation like 'Musketeer' again. Britain's main defence problems, it postulated, were related to the nuclear bomb and if the Western World was threatened, the only real security attainable was through the medium of an alliance. Under these circumstances the three services could be organized on a basis of retaliation with nuclear weapons. This would enable our multipurpose forces to be cut to a level which would provide a reduced shield force for N.A.T.O., sufficient troops to maintain the few remaining garrisons to which we were still committed, and a small central reserve. The shield force would be just sufficient to ensure that no attack by satellite armies could be successful without the Russians, and if the Russians did help it would be a case for unleashing the nuclear deterrent. The garrison troops would cope with local security problems and in the event of a brushfire war developing our alliance arrangements would ensure that only a modest British contribution would be necessary. On this basis a central reserve of a single parachute brigade group, one infantry brigade group and an armoured regiment should be sufficient.

The reorganization offered certain attractive returns: the end of

13

conscription would mean savings which would help to offset the increased expenditure on the nuclear deterrent and to replace the old equipment which all three services had struggled along with since 1945. The manpower problem should resolve itself; a reduction of the forces to 375,000 men, allied with more interesting and attractive careers, should ensure a volunteer army which would carry reduced overheads in the way of training facilities necessary for a large conscript army. Even the commitments which still remained seemed to fit in admirably, because they added up to this same figure of 375,000 which the planners estimated would be forthcoming if conscription were abolished.

There is no need to stress the manpower difficulties which have grown worse with the abolition of conscription and which are still with us. The commitments which we expected would diminish still seem to be with us, indeed we seem to have collected others along the way, and our voluntary army is strained to the limit. Nor is there any need to restate our deficiencies in equipment: the recent actions in Malaysia, Africa and Cyprus have shown that much can be attained with few resources when they are mobile and handled boldly, and the Services certainly seem to have retained their old knacks of adapting and improvising. Nobody seriously believes now that we could ever conduct a conventional campaign of any length—even against Indonesia—without invoking U.S. help, particularly if our reserves are fully committed (as they are at the time of writing). Nevertheless, if we are to accept the world-wide responsibilities which we have inherited from our Imperial past, we still have a role to play in international affairs—even if we act as agents of U.N.O. To do this, the Royal Navy and Army both need more men and better equipment, our amphibious forces need to be built up, and the R.A.F. needs more and better aircraft.

Because the Suez operation was indeed the end of an era and because all the pointers on what was needed for the future were there, I have always thought that an account of its purely military aspects would be worth while. I hope others will think so too, and that they will give as much thought to the military issues as has been devoted to the political ones. Finally, because it is considered desirable for the writer to declare his interests, I should add that I did not take part in the operation; though I might claim to be a 'casualty' of the operation consequent on the reorganization of the Army which followed.

Acknowledgements

Writing this book would never have been possible without the help, advice and criticism of the many friends who took part in Operation 'Musketeer'. Though the book has benefited from their experiences and opinions, responsibility for any errors still rests with me and any assessments which I have made are not to be interpreted as held by those whose courtesy and assistance is acknowledged here.

Major Michael Gray, my old comrade-in-arms, was primarily responsible for triggering the idea that I should try to make an appraisal of the military side of the operation and I am very grateful for the help that he has given since then. In thanking him I must also express my gratitude to all those whose aid he has enlisted on my behalf.

Many others, some of whom prefer to remain anonymous, have made valuable contributions or suggestions but I should like particularly to mention Général de l'Armée André Beaufré; Admiral Sir Manley Power, K.C.B., D.S.O.; Major-General R. W. Madoc, C.B., D.S.O., O.B.E.; Major-General N. H. Tailyour, D.S.O.; Major-General D. H. V. Buckle, C.B., C.B.E.; Brigadier J. C. de F. Sleeman, C.B.E.; Captain A. W. F. Sutton, D.S.C., R.N.; Colonel A. Cameron, O.B.E.; Lieut.-Colonel N. G. Kirby; Lieut.-Colonel F. W. E. Fursdon, M.B.E.; Major J. M. Franklin; Major F. E. Bardell, E.R.D.; Major G. R. Ewart and the Port of London Authority; Captain G. H. Hennessey, R.M., the Royal Marines Historian; Captain H. A. J. Stacpoole, M.C.; Captain T. Green; Lieut. P. Harvey, R.N.; and Messrs. R. B. Allin, C. R. Butt, G. Knight, R. Morrell, R. F. Pearman, B. R. Ward. I am also indebted to various Corps and Regimental Associations who loaned copies of their regimental journals.

Of those who kindly loaned photographs and gave me permission

ACKNOWLEDGEMENTS

to publish them, I must thank the Regimental Colonel of The Parachute Regiment, the Defence Attaché of the Embassy of Israel in London, *The Times of Malta*, The Associated Press and the individual officers who ransacked their photograph albums in order to provide suitable illustrations. Finally I must thank Miss S. M. White for her work deciphering my writing and converting it to typed form and Mr. C. G. Lovegrove for his help with some of the drawings.

Prelude

In the course of a speech of welcome to Ferdinand de Lesseps on the occasion of his election to the French Academy in 1884, the President of the Academy said prophetically: 'The Suez Canal . . . will be a gateway to the oceans. So great is its importance in a maritime war, everybody will compete for its possession. You have thus marked the site of a great future battlefield.'

In Alexandria's Liberation Square on the evening of Thursday, 26th July 1956, Gamel Abdel Nasser, President of Egypt, made a frenzied and fateful three-hour speech to a large and enthusiastic crowd estimated to be more than 100,000 strong. His speech started calmly but when he came to describe how the United States, and to a lesser extent Britain, had thwarted Egyptian plans to build the Great Aswan dam by withdrawing their offers of financial assistance, the pitch of his voice rose and he became almost hysterical. After a description of the events leading up to the cancellation of the dam offer, he spoke of the Suez Canal, making a number of strange and repeated references to Ferdinand de Lesseps as he developed the theme of his announcement. Finally came the dramatic climax to his speech, when he declared: '. . . Egypt will run the Canal. The Suez Canal belongs to us. . . . The Canal will be run by Egyptians! Egyptians! Egyptians!' The crowd went wild with enthusiasm, fezzes were flung into the air and some of the men linked arms and began to dance. Not only had El Rayis got rid of the British troops occupying Egyptian soil, now he was freeing Egypt from economic domination; the mob screamed its approbation as the speech continued into the hot night. Some said later that it was only the presence in Alexandria harbour of the British cruiser H.M.S. *Jamaica* that restrained them from more turbulent demonstrations against the British.

Meanwhile the reference to 'de Lesseps' had been a coded signal for action in Port Said, Suez and Ismailia. Men listening to the radio waiting for this signal, knew what they must do. Within minutes, Egyptian security police had taken over the Canal installations and occupied the headquarters of the Canal Company in Port Said. The staff, most of whom were British or French nationals, were given the alternative of working for the 'Nationalized' administration, or of facing prison sentences of up to fifteen years. The operation—described by an American reporter later as '*a masterpiece of staff planning, secrecy and discipline*'[1]—was ruthless, quick and successful. Western reaction was equally quick, but its early manifestations could hardly be described as either ruthless or successful.

In Britain, in late 1955, a 'New Look' Defence Policy had been declared. It was a policy that appealed to politicians since its reliance on nuclear weapons postulated a denuded battlefield; with a tactical threat of nuclear annihilation it was positively desirable to reduce battlefield densities. Such a reduction clearly meant a smaller army since all that would be needed to maintain British prestige would be to guard against a surprise nuclear attack and to retain a capacity for a massive retaliatory blow. No longer was there the need to keep a large strategic reserve in Britain, the Army could be reduced to a size just sufficient to meet her overseas commitments with N.A.T.O. and those areas that still remained her responsibility—Hong Kong, Malaya, Cyprus and a few scattered garrisons. As recruitment, the future of National Service, and the provision of new equipment was then—as always—the subject of considerable political concern, the 'New Look' was generally regarded with favour from both Government and Opposition benches. Yet it cannot be said that this new policy was primarily responsible for any lack of effectiveness of the strategic reserve; since the end of the war its strength had been dropping and its weapons steadily becoming more outmoded. All the 'New Look' did was to set the acceptance seal on a state which already existed. Now if a situation arose which demanded military intervention of a 'limited' nature precluding the use of nuclear weapons, recourse would have to be made to the call-up of reservists. Within six months this was the very problem that the British Government was to face.

[1] The U.S. fortnightly magazine *The Reporter*, September 1956. According to the writer, a Mr. Simon Malley, the plan for the take-over was conceived in 1954, nearly two years earlier.

For France the situation was somewhat similar. Her contribution of five divisions to N.A.T.O. had consisted almost entirely of conscripts serving for eighteen months. The war in Algeria had steadily required ever-increasing numbers of troops, and because of this she had been compelled to withdraw three of these divisions from N.A.T.O. and redeploy them in North Africa. Thus, at the time of Nasser's seizure of the Canal, the flower of the French Army was mostly serving overseas, and there was no reserve striking force with which she could act quickly at the onset of the crisis. When the moment was opportune—in the period immediately following the Egyptian coup—neither country had either the trained men available, aircraft, or amphibious means with which to transport them to Egypt in order to enforce their policies. It was doubtful also whether the services necessary to support a task force in such a role were sufficient either; the Movement and Port Operating Services in particular— most of which are not included in the peacetime order of battle— serving as one small but vital example.

President Nasser may not consciously have recognized the military weakness of the two nations he seemed so intent on antagonizing, but he unquestionably appreciated the possibilities open to him by pitting the East against the West. His open support of the Algerian rebels in his game of 'positive neutrality' was more than sufficient to upset the French. Tunisia and Morocco had already achieved independence, Algeria was the last French territorial foothold in North Africa; its loss could not be contemplated. Yet Nasser, from Cairo, was openly supporting Algerian rebels. It seemed more than clear to the French Army, let alone the French politicians, that Nasser's downfall was the key to Algeria continuing as a French possession. Britain too, was concerned about Nasser's fervent pan-Arab activities. His hand could be seen in the failure to persuade Jordan to join the Baghdad Pact in March and the subsequent dismissal of Glubb Pasha. His scarcely veiled hostility towards Britain was apparent even as the last British troops stationed in Egypt under the 1936 Treaty of Alliance embarked from Port Said in June; his attitude towards Iraq was contrary to British interests in that country.

The critical issues were much more fundamental. Both Britain and France regarded Nasser's Nationalization Act as being a direct threat to their strategic and economic interests, and considering the importance of the Canal and the fact that they were also the two principal shareholders in the Canal Company, this is not surprising.

19

The strategic interests require little explanation; Britain and France both had obligations in the Far East which might well necessitate the quick passage of troops or naval units to that area. Whilst light mobile forces can be air transported to a trouble spot—even though there may be difficulties in regard to over-flying the territory below— their heavy equipment, stores, ammunition and the like still have to go by sea. The Suez Canal is the shortest sea route to the Far East and the International Convention of 1888 had provided that 'the Suez Maritime Canal shall always be free and open in time of war as in time of peace, to every vessel of commerce or of war without distinction of flag'. The possibility of the Canal being closed to Anglo-French shipping in the same way that ships bound for Israel had been denied passage, was a vital consideration that now had to be faced.

Economic interests in the Canal even today are perhaps more important than the 'strategic interests'; apart from the holdings of Canal Company shares, both nations are among the main users of the waterway. From the Middle East at least 60 per cent of the crude oil used by Britain and France comes through the Canal, and Europe still remains industrially dependent on oil; Britain is particularly susceptible to any interference with this traffic and in July 1956 the seizure of the Canal appeared to be an acute danger signal. In each of the two years preceding the nationalization, British tonnage of ships using the Canal averaged 33 million. About half of this consisted of tankers, carrying 20·5 million tons of oil, which represented about 65 per cent of Britain's requirements. On the Government's declared basis of a 3 per cent increase in Britain's standard of living, the 20·5 million tons of oil could be expected to be doubled by 1985 (and, in fact, the demand has risen at approximately this rate). The increase then, as now, depended on Middle East oil reserves since the oil exports of Latin America and the Caribbean go to the United States and can be obtained only for dollars. Every drop of the Middle East oil coming to Britain has to come via the Suez Canal, by pipeline to the Mediterranean coast or by the long haul round the Cape. It was not enough for Egypt to affirm that she had no intention of changing her attitude to passage through the Canal; arbitrarily, she had already done so: Israeli vessels were debarred from using it. Soon, other nations who were not politically in accord with Egypt might be denied passage, whilst the Canal dues could be raised selectively according to the whims of the Egyptian Government.

First Anglo-French reactions to the Egyptian take-over came in the afternoon of the day following Colonel Nasser's speech. Both countries lodged formal protests in Cairo, and the attitude of the French was distinctly belligerent. Simultaneously, with the announcement that both countries were taking 'certain precautionary measures of a military nature',[1] their Embassy in Cairo ordered all French women and children to leave Egypt immediately—an order which had clear military significance. The British instruction was less exacting: those British subjects in Egypt 'who had no compelling reason to remain should consider the advisability of leaving whilst the situation is quiet'. Similar advice was given to Egyptians in Britain, and the blockage of all Egyptian accounts in the U.K. by the British Treasury compelled many Egyptian students to drop their studies and look for passages home. (British residents in Egypt who chose to ignore the Foreign Office instruction, were to suffer considerable hardship later, and many have been poorly compensated for the losses they incurred.)

The number of ships using the Canal sharply declined. British and French vessels approaching the Canal from either end were ordered to change course, the British Army troopship *Asturias* on her way home from the Far East, was told to go round the Cape, and the *Dunera* outward bound for Hong Kong was recalled to the U.K., from Malta, the courtesy visit of H.M.S. *Jamaica* to Alexandria was abruptly terminated and leave for men of the Home Fleet was cancelled. The French, engaged in similar preparations, put their Mediterranean Fleet on a war footing and its ships began to collect at Toulon in readiness for an operation at an undisclosed destination. Under what *The Times* described as 'a smoke screen of security' it was obvious that preparations were being made for a military operation in the Eastern Mediterranean. This operation *when launched thirteen weeks later, was to estrange the American and British Governments* and achieve a result which was the exact inverse of its object. Instead of keeping the Canal open, ensuring the flow of oil to Europe, curbing Nasser's activities and the growing power of the Soviet Union in the Middle East, by mid-November the Canal was blocked, Western Europe was suffering from a shortage of oil, Nasser's prestige and that of the U.S.S.R. had been considerably strengthened, whilst the prestige of the Anglo-French had just about disappeared.

The account of it which follows is an attempt to describe and appraise the practical side. It is not concerned with the political or moral issues by which the operation was constrained, although it is

[1] Sir Anthony Eden to the House of Commons, 30th July 1956.

impossible to give a true picture or assess the lessons without some reference to the political background. Attention is drawn to the military failings because of the lessons they contain for future British defence policy; many of them have been corrected but it would be a bold man who would say that all of them—so apparent in 1956— have now been set right.

An Aide-Mémoire to the Dates of Events

(A detailed Chronicle of Events will be found at Appendix C)

Early 1956 British Forces finally evacuated the Suez Canal Zone.

July

26th Suez Canal nationalized by Egypt.

27th Britain and France lodge formal protest.

30th Britain and France start taking 'precautionary military measures'.

August

11th General Sir Charles Keightley appointed Supreme Commander of the Franco-British forces for Operation 'Musketeer'.

12th Egypt refuses to join London Conference on the future of the Suez Canal.

September

7th The first contingent of French troops disembarks in Cyprus.

October

26th Israeli forces start mobilizing.

27th Warning order given for Operation 'Musketeer'.

29th Operation 'Kadesh' is launched and the Israelis attack Egyptian troops in Sinai.

30th Franco-British ultimatum to Israel and Egypt to cease operations within forty-eight hours.

31st Ultimatum rejected and go-ahead for Operation 'Musketeer' ordered.

Seaborne assault force sails from Malta.

First allied air strikes against Egypt.

AN AIDE-MÉMOIRE TO THE DATES OF EVENTS

November

4th/5th	Israeli operations against Egypt cease.
5th	French and British paratroops drop on Egypt.
6th	Seaborne assault force lands. Demand by United Nations Secretary General for cessation of hostilities. Ceasefire ordered for midnight. United Nations agree to provide Emergency Forces.
21st	First U.N. troops arrive in Port Said.

December

3rd	Franco-British troops start to leave Egypt.
22nd	Evacuation completed.

CHAPTER 1

The Plan

The conquest of Europe, which began with an amphibious invasion in the face of an able and resolute enemy, was undoubtedly the greatest and most complex military operation of history. Great numbers of men and vehicles, huge masses of highly diversified stores and a wide scale of new and intricate techniques were involved. The whole operation ran like clockwork; it was one of the best planned and best executed military ventures that has ever been undertaken. Co-ordination was perfect; the allied nations worked together smoothly and effectively, timing was magnificent and the elements of surprise and deception were utilized to the fullest extent, the military commanders were given the support and backing that was essential to success, and the forces involved were properly trained and adequately equipped. Why then did we seem to be incapable of planning and executing an operation of incomparably smaller scale, against a nation hardly worth a rating as a military power? The answer will be seen to lie in the fact that the preparations for an armed descent on Egypt were conducted in a peacetime atmosphere devoid of the urgency or the bonds of union that existed in the years between 1939 and 1945 and—worst of all—in a political arena.

On Friday, 27th July, when the climate of opinion was ripe for joint Anglo-French action against Nasser, neither Britain nor France was in any position to apply force; both countries were in a state of military unpreparedness. It was true that their Mediterranean fleets were available and could have been off the coast of Egypt in less than a week but the French aircraft carriers then operating in the Mediterranean were all inadequately equipped with piston-engined aircraft and even the jet planes of the only British carrier immediately available could be outflown by Nasser's Soviet MIG's. Britain had two squadrons of Canberra bombers based in the Mediterranean but their airfields were in Arab countries which were certain to oppose their use to attack another Arab state. In any case there were no long-range fighters in the Middle East to support them. France had three squadrons of long-range Mystères in Germany but it would take upwards of ten days to transfer them to the Mediterranean and the only area they could operate from would be Cyprus. In that island, the war for self-determination had absorbed a large proportion of the British Army's meagre reserves. Two of the 16th Parachute Brigade's battalions, two of the Commandos of the Royal Marine Commando Brigade, and eight infantry battalions were deployed in anti-terrorist roles; the parachutists had done no parachute training for months, the Commandos had not practised amphibious warfare or co-operation with tanks for over twelve months. There were no transport aircraft and none of the base organizations or specialists required for an amphibious operation were readily available. There was in Malta an Amphibious Warfare Squadron of only two tank-landing ships (LST's) though both of these were equipped to carry eight assault landing craft (LCA's) each and two tank-landing craft (LCT's); this was totally inadequate for the size of an assault force required for a seaborne invasion of the magnitude necessary for an effective invasion of Egypt. Such equipment as remained from the Normandy landing was in 'mothballed' storage, the remainder had either been sold or destroyed. The French Army was little better off, the Algerian struggle had drained off their reserves and like the British they had only a few landing craft available—and these were old British craft sold to them after the war. Yet whilst both countries were incapable of taking any immediate forceful action against Egypt, their Governments were grimly determined that Nasser's Nationalization Act was not going to remain unchallenged.

On the 2nd August the Queen approved a Royal Proclamation recalling a limited number of reservists to the Colours and the retention of those regular soldiers due for discharge. In the House of Commons Sir Anthony Eden explained that these would be mainly specialists and technicians from Sections A and B of the Army Reserve and Categories 1 and 2 of the Army Emergency Reserve.[1] He also announced that extensive troop movements and other 'pre-

[1] At this time, the total number of men liable to recall comprised: 24,000 in Section A and 100,000 in Section B of the Regular Army Reserve; 3,000 of Category 1 and 150,000 of Category 2 of the Army Emergency Reserve. In the event, a total of about 25,000 were called up.

cautionary measures' in the Mediterranean might well delay the return home of National Servicemen from overseas. Meanwhile, whilst the French fleet was assembling at Toulon, three British aircraft carriers—H.M.S. *Bulwark* (22,000 tons), H.M.S. *Theseus* (13,190 tons), and H.M.S. *Ocean* (13,190 tons)—were hurriedly prepared for despatch to Mediterranean waters, a squadron of Canberras was ordered to Malta, the scheduled services of R.A.F. Transport Command were cancelled, and it was announced that a number of Army units including the Life Guards and the battalion of Grenadier Guards which were stationed at Windsor were under orders to move to an unknown destination. Despite the enforced postponement the Anglo-French military preparations appeared to be going ahead with all speed.

In Cairo, Colonel Nasser had reason to feel disquieted. The Anglo-French military preparations, discouraging enough in themselves, were perhaps less effective than some of the economic difficulties that were beginning to be felt. Both the British and French Prime Ministers had publicly denounced him as a Hitler-like figure: 'a menace to peace'; several clandestine radio stations broadcasting on wavelengths close to that of Cairo's 'Voice of the Arabs' were openly trying to provoke revolution, and a series of enigmatic messages issuing from them suggested a Maquis-like organization was operating within the Egyptian boundaries. In less than a week he had ordered the Egyptian Army to mobilize and had authorized the formation of a volunteer National Liberation Army of men, women and boys.

Back in London, between the 7th and 9th of August, the British and French military staffs conferred and Lieutenant-General Sir Hugh Stockwell, Commander of the British 1st Corps, was recalled from Germany to take part in the talks. Under a cloak of secrecy—a cloak with rents through which many people were able to appreciate what was afoot—the planning for an assault on Egypt was being worked out. There could be no question of using the facilities of N.A.T.O. and the formation of a combined Anglo-French headquarters to plan and control the operation had to be agreed first. Who would command, and what each country would contribute, also had to be decided. As Egypt had been so long in the 'Zone of influence' of the British, Cyprus would be the operational base, the long-range bomber force would be British and, as the British could fairly claim a 'special relationship' with the Americans by which they would hope to maintain the neutrality of the United States in the period of the operation, Britain was the obvious choice for leadership. The task force would be 'integrated' under a British Supreme Commander with a French Deputy; their staffs would follow the same system: each service would be under a British commander with a French deputy—a *commandant interallié adjoint*.

By welding the British and French staff officers into a single command system, following the pattern that had proved so successful in the war and which had been established in N.A.T.O., it was hoped to avoid the friction and rivalry which might arise between forces separately controlled by national commanders of equal rank and different outlook. The integrated system ultimately agreed could be said to have made little impact on the naval forces although it was eminently successful with the air forces; because of political influences and the differing temperaments of the Commanders concerned it failed with the land forces. So long as the British were leading the French were content to follow, but once the British feet began to drag the French found the system intensely irksome.

On the 11th August, the Commander of the British Land Forces in the Middle East—the genial ex-cavalryman, General Sir Charles Keightley—was appointed to be the Supreme Allied Commander and the dynamic little Vice-Admiral D'Escadre Barjot, Commander of the French Mediterranean Fleet, was named as his deputy. Lieutenant-General Sir Hugh Stockwell with General André Beaufré as his deputy, had already been nominated to command the land forces; the latter's job was to be the least envied of all since the circumstances of the operation soon put him in a position where he was in permanent disagreement with either Stockwell or his own Government. Vice-Admiral M. Richmond—later to be replaced by Vice-Admiral D. F. Durnford-Slater—was given command of the Naval Forces, and the silver-haired Contre-Amiral Lancelot was made his second-in-command. Air Marshal D. Barnett, with General Brohon as his deputy, was made responsible for the air element.

The scope of the proposed operation was much greater than was generally realized. The initial contribution of each country decided upon in the early London consultations was for 50,000 men from Britain and 30,000 from France; this 5 to 3 proportion was amended later when France agreed to increase her contribution. For an expedition force of this size the naval and air force backing would be considerable: over 100 British and 30 French warships, as well as

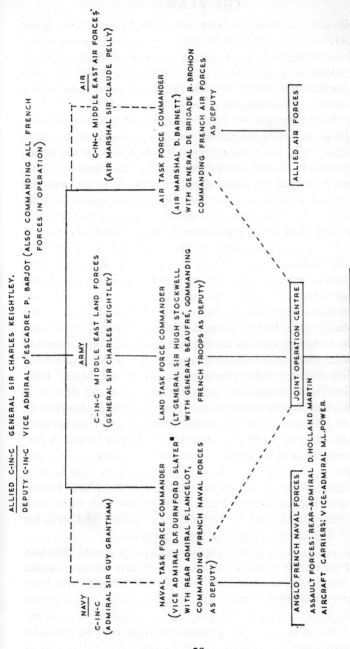

ALLIED C-IN-C   GENERAL SIR CHARLES KEIGHTLEY.
DEPUTY C-IN-C   VICE ADMIRAL D'ESCADRE. P. BARJOT (ALSO COMMANDING ALL FRENCH FORCES IN OPERATION)

NAVY
C-IN-C
(ADMIRAL SIR GUY GRANTHAM)

ARMY
C-IN-C MIDDLE EAST LAND FORCES
(GENERAL SIR CHARLES KEIGHTLEY)

AIR
C-IN-C MIDDLE EAST AIR FORCES
(AIR MARSHAL SIR CLAUDE PELLY)

NAVAL TASK FORCE COMMANDER
(VICE ADMIRAL D.F. DURNFORD SLATER *
WITH REAR ADMIRAL P. LANCELOT,
COMMANDING FRENCH NAVAL FORCES
AS DEPUTY)

LAND TASK FORCE COMMANDER
(LT GENERAL SIR HUGH STOCKWELL
WITH GENERAL BEAUFRÉ, COMMANDING
FRENCH TROOPS AS DEPUTY)

AIR TASK FORCE COMMANDER
(AIR MARSHAL D. BARNETT)
WITH GENERAL DE BRIGADE R. BROHON
COMMANDING FRENCH AIR FORCES
AS DEPUTY

ANGLO FRENCH NAVAL FORCES
ASSAULT FORCES: REAR-ADMIRAL D. HOLLAND-MARTIN
AIRCRAFT CARRIERS: VICE-ADMIRAL M.L. POWER.

JOINT OPERATION CENTRE

ANGLO FRENCH LAND FORCES

ALLIED AIR FORCES

* SUCCEDED VICE-ADMIRAL M. RICHMOND.
ON 24 TH OCTOBER 1963.

29

Chain of Command for an Operation against Egypt in 1956

hundreds of other vessels ranging from tankers and auxiliaries to landing craft of all types were required. The distances involved and the fact that the airfields in Jordan and Libya might not be available, meant that much of the air support would have to come from naval carriers, and seven carriers in all—five British and two French[1]—were used eventually. From the first, it was quite clear that the majority of the expeditionary force would have to be transported by sea. Whether or not the airborne troops were used in the initial assault—and both aircraft and airfield space shortages limited the numbers which could be used even if the men were made available—they could not be left for long without armoured support. The Egyptian Army was known to have large quantities of modern Soviet tanks and there was every reason to suppose that these would be used against the invaders. And so, although this would be a slow tedious process, with little hope of any element of surprise, there was no alternative to a seaborne assault. Yet only poor base port facilities existed. Cyprus, a day's sailing from the Egyptian coast, has only one small harbour at Famagusta and this was completely inadequate to cope with the assembly of a great armada; the other major port of Limassol has no wharf facilities and both men and material consequently would have to be loaded from lighters. Apart from the inadequate capacity and limited quayside capacity of the Famagusta harbour, it is also so shallow that ships of more than 5,000 tons have to remain outside the reef about a mile away from the land. During the emergency Famagusta's docks would also have to cope with the normal shipping trade on which the economy of Cyprus is so dependent.[2] The only other ports in the island are scarcely worth consideration; Larnaca, Kyrenia and Paphos were all so small as to be out of the question.

[1] H.M.S. *Eagle* (36,800 tons), H.M.S. *Albion* and H.M.S. *Bulwark* (each 22,000 tons). H.M.S. *Theseus* and H.M.S. *Ocean* (each 13,190 tons); the French *Arromanches* (13,190 tons) and the *Lafayette* (11,000 tons).

The British vessels carried a total of about 150 aircraft, the two French vessels about 65.

[2] Where there is no quay or where the dockside facilities are inadequate large ships may be conveniently discharged by ferrying their cargoes ashore in special landing ('Z') craft. The shallow draught of these boats enables them to get well inshore where they drop their ramps. To perform this function repetitively and efficiently there are two requirements: first, that the beach where they go ashore should have a suitable slope and shelf, so that the ramp is on dry land; second, that the land where the loading is to take place should be 'hard', i.e. capable of being used again and again without deterioration.

Malta, the next nearest base, is 936 miles or six days' steaming from Port Said; it has a good harbour but the island itself is really too small for the assembly of an expedition of this size and certainly it could not provide adequate training areas for the troops waiting in readiness. Libya appeared to offer an attractive half-way solution, particularly as the skeleton 10th Armoured Division was stationed there on Egypt's flank already. Any ideas of mounting the expedition from here were subject to the agreement of the Libyan Government, however, and it soon became plain that they would be reluctant for another Arab state to be attacked from within their boundaries. With bases in N.A.T.O. countries which had a Mediterranean seaboard out of the question also, there was no alternative but to fall back on Malta—a decision which meant that once it had been decided that force was to be used, the main assault force would have a long and slow sea journey before they could be got into action. The time taken on this journey would be decided by the speed of the slowest ships involved and could be expected to be about six days.

The declared aim of military intervention in Egypt was the 'safe-guarding' of the Canal; in effect this meant its occupation. To a military-minded individual such an aim will appear to fulfil all the requirements for the simple expression of a single purpose: there are no dependent objectives, no limitations; the military aim was soon fogged by political considerations of overthrowing the Egyptian Government and deposing Colonel Nasser however. Without any detailed consideration of such complications, it was apparent that there was a number of ways that the aim could be achieved. These ranged from the seizure of strategic points along the Canal to the complete occupation of the country and the annihilation of the Egyptian armed forces. The first consideration was where the troops were to land. If the operation was aimed directly at Egypt, or intended to topple Nasser, there was good reason for making Cairo the objective. In this case, Alexandria offered the best foothold. It is a well-equipped port —much more so than Port Said—and once a bridgehead was estab-lished, troops and equipment could be poured in very quickly. Com-bined with an armoured advance from Libya, Cairo should soon fall. The main objections to Alexandria as the first objective stemmed from the fact that the operations would be remote from the Canal and on the wrong side of the Nile. The most direct advance towards the Canal would have to cross the densely populated area of the Delta, well suited to guerrilla operations, and although the original plan was to move on Cairo by the desert flank there was still the river obstacle before the advance could continue via Abu Sueir. Libya's refusal[1] to allow the use of the British bases in that country precluded a thrust by the 10th Armoured Division back along the old 8th Army's Western Desert routes although this decision did not in itself rule out the possibility of Alexandria as the landing site.

The alternative was Port Said. A landing here would put the invasion force at the very top of the Canal and an advance to Suez should split Nasser's army right down the middle. But Port Said is a port only in name. At the end of a low-lying sand depression, it acts as the marshalling area for the convoys in transit through the Canal and the short length of quay which it possesses is totally unsuited to normal loading or unloading operations, these are carried out from lighters in the harbour. The capture of Port Said would mean that provision would have to be made for all the attendant complications resultant on this lack of facilities. Adequate specialist labour and equipment would have to be put ashore very early in the initial landings and even when the Port had been secured, there were still many obstacles to further progress. Its peculiar geographical position on what is virtually an island almost isolates it from the mainland; in consequence the few routes out of it are vulnerable and exposed. The main roads and the railway all run south to El Qantara and Ismailia; up to Qantara, where the mainland proper begins they all follow the Canal along a 25-mile neck of land, forming a narrow defile over an area of salt marsh and lake. In some places the causeway is a thousand yards wide but mostly it is much less. At El Raswa at the Port Said exit, the roads and the railway cross two bridges, which join the island of Port Said to the causeway. These bridges being a vital link in the routes to the south would either have to be captured, or if they were destroyed be replaced, before vehicles could cross to the mainland. The larger of the two, though a swing bridge, was just capable of carrying Centurion tanks. Once across the bridges the break out from Port Said would be restricted because of lack of space to deploy and there would be many difficult moments if the defile were defended. Mines could be expected, tanks and self-propelled guns might be dug-in along the route; all would mean considerable delay.

[1] The Libyan Government finally vetoed the movement of the 10th Armoured Division on 4th November: it had been known for some time that it would do so.

The problem of water and the responsibilities attached to administering the huge population of Port Said would also have to be considered. The town's only water supply comes from the Sweet Water canal, a waterway bringing the waters of the Nile into Port Said along the causeway and which runs parallel to the main road. Because it is Port Said's only water supply and so easily interfered with it may justifiably be considered the town's Achilles heel. With the Sweet Water canal out of commission, sufficient drinking water for the 170,000 inhabitants of Port Said, as well as the men of the invasion force, would have to be imported. (In the event, French wine tankers were requisitioned expressly for this purpose. It was planned that these ships, their wine tanks filled with Cyprus water, would shuttle between Cyprus and Port Said and maintain a barely adequate ration of two gallons per head per day.) On balance, Alexandria seemed to offer the best solution, though the planning staff were compelled eventually to revert to Port Said.

Planning any major operation is always a monumental task; planning this one was not made any easier by the wide geographical dispersal of commanders and troops alike. General Keightley, as Commander-in-Chief of the Middle East Land Forces, had his headquarters at Episkopi in Cyprus; Barjot shuttled between Toulon where his fleet lay, Algiers and Paris. Most of the planning was done in London, this location largely being determined by political expediency. In consequence, 'a great deal of travelling was required by all commanders' between London, Cyprus, Toulon, Paris, London, Malta, Algiers and Libya'[1] this often meant that commanders had to leave their formations for long periods at a time when their presence during the intensive training that was now being undertaken, might have been preferable.

At this point it is as well to be clear that the integrated planning and command system which had been agreed did not mean an integrated or combined supply organization. The latter would have been impossible; British and French equipment was—and is—of different design; ammunition is not interchangeable, techniques are not common to both countries and little has been achieved in the way of standardizing even minor components, let alone techniques. No one country is going to accept what is to them a second-best solution, the result is that even screw threads remain particular to individual nations. With rations it is the same. Despite M. Mendes-France's

---

[1] General Keightley's Despatch 12th September 1957.

'Drink more milk' campaign, the French Army still persists in an issue of cheap red wine; British troops like tea, and a French 24-hour ration pack comprising a tin of herrings in tomato sauce with some sugar and little else besides would be regarded with scorn by Thomas Atkins. Even nursing and medical techniques are not standardized; for instance the French with their thermometer graduated on a Centigrade scale, do not take the patient's mouth temperature. Fortunately no one suffered any hardship from differences of this nature. More serious were the complications which could be expected to evolve across the barrier of language. A need for British soldiers to be able to call urgently for the fire support of French sea-borne ground-attack aircraft was vital; this meant that their signals should be clear, unambiguous and capable of being understood. British signallers knew no French, few of the French signallers knew any English and there was no question of either replacing them or of one learning the other's language. The improvised solution was an interchange of signallers and wireless sets, an answer which proved clumsy and only just adequate.

Following the appointment of the Supreme Commander, the joint staffs' work began in earnest and by the middle of August the first tentative plan had taken shape. The operation was to be known as 'Hamilcar'—an esoteric reference to the Carthaginian general who had had a record of successful invasions. It had been estimated that at least six weeks' preparation were needed to mount an operation and as two of these had already elapsed everything should be ready for an attack about the middle of September. In preparation for a move to Egypt, troops assembling in Cyprus and Malta were ordered to paint a single, large, white letter 'H' denoting 'Hamilcar' across the bonnets and roofs of vehicles as aircraft recognition signs —an action which in itself revealed one of the peculiar differences which militated against British and French integration. The British painted 'H' ('H' for 'Hegypt' according to the British troops!), the French, whose spelling of the name is 'Amilcar', painted 'A'. The paint was hardly dry, when a new plan was christened 'Musketeer'— supposedly at the instigation of General Stockwell,[1] who had a weakness for Dumas's dashing characters.

[1] General Stockwell was an ex-Parachute General, having commanded the 6th Airborne Division in Palestine in the difficult days of 1947-8. He was well known to many of the younger Army officers who took part in 'Musketeer'; they remembered him as their Commandant at the R.M.A.

'Musketeer', like its predecessor 'Hamilcar', was based on the combined British and American methods used in the Mediterranean landings of the last war. First, air superiority was to be attained by a series of strikes at Egyptian airfields; airborne landings would then precede a seaborne assault designed to seize the base through which men and material could be poured in; the whole operation would be supported by the guns and aircraft of the combined fleets. The method was slow but sure; it was to prove unsure by being too slow. In the wartime landings, time for careful preparations had not been limited by political considerations; a successful solution to the Suez crisis demanded quick decisive action and from the beginning there were rumours of differences between the French and British High Commands over the pace and magnitude of the operation. The French were impatient, saying 'Commettant une erreur d'appréciation sur l'adversaire, nous montons une nouvelle opération. Overlord du petit pied'. British arguments were based on the premise that there was no reason why the actual landing operations should not be preceded by up to six days of air bombardment. The main assault force which it had been agreed must come from Malta would be six days at sea and the convoys could not set out until all hopes of a political settlement had disappeared. An airborne assault, without the support that could only come by sea, could only function for a limited period, since to leave an airborne force without armour for more than twenty-four hours in hostile territory where the enemy was known to be well equipped with modern tanks, was completely unacceptable. In any case, there were airmen who said that five days might well be sufficient to break the Egyptian will and so win the land battle without any actual invasion of the land: this, despite the evidence of the United States Strategic Survey on the Ruhr bombing and the lessons of Korea.

The original plan postulated the capture of Alexandria as the prelude to an attack on Cairo; for this operation a seaborne assault would be preceded by an airborne drop on a ridge south-west of the town. By mid-September, however, the intention had been changed to concentrate on the Canal, and the final plan designated Port Said

Sandhurst. There his tall elegant figure was often seen riding about the Academy grounds on a decrepit old Corgi motor-scooter which frequently broke down. A man of great colour, his 'Who's Who' entry emulated Sitwell (Education: 'during the holidays from Eton'), in recording his 'recreations' as 'befitting age and rank'.

THE PLAN

as the initial objective. The very complexity of the operation made the series of revisions which the plan was to undergo before its final form a veritable Staff College student's nightmare; any combined operation is a difficult form of jigsaw and the instructions for it have to be compiled in detail analogous to that of a London telephone directory —'Musketeer's' Naval disembarkation plan was equivalent to this in both size and shape.

The forces finally allocated to General Keightley for the Egyptian expedition consisted on the British side of about 45,000 men, 12,000 vehicles, 300 aircraft and 100 warships of the Royal Navy, including 3 conventional aircraft carriers, 2 obsolete carriers converted as heli-copter-carrying troopships and 3 cruisers; on the French side, about 34,000 men (not including Marines and Air Force personnel), 9,000 vehicles, 200 aircraft and about 30 warships, including 2 aircraft carriers, a battleship and 3 cruisers. Of the land forces, the British 16th Independent Parachute Brigade and the hard-bitten French 10th Airborne Division commanded by General Massu were to provide the airborne spearhead; the British 3rd Commando Brigade, sup-ported by armour from an armoured regiment of the 10th Armoured Division (totalling 48 Centurions)[1] would form the backbone of the seaborne assault, whilst the British 3rd Infantry Division sailing from the United Kingdom, and the French 7th Division Mécanique Rapide would follow up from Algeria. The administrative arrangements for a combined force of this magnitude presented enormous planning problems and as the operational plan changed, revised logistic ar-rangements had to conform with the changes. And whilst considera-tion of the operational aspects of 'Musketeer' could be undertaken *in vacuo* since the planning team needed to give little consideration to the current commitments of the Supreme Allied Commander, the administrative arrangements could not be resolved so easily. The same resources, many of which would be in short supply when the troops started to collect in Cyprus and Malta would have to provide for the many and varied commitments existing in the Middle East as well as 'Musketeer' and in the light of this consideration it seemed preferable for the existing administrative staff of the Middle East headquarters to remain in control of these resources. But so far as 'Musketeer' was concerned, the work of the administrative staff began

[1] In the event, the 6th Royal Tanks, which, with the 1st Royal Tank Regiment had been mobilized in the U.K. to function with 3 Inf. Div., was shipped to Malta and provided the armoured support for the assault.

in London in common with their colleagues[1] planning the operational aspects. Logistical planning information had to be passed back to General Keightley's headquarters and long-term plans had to be made for the occupation of all or part of Egypt although this was not such a problem as might be supposed since British troops had occupied the Canal Zone until four months previously and their old installations were still largely intact; all that would have to be done would be to reactivate them.

In Cyprus and Malta, arrangements had to be made for a vast influx of those connected with the naval and air task forces. More men on the island would mean greater quantities of food, petrol and other stores as the task force assembling in Cyprus and Malta had to be fed at the same time as the reserve stocks necessary for the operation had to be built up. Once established in Egypt the troops might well get their supplies direct from the United Kingdom but the distance between Port Said and Britain was such that buffer stocks would still have to be held in Cyprus to cope with an emergency. Then there was the nagging problem of providing water for Port Said in the likely event of Nasser turning off the tap of the Sweet Water Canal. Finally, as the airborne assault would have to be made from Cyprus, the airfields would have to be ready to accept a large number of both British and French aircraft which would consume vast quantities of fuel, though this was less of a problem than preparing the airfields themselves.

Cyprus had only three airfields suited to the needs of the Allied Air Task Force and in August only one of these—Nicosia—the island's only civilian international airport was working. And the traffic which it was able to take was limited by the extensive reconstruction work that had been undertaken before July. Akrotiri, which was the island's R.A.F. base, was still under construction and a favourite sabotage area of E.O.K.A.; Tymbou was a neglected field which needed considerable development before it could be classed as fit for use as an operational base. It was not until late October that they were both fully operational. Nicosia and Akrotiri were both designated Royal Air Force bases since Britain was making the largest contribution to the air task force and these airfields were supposedly best suited to the

---

[1] Under the direction of Major-General R. G. S. Hobbs who was appointed Chief of Staff to the Supreme Commander and charged with the planning responsibility of 'Musketeer'.

requirements of the British machines;[1] this left Tymbou, five miles outside Nicosia on the main Nicosia–Famagusta road, for the French. Prior to its speedy development from August onwards, Tymbou had been used only as an emergency landing ground for the R.A.F., or other aircraft unable to land at Nicosia. Built originally by German prisoners-of-war, it was rumoured that the German colonel who surveyed the site had failed to point out a treacherous dip in the runway and its detection later resulted in further development being stopped—until the advent of 'Musketeer'. Tymbou appeared to satisfy the French requirements however, they had no accidents and made the maximum use of it during the operation.

If limited airfield facilities seemed to be a problem in August other much worse problems were to present themselves as the weeks slipped past. As the plan evolved, the troops collected: they were assembling not for a war—as politicians and senior commanders took pains to point out—not for a war, but for a 'police' action. And what might be generally considered as an academic difference in terminology really meant that the initiative of the field commanders was to be constrained within narrow limits by the political masters; a military machine was to be launched but its engines were to be governed from start to finish. As one commanding officer said, to the delight of the Press, 'War is a pretty simple thing. It only becomes complicated when the politician takes a hand.'

Clearly, political issues will always govern the formulation of a military undertaking of this nature. Much of the interest in the operation has stemmed from the fact that so many of the issues were not clear cut. These have been—and will continue to be—debated *ad nauseam:* it is not proposed to reiterate the arguments here. Reasoning as to whether or not the operation should ever have been undertaken is outside the scope of this book. Certainly the decision to conduct it as 'cleanly' as possible so causing as few Egyptian casualties as was commensurate with attaining the object was a commendable limitation, though a somewhat restrictive practice militarily. In the event, most of the Egyptian casualties were in the British zone, since the success of the French airborne operation on Port Fuad eliminated the necessity for the French fleet firing in support of their seaborne assault.

[1] Not altogether suited: the short clearance between the ground and fuselage of the Canberras necessitated pits being dug to enable bombs to be loaded into the aircraft bomb-bays.

THE PLAN

The combined Anglo-French plan for 'Musketeer' was evolved *without* consideration of Israeli action; a discussion on the question of the collusion with the Israelis has no part in the story but one issue is worthy of consideration. From a purely military standpoint, the British intelligence staff ought to be regarded as having failed in their duty if they had no inkling of Israeli intentions. The August plan was worked out on the basis of occupying the Suez Canal Zone, utilizing only French and British troops and resources; the possibility of the Israelis being concerned with the operation was not taken into account. The final plan was still a workable proposition in separating the Israeli and Egyptian forces when the Israelis invaded Sinai however, for by using the same technique they would be separated once the Canal was captured. Politically, of course, Israel's Operation 'Kadesh' presented an opportunity in which duty and self-interest were happily combined; the refusal of either country to cease hostilities and withdraw from the Canal area merely provided a valid reason for unleashing the preventive military action which had first been envisaged in July.

Through August into September and then October, the details of the plan varied as preparations continued although the basis remained the same: bombing to eradicate the Egyptian Air Force, then a co-ordinated land assault by airborne and seaborne forces, followed by a quick exploitation of an armoured column whilst the Anglo-French Air Forces and the British and French naval aircraft continued to bomb military targets and support the move of the column. If all went well it was reckoned that the Canal Zone should be quickly occupied: the French said four days, the more cautious British estimate seven to ten days from the word 'go'.

The code word 'Toledo' was to be the signal for the operation to start. On the day set for landing, the seaborne assault force would touch down on Port Said beaches, at an H hour thirty-five minutes after sunrise. For close on an hour prior to this, the coast defences would have been under bombardment from the guns of the combined fleets and before this they would have been subjected to a number of heavy air attacks. Seaborne landings would be made at H hour and thirty minutes after the first wave of troops had arrived on the beaches, British and French parachutists would drop near selected vital installations on the outskirts of the town. Then, whilst Port Said's Egyptian garrison was being subdued, minesweepers accompanying the fleets would sweep a passage into the harbour and in three hours it was hoped to land the first tanks. By this time it was reasonable to suppose that the seaborne assault troops should have linked up with the parachutists and a route through the town opened up, so that when the armour was put ashore it could roll on down the Canal road towards Suez. Long lists of code words covering every eventuality and most of the places likely to be involved were compiled; ironically the eventual operational limit of El Cap was nicknamed 'Love Knot'.

It will be apparent, in retrospect, that the 'Musketeer' plan which was used in the event may be faulted on two counts: for the overestimate of the military worth of the Egyptian Forces which was inherent in it, and for a lack of flexibility partially conditioned by the state of training and the poor equipment of the troops allotted to the operation. Yet it is difficult to see how operations may be planned efficiently if time, equipment and men are limited by political motives. If Britain is to face the possibility of so-called 'limited' warfare operations, her fighting forces must be sufficient, equipped, and trained in readiness for such eventualities. As will be seen, the planning of Operation 'Musketeer' drew attention to the military hollowness of our defences, preparations exposed it, and the actual operation paraded our inadequacy before the whole world.

CHAPTER 2

Preparation

In February 1954, Royal Assent was given to a piece of new legislation, which appeared on the Statute Book under the concise title 'The Navy, Army and Air Force Reserves Act, 1954'. Its provisions were intended to cover the requirements of a national emergency and to bring order to a muddle that had been developing since 1945. If an emergency faced Britain, the problem was expected to be one of quickly bringing the regular forces up to strength, getting the Territorial Army on a war footing and providing the mass of ancillary units not available in peace but essential in war. As in the Second World War, national service would eventually provide a steady stream of men from civilian life afterwards but the initial difficulty was to provide trained men in sufficient numbers at the outset of the emergency. There were no special provisions for a 'limited' emergency such as was to arise two years later.

In 1939 the reserves which were called up had been those of the Regular and Supplementary Reserves for other ranks,[1] the Regular, Territorial and Supplementary Reserves of Officers and the Officers' Emergency Reserves. At the end of hostilities, reserve officers reverted to their former reserves; Territorial Army officers were released but held in the Territorial Army Reserve of officers; Emergency Commissioned officers, who then formed the bulk of serving officers, were 'released to unemployment'; other ranks were released to newly formed classes of the Royal Army Reserve, renamed Classes 'W' and 'Z' for men retained beyond the period of their Regular and Supplementary Reserve engagements, and Classes 'W(T)' and 'Z(T)' for those who had been 'emergency only' or members of the Territorial Army. Subsequently, regular soldiers of the post-war army were

[1] Militiamen, who have no counterpart in the post-war reserves, were also called out.

released to Class 'Z' after completion of their service, none being discharged except on medical grounds.

In the immediate post-war years, National Service kept the Army up to strength, the Royal Air Force also relied on its National Servicemen to a lesser extent; the Royal Navy was little affected and reverted to its pre-war system.

When Colonel Nasser announced the nationalization of the Canal and it was apparent that the services were faced with a manpower crisis, mobilization problems and states of readiness in the three services followed the same order of dependence on National Service, the Army being faced with most difficulties, the Navy least. Nevertheless, in 1953, five years after the first call-up, since both the Territorial Army and the Supplementary Reserve (renamed later the 'Army Emergency' Reserve) had been swelled by young men who had completed their national service with the Colours, it had become clear that the Reserve Army required tidying up and reorganizing in order to dispense with the services of older men still held on the books by the 1939 emergency legislation. The effect of the reorganization was to discharge men in Classes 'W', 'W(T)', 'Z' and 'Z(T)' from their engagements but to impose a new liability on those who were below the age of 45.[1]

At the end of July 1956, the manpower crisis followed the anticipated pattern: men were needed to bring regular units up to strength and specialized units, such as those concerned with operation port and dock facilities which were not included in the peacetime Order of Battle, had to be mobilized. On paper these specialized units already existed as part of the Army Emergency Reserve although invariably they were below the strength required. Following the Queen's Proclamation on the 2nd August the reservists began to report according to their instructions; the regular reservists going to make up the strength of units of the regular army and the emergency reservists to the depots and training regiments which had the responsibility of reconstituting the Army Emergency Reserve units. As the reservists had been called up selectively and there was no apparent urgency after the first few days, their morale was soon affected. Personal economic problems, with an apparent lack of purpose combined with the irksome confinement to camp attendant on the mobilization routine, all had an adverse effect. So did the

[1] The Army reserve organization and a note on its function is given at Appendix A.

realization by some reservists that they were surplus to the requirements of the unit to which they had been recalled, and instances of
over-posting to units were not uncommon. Nor had administrative
arrangements for recalling the men always kept abreast of developments; in the case of the armoured regiments, reinforcement tank
crews were called up on a basis of five men per tank although the
Centurion has a crew of only four. A surfeit of regular reservists,
embarrassing enough during the period of mobilization, almost
proved to be a disaster when a political decision was taken that they
should all accompany their units overseas even if it meant their
displacing regulars and serving national servicemen—many of the
latter finding themselves displaced by individuals less well trained,
less keen and often less fit. With stores, instructors and equipment
gone when once their regiments had departed overseas, often the only
employment that could be found for such individuals was on garrison
fatigues and they were denied the operational experience that they
would have gained by participation in 'Musketeer'.

The calibre of those recalled to service varied. Some, who had only
recently gone to the reserve, were well trained and found no difficulty
in resuming their duties; most of the parachutist reservists were in
this category. Others, also recently discharged to the reserve, resented
leaving recently found—sometimes lucrative—civilian employment
to return to the Colours for an unspecified period. There were others
who had been so long out of the Army that they were completely out
of touch with modern equipment and techniques; one officer, on
being shown a Centurion, is reported to have said in all seriousness
that 'it was very nice, but what was it?' Other reservists were found
to be not physically fit for active service and had to be sent home. But
these were all minorities; most of the men recalled took their places
without complaint and served well. It was only the misdemeanours of
a few that led to rumours of disturbances and unrest; the majority
resigned themselves to the situation and settled down to seeing the
emergency through. Such disturbances as did occur took place during
the period of waiting in September and October; when the time for
action came, even the malcontents acquitted themselves well.

Of the troops destined for the operation in early August, most of
the 3rd Commando Brigade[1] and two battalions of the 16th Parachute

[1] The 3rd Commando Brigade, under the command of Brigadier R. W.
Madoc, O.B.E., A.D.C., had two of its Commandos in Cyprus. The third

Brigade Group were in Cyprus, committed to internal security duties. The Commandos had had no opportunity for some time to do any training in assault landing techniques, nor had the parachutists been able to do any parachuting; what is more, neither formation had anti-tank weapons capable of dealing with the Egyptian army's modern Soviet tanks. The main strategic reserve force of the 3rd Infantry Division was in the United Kingdom and its units would have to be brought up to strength and draw their mobilization stores before they could be ready for war. Considerable training was also desirable since the formation was a division in name only—many of the units being deployed in roles completely unrelated to their tasks as part of the strategic reserve, indeed some were serving in Cyprus. In Libya, the regiments of the 10th Armoured Division—also a division in name only since it was little more than an armoured brigade—were trained, acclimatized and reasonably well equipped but, as has already been mentioned, their use from Libyan bases had been in doubt almost from the outset. (Subsequently the division was removed from General Keightley's Order of Battle before 'Musketeer' was actually launched, their place being taken by the 3rd Infantry Brigade who had been flown to Malta in August and were originally destined to relieve the 10th Armoured Division.)

From almost the beginning of the crisis, Keightley's staff had recognized that a quick 'domination' of the Canal Zone could only be achieved by the use of tanks. The various plans had all been based on the landing of an armoured regiment with the assault force, this being followed up by a second regiment. If the 10th Armoured Division were to be denied to the operation, armour would have to be found from elsewhere and early in August it was decided that an armoured brigade would have to be raised in the United Kingdom as part of the 3rd Infantry Division; it was the 6th Royal Tank Regiment of this newly raised brigade that was eventually used in the battle. No armoured brigade headquarters existed with the division and only one regiment of the three which were ostensibly included in the divisional Order of Battle could feasibly be considered available or suited to the task. The armoured brigade commander-designate faced a mammoth undertaking and his difficulties in the *laisser-faire* atmosphere of an England at peace during those summer months, were typical of those experienced by almost everybody trying to

functioned as a training unit in the United Kingdom. At full strength—with its three Commandos it totalled approximately 2,800 men.

prepare for a war that was not a 'proper' war in an atmosphere that was not properly peace.

Orders for units to mobilize were issued simultaneously with the notices recalling the reservists. In some cases these orders meant that whole units—such as those who would be concerned with the operation of the port facilities or the essential services in Port Said town—had to be completely reconstituted. Other units, like the amphibious observation regiment of the Royal Artillery, which would be controlling the naval bombardment of an immense fleet, and which existed only in cadre form, would have to be rapidly expanded. Battalions and regiments short of the numbers prescribed in their war establishments started to receive their quotas of reservists. These men all had to be clothed and equipped and the units, whose role necessitated their reservists reporting direct from civilian life rather than along a buffered channel of regimental depot to training regiment to unit, soon found themselves in a frenzy of feverish activity whilst they re-equipped, trained for the ordeal ahead, and moved to the stations from which they would deploy for battle.

At the military depots responsible for the specialist units of the Army Emergency Reserve, the mobilization drill rapidly converted the heterogeneous collections of reservists into a semblance of martial uniformity. The men, whose civilian jobs approximated to their service employment, were soon clothed and equipped and all that was necessary now was for them to train in their collective role. It was at this stage that the real difficulties set in. Up to now the majority of the reservists had been carried along on a flood of excitement and anticipation but as training continued, punctuated by periods of stand-to and stand-down, and as politicians expressed doubts about the feasibility, desirability and British capability of undertaking an operation against Egypt, morale really began to suffer. Harassed commanding officers, perturbed by considerations of keeping their men occupied, sought ways of utilizing the specialist trades which they possessed. Service utilities were overhauled by capable maintenance engineers; a bridge near Portsmouth was dismantled; electrical cables were stripped from the old forts near Weymouth and the lighting, plumbing and accommodation of a number of camps were reorganized. Men of 81 Port Regiment, flown to Cyprus at the end of August, were employed during the months of uncertainty in discharging stores at Famagusta. Some of the work had no direct bearing on the forthcoming operation, although the stevedore work of the

Port Regiment clearly helped in the build-up of the Cyprus base, but it did have training value. And collective training was what many of the units needed. Limited by the facilities available and often restricted by lack of the equipment with which they would be expected to fight, regiments and battalions all endeavoured to use the period of waiting to train in the role to which they were assigned.

Mobilization of the armoured brigade generated its own special sort of problems. Since it was not considered feasible to employ either the Royal Scots Greys or the Westminster Dragoons, only one of the three armoured regiments in the original Order of Battle was to be included in the new brigade; even this regiment, the 1st Royal Tanks, was in no fit state in August to go to war. One of its squadrons had been detached for demonstration duties at the School of Infantry, the men of another, without their tanks, were working as mechanics with the Territorial Army, and the rest of the regiment was mostly employed on garrison duties in and around the home base of Tidworth. For months, the commanding officer had had no opportunity to get his men together with their equipment to train them collectively and shooting practice had been completely out of the question. The second regiment[1]—the 6th Royal Tanks—was little better off; it had returned from Germany only about five months previously, leaving many of its trained men in B.A.O.R. on extra-regimental duties. Since then the remainder had been working with the Territorial Army throughout the length and breadth of the United Kingdom, and as no role in the Strategic Reserve had been prescribed for the regiment, it too, was unprepared for the sudden call to mobilize. Inadequately equipped with old vehicles, short of the stores that were required for war, their men sadly in need of training, particularly in shooting on the open ranges, both regiments were committed to a hurried programme of reorganization, resupply and retraining.

Refurbishing and making up the shortages and deficiencies might well seem to be a comparatively simple issue but the system for collection of the vehicles, ammunition, technical stores and myriad other necessary items proved to be archaic. Collection had to be

[1] Although the Life Guards, who moved to Cyprus in August, were subsequently included in the Order of Battle, for practical purposes only two regiments were allotted to the brigade. It was considered that a shortage of shipping would preclude the move to the Middle East of the customary three regiments. In the event only the 6th Royal Tanks took part in the operation.

made from different depots scattered about the country and as most of these downed tools at the week-ends, there was often an added factor of frustration. The vehicles which were issued came from mobilization reserves earmarked for just such occasions as these—many of them often proved to be unsuitable. Sometimes they were of the wrong type; sometimes their fittings—wireless aerials, canopies, ammunition racks and the like—were missing. Against a scale which clearly required some revision, ancient trucks of 1940 vintage, quite useless in the role for which they were intended, were solemnly handed over by the vehicle depots. Consequently, at the eleventh hour, as the two regiments frantically prepared to embark for an unknown destination—clearly not unassociated with the troubles precipitated by Colonel Nasser—an unprecented amount of improvisation had to be undertaken. Not even the armament of the Centurions was wholly satisfactory. Changing the original armour-piercing ammunition for more modern discarding sabot shells proved relatively simple although its need for use against Soviet-type tanks might have been predicted. But the fact that the smoke grenades with which Centurions were equipped had proved to be unsafe and had to be withdrawn was anything but a comforting reassurance to the regiments contemplating the action ahead.

Concurrently with the flurry caused by this re-equipping, efforts were being made to embark the armoured brigade. Less than a week after their being told to mobilize, a whole series of warning orders for the two units to move began to descend on the unfortunate regiments. Often contradictory, these orders came from innumerable head-quarters—all of which had the best of intentions, no doubt—to add to the general confusion, bewilderment and concern of the families of those who were to go. Through the chain of command and district headquarters which lay above it, the armoured brigade headquarters located in Colchester, received its orders from the War Office through Eastern Command, East Anglian District, and the headquarters of the 3rd Infantry Division. The two regiments who were both at Tidworth received their orders through Southern Command and Salisbury Plain District and at one time six different sources were found to be issuing orders to them, many of the orders conflicting with each other. It was the old business of the man underneath feeling the weight of those on top.

Early in August the brigade commander—Brigadier J. de F. Slee-man—had decided that the 1st Royal Tanks were best suited to support the commando assault and it was generally understood that they should move first and have priority in everything from tanks and equipment to transportation to the ports. In the expectancy of their being first into battle he even went so far as to load his own headquarters on to their ships; his keenness, planning and foresight were to be thwarted however, he had not reckoned on the embarkation authority changing his plans. Priority in tank transporters which the regiment enjoyed ensured that their tanks were loaded into the LST's waiting at Portland before those of the 6th Royal Tanks had completed the journey to their embarkation port of Plymouth, but once they had been loaded the situation changed and the brigade commander found himself completely powerless to do anything about it. It was as if an unknown, untraceable hand was feeding difficulties into the operation. Compelled to leave three Centurions behind because of the shortage of LST's, the 6th Royal Tank Regiment sailed for Malta on the 4th September; nearly two months was to elapse before their sister regiment and the brigade headquarters followed them. None seemed to know why they sailed on that date; that the decision was an arbitrary one may be concluded from the fact that the arrival of the regiment in Malta was unscheduled, unheralded and unforeseen.

Since it highlights the chaotic core of the preparatory period which damned the military aspects of 'Musketeer', the unhappy story of the armour would not be complete without an account of the move from Tidworth to Portland and Southampton. To those who were intimately concerned, it must have seemed then that the British Army had lost the art of moving tanks in Britain; the weight and size of these monsters precludes their moving by train and their movement by road under their own power is virtually prohibited, sometimes undesirable. Moving them by road, off their tracks, means their being carried on wheeled transporters and only a few military transporters existed in 1956. The well-known removal firm of Pickfords who use these enormous roadsters to transport heavy engineering components was the only source that could be called upon, and being a civilian firm, Pickfords was governed by civilian rules. Consequently the move proved to be not only expensive and inconvenient, it was also slow and wasteful. Transporter crews, tied to trade union hours of work and restrictions never intended to cope with an emergency or the needs of the Services, took a week to do a journey which a military unit would have covered in three days, and behind each convoy

trailed a fantastically disproportionate number of empty spare transporters which the regulations of the British Road Services said must
always be held in reserve. Between the time that the first tank was
loaded on to its transporter and the last tank was stowed in its LST,
there was a lapse of four weeks; valuable time, which could have been
spent in hard training, had been lost.

Eventually a total of 93 Centurions—something less than two armoured regiments as there was no room for one fighting troop and
the reserve tanks—was loaded on to 14 LST's, albeit in the wrong
order.[1] It was all that could be managed, since it had just not been
possible to muster enough suitable ships—a sure indication of Great
Britain's declining maritime power. Articles which appeared in the
September newspapers carried stories of other deficiencies, muddles
and lack of foresight. Of the thirty-two tank landing ships available
to the services, only two were actually commissioned; the remainder
were in 'moth-balls' and even these, when their cocoons were removed, were not fully seaworthy. (Eighteen LST's actually took part
in the operation; eleven smaller assault craft were also used.) Wooden
hulled minesweepers were said to have been dried out on the inside
and left wet on the outside so that they had then rotted; steel plates
on vessels that were taken from reserve buckled under the testing
hammers of the men in the dockyards. And when it came to the
loading and the voyages of the ships, there were errors that even
rivalled those of the Gallipoli expedition of 1915. The operational
problems which resulted in the unexpected precipitation of the 6th
Royal Tanks on Malta when all arrangements had been made for
their sister regiment to spearhead the assault may be imagined.

Confusion was not confined solely to the armour and much of the
muddle undoubtedly arose from the political machinations which
kept the 'Musketeer' plan 'fluid'; long after the assault, the stores and
equipment of many units which had followed up the invasion force
were still arriving in the wrong order. That an amphibious force
should be tactically loaded is a fundamental principle. It seems almost
elementary to expect that the men and equipment needed first should
be loaded in such a fashion that they disembark first, and once the
loading is complete, that there should then be no change in the plan

[1] One officer responsible for loading the tanks is reputed to have said
as he surveyed the laden LST's: 'Well, we've got them all on, it's up to
some other —— to get them off.' This despite the fact that they probably
had to be unloaded under fire!

unless everybody concerned is well aware of it, so that the cargo arrangements can be altered accordingly. In November, when ships were unloaded at Port Said, some were carrying stores which bore little relationship to the tactical order of disembarkation of the units for which they were intended—some even for units which never reached Port Said at all. This was due to some of the ships being loaded in accordance with the earlier plan which had Alexandria as the objective.

The only aircraft carrier with the British Mediterranean fleet at the time of Colonel Nasser's fateful speech was H.M.S. *Eagle*. Her complement of about a hundred planes formed a composite air support group of fighters and ground support aircraft; the latter being of older types which were not fitted to carry rockets. Two light fleet carriers, H.M.S. *Ocean* and H.M.S. *Theseus*, which were serving in home waters, had been converted at the end of 1954 from their role of operating aircraft into floating schools for new entry officers and seamen, and as a result they had lost their ability to launch or land conventional aircraft. (Another training ship, the 22,000-ton H.M.S. *Bulwark*, was also in home waters; being the training ship of the Fleet Air Arm she could operate aircraft.) With the hasty embarkation of a few thousand camp-beds, *Ocean* and *Theseus* underwent a further conversion to become the first emergency troopships of the crisis. Carrying reinforcements and heavy equipment, they sailed for Cyprus at the end of July[1] and were subsequently engaged on the re-

---

[1] One anecdote relating to this period is worth repeating.

In July, a troopship flew the flag of a certain Rear-Admiral, who, with his wife, is well known for his attachment to the beauties of Devonshire. As Flag Officer in command of a Squadron, this Admiral was entitled to a band which duly embarked before the ship left Plymouth. According to custom, the troops, ships company and band were paraded whilst the ship steamed out of the harbour. As the band remained inactive the Admiral relayed a sharp inquiry to the ship's Commander as to why his band was not playing. The Commander, who, till now, had been unsure of protocol, hesitated no longer and over the loud-hailer a crisp instruction to the bandmaster prompted the band to bestir themselves. As the ship passed Drake's Island, running close by where the families had assembled to wave goodbye, the first notes of a dirge sounded across the water. There was no hesitancy about the Commander's action now, and a repeated 'Stop, Stop, Stop' over the loud-hailer brought the band's performance to a ragged conclusion. 'Bandmaster,' said the loud-hailer, 'play something cheerful,' and after a few moments the familiar strains of 'Colonel Bogey' wafted across the

deployment programme which will be discussed later. *Bulwark*, meantime, with equal haste had embarked three squadrons of the latest Mark VI Seahawks and also sailed for the Mediterranean, arriving at Gibraltar on the 9th August for a two-day stay, whilst her hull was scraped. She finally joined the rest of the fleet at Malta six days later and, with *Eagle*, started in on an intensive training programme designed to fit her squadrons for the task in view. The knowledge that Nasser's MIG's were, in theory, superior to the British naval aircraft suggested that daylight attacks deep into Egypt would be fraught with danger and so consideration was given to confining the attacks to the hours of darkness. The development of a night attack technique using flares to illuminate the targets soon showed that this alternative was not feasible, however and that the first phase of the operation would have to be carried out in daylight. From then on, the training was based on the idea that the Egyptian installations and airfields would struck repeatedly as soon as there was sufficient light for them to be identified. By this means it was hoped that the threat of the MIG's would be reduced to a minimum. In addition there was the usual round of pre-dawn launches, air to air combat, photo-reconnaissance missions and later, in co-operation with the Royal Marines of the 3rd Commando Brigade on the north island of Malta, air support strikes. Dummy night strikes against the frigate H.M.S. *Ulysses* and the French carrier *Arromanches* completed the training of the aircrews and in mid-October both *Eagle* and *Bulwark* returned to Gibraltar where, with the arrival of H.M.S. *Albion* at Malta the rumour was circulating that *Bulwark* would return to England. Following a refit, *Albion* had recommissioned and sailed for Malta where she arrived in record time. Now she was busy working up her complement of Seahawks and Sea Venoms to operational efficiency before joining the other two carriers in their general training.

By this time, *Ocean* and *Theseus* had finished their initial round of trooping and had got back to England in the first week of September. For the two weeks in the middle of the month rumours of changes in plan kept the crews scurrying round to cope with the changing

waves towards the families. No sooner had the ship cleared Plymouth Sound than the Commander received a summons to the Admiral's cabin where he presumed he was to be congratulated for the masterful way he had handled a crisis. 'The tune which you prevented MY band from playing', said the Admiral curtly, 'is entitled "Widdicombe Fair" and was composed by my wife especially for the occasion of leaving harbour.'

roles of their ships. Improved accommodation arrangements were made for further trooping runs and tiered bunks were welded into the former hangars and classrooms; an operating theatre and other hospital facilities were also installed to face the possibility of *Ocean* being used as a hospital ship. However, on Wednesday the 26th September, both ships were ordered to revert to an aircraft carrying role—of a somewhat unusual nature—and *Ocean* embarked 845 Naval Helicopter Squadron which were equipped with Whirlwinds, and *Theseus* the Joint (Army and R.A.F.) Experimental Helicopter Unit with its mixed complement of Whirlwinds and Sycamores. Stores, loaded but a few days before, now were hastily unloaded and the recently erected bunks had to be cut out with oxy-acetylene burners. Both ships sailed on the 31st for a trial cruise to practise the working of helicopters from the carriers but at the end of a fortnight *Ocean* was ordered to return to her original duties of seamanship training whilst 845 Squadron transferred to the *Theseus* and sailed for Malta. There the Commandos saw their helicopters for the first time and were able to work out the drills they would have to use in the forthcoming operations. *Ocean*'s reversion to her 'normal' duties was shortlived. In less than a week she had re-embarked the Joint Experimental Helicopter Unit and sailed for Malta, arriving there on the last day of October; thirty-six hours later the men of 45 Royal Marine Commando were embarking in her and on Saturday the 3rd November, together with the *Theseus* and an escort of frigates and destroyers, *Ocean* steamed out of Valetta's Grand Harbour *en route* for a destination which was known to be in the Eastern Mediterranean but which was not yet generally known to be Port Said.[1]

Back in the United Kingdom, in August, considerable publicity had been given to a 'great airlift'—largely by chartered aircraft—of reinforcements to the units stationed in Cyprus. On the 7th, the Government publicly warned the independent air lines that they must be prepared to move troops to the Mediterranean, and the Chairmen of British Aviation Limited and Airwork Limited, replied in a joint statement which expressed their satisfaction at 'having a real place in the defence of the country's interests'. Doubtless they were also satisfied with the business it promised for the future. Between them the independent air line companies could muster a fleet which, including

---

[1] The uncertainty as to who the operation was to be directed against may be judged from the fact that at the last minute those who held the Jewish faith were given the option of remaining behind. Several did.

the Bristol freighters employed on the cross-channel car ferry, totalled about two hundred aircraft, half of which were four-engined machines. The first real call on their services came on 9th August when aircraft of B.O.A.C. and the air charter companies started to evacuate 900 British wives and children from Egypt; this operation—Operation 'Nursery'—was completed in ten days and was probably the most significant part of the so-called 'great airlift'. (By what standards an airlift of seventy-five plane loads per week could be called 'great' is difficult to understand since the total number of troops carried only accounted for about a quarter of a division. Operation 'Nursery' added only marginally to these moves.) The need to employ civilian airlines did draw attention to our lamentable lack of military transport aircraft; this combined with the lack of ships, might be considered to be a sobering thought for a nation with so many overseas commitments.

Among the first of the major redeployments which have been referred to were those of the 40 and 45 Royal Marine Commandos from the 3rd Commando Brigade, who returned to Malta from Cyprus in August. There they were made up to a strength of about 2,800 by 42 Commando, the training unit from England, which travelled out on the cruiser H.M.S. *Cumberland*. Once in Malta, Brigadier Madoc thrust the whole brigade into an intensive refresher training course which included assault landings, street fighting and house clearing, and—towards the middle of October—a brief and elementary exercise in infantry–tank co-operation with a squadron of the 6th Royal Tanks. Until this exercise the tanks had not been allowed to move about in Malta, the roads being considered too narrow and the island too restricted. Consequently, this for them was also the first real training which they had had in co-operating with the troops whom they were to support in a few days time; other than this their training had been confined to wireless exercises. Several landing practices on to the assault craft which would carry them to their objectives followed, and both forms of training were to pay dividends in 'Musketeer'. Supposedly for security reasons, no mention was made of the possibility of a helicopter assault, and as has been seen, it was not until the end of October that the commandos even saw a helicopter, let alone rehearse a landing.

Meanwhile the 16th Parachute Brigade Group had concentrated in Cyprus and had been brought up to strength by an intake of reservists. The 1st and 3rd Battalions, which were already there, were joined by

53

the 2nd Battalion and the supporting arms of the brigade group, who were either flown out or travelled in H.M.S. *Theseus*. Then, in September, the two parachute battalions which had been in Cyprus since before the emergency were flown back to the United Kingdom for a rapid refresher course in parachuting following which they returned to Cyprus once more. Slowly the assault force was taking shape.

To turn briefly to the French. On the 29th August the Foreign Office announced that the French Government had asked permission for facilities to station troops in Cyprus and that this had been granted; ostensibly the request was made so that the French would be in a position to 'protect' their Nationals in Egypt 'if the occasion arose'. Following the announcement, 2,700 Frenchmen disembarked at Limassol on 7th September, having been preceded about a week before by an advance party with large quantities of stores, which had been off-loaded at Limassol and Famagusta. Despite the fact that their arrival had been expected, the Frenchmen were still something of a novelty, it was even more of a novelty to find that few of them spoke much French, being Germans serving in the Foreign Legion; or men from Alsace. On landing in Cyprus almost the first action of their advance party was to mob the sandwich stalls and small cafés just outside the dock gates; apparently the merchant ships in which they had travelled from Marseilles had been hastily requisitioned and barely provisioned and some of them claimed that the rations had run out three days before arrival. The British troops, sympathetic and, in the way of soldiers quick to appreciate the problems of others, soon responded and in no time those sent to help in the disembarkation were cooking sausages and handing out hot drinks.

Arrangements had been made for the main body to be quartered near Tymbou in Camp 'X', the very name of which had already excited considerable curiosity. With the arrival of the main body, the docks quickly filled with French troops and vehicles and 'Tenez la gauche' signs were posted along the route from the docks to Camp 'X'. Apparently these meant little to the Foreign Légionnaires and 'Les Paras', accustomed as they were to driving on the right. Their huge Mercedes 'camions' were almost too big for Cyprus roads and were driven, often at breakneck speed, without any consideration for the convoy discipline which is inculcated into British service drivers. If a breakdown occurred the driver would set up his camp-bed by the side of the road, to doze and await the arrival of a 'depannage' truck. With E.O.K.A. terrorists active, this practice had definite security limitations. The drivers of camions which broke down were in the habit of leaving their rifles in the clips in the cab, so presenting unique opportunities to prowling Cypriots who were not particular from whom they got their weapons and ammunition. During the first few days, E.O.K.A. appeared to have a special interest in the new arrivals, since attempts were made to subvert them by the planting of leaflets, in French, calling on them to assist E.O.K.A. by not helping the British, by giving up their weapons, and praising their love of freedom. There is no reason to suppose that the Légionnaires took the slightest notice. Most of them were veterans of Indo-China and Algeria and had firm ideas on the subject of terrorist activities. On at least one occasion they showed themselves to be decidedly averse to delivering their weapons over to the Cypriots[1] and it soon became clear that they were apt to be trigger happy as well.

The number of women who had accompanied the French to Cyprus was noticed very quickly and this led to a number of rumours explaining their presence variously as nurses, secretaries, or camp followers.[2] The British troops were most intrigued.

With the establishment of good relations, there were parties and games, and despite the language barrier everybody got on well together, the French entering into the party spirit with gusto. The British, taking upon themselves the role of hosts, leaned over backwards to ensure that their French guests should have their share of the Island's amenities and often provided facilities which were not even available to themselves. But the French, who came to Cyprus to do a job of work, were stripped for battle. A visit to their headquarters was something of a revelation in itself. The Regimental Officers' Mess and Orderly Room were one and the same place: a big tent with a telephone exchange in one corner, a large map board in another, with the rest of the tent filled with numerous planning tables strewn with aerial photographs, chinagraph pencils and half-empty glasses. Amidst all this confusion the inevitable telephones, and the remote controls of radio links to the various units were dotted

[1] One story was reported of a Greek Cypriot youth attempting to abscond with a driver's pistol. The Frenchman gave chase, caught up with the thief and proceeded to box his ears.
[2] Following the assault on Port Said a British officer commented on the number of casualties that the French had seemed to expect, as evinced by the number of 'nurses' seen in Port Fuad. With a Gallic smirk a French Liaison Officer explained: 'They are not nurses, they are "ores".'

around. In the middle of the tent a large table holding vast tureens of steaming stew surrounded by loaves, bottles of wine, tin plates, mugs and an odd collection of cutlery provided the centre-piece of the operations centre. Meals would be taken as and when they could be fitted in and officers would go up to this table. There, they would take up any tin plate or any mug, whether used or not, and ladle out some stew, which they would eat and wash down liberally with wine, whilst continuing to talk volubly on the subject of the forthcoming operation. Plates then would be perfunctorily cleaned by wiping with the remains of the bread, before they returned to their duties; this performance went on throughout the day.

Only in one respect were the British superior; British rations were better than their French equivalents despite differences in taste. The same could not be said about weapons and equipment however, and those who are apt to assume that the motto 'British is best' invariably applies would have been surprised. The design of the French equipment showed considerable originality and there was nothing cheap or makeshift about any of it; even their surgical packs had been standardized, pre-sterilized and pre-packed for use in a single treatment and were ideally suited to the type of operation about to be launched. British medical officers struggling to collect and improvise their kit were justifiably envious.

According to General Keightley's despatch, the Royal Air Force was most easily prepared for action. Canberras, Valiants and Hunters flew to join the Venoms and Shackletons in Malta and Cyprus, carrying the bombs without which they would be unable to go to war. Their first task was to ensure that the Egyptian Air Force did not attack the seaborne convoys moving towards the Eastern Mediterranean and Malta, or interfere with the air transport routes to and from Malta; in addition, the airfields in Cyprus, crowded now as the expeditionary force built up, also had to be safeguarded from attack by Nasser's Soviet-built bombers.

As September passed and there was little progress towards a political settlement, General Keightley was warned that he might have to reckon on the operation being deferred until sometime during the winter months. With preparations almost at their zenith, this presented a further series of problems; neither men nor machines could be kept tied up indefinitely awaiting an operation which might never take place. Most of the reservists—some now serving in the Middle East—had been called up at short notice and would have to be sent on leave, the vehicle batteries and other equipment were deteriorating as they lay idle in the loaded ships, the ships themselves could not be kept hanging about for long. Yet the fact that nothing had happened produced a general impression that the political tension had actually lessened. With this relaxation came an easing in the tempo of training and quickening of the social life in places like Malta[1] whilst in the United Kingdom the newspapers began to campaign for an early release of the reservists.

For the sailors, soldiers and airmen who had been hurried out to the Middle East in particular, these days were not comfortable ones. Both in tiny Malta and on the uneasy soil of Cyprus the men were living in crowded barracks, hastily requisitioned buildings, or, more generally, tented camps. Conflicting reports on demobilization, leave, and welfare problems, complicated by the distance from the United Kingdom and the inevitable rumours, all tended to cause unrest first among the reservists and subsequently by contact with them, amongst the National Servicemen and regular soldiers of some of the units. In Cyprus, for example, the Port Squadrons of the Reservist Port Regiment were quartered under canvas in the Golden Sands leave camp at Varosha just outside Famagusta. Being deprived of their leave camp was itself sufficient to irritate all of the troops in Cyprus; the reservists by their behaviour soon dispelled any sympathetic feelings that others might have had for them and this quickly added fuel to the flames of resentment. With the passage of time, men became more and more frustrated, morale deteriorated, and the pessimists began to fear a long deadlock. As the negotiations dragged on, and the days of training passed one after another, with little in the morning and evening news to produce hope of an early solution, eyes turned towards the 25th December on calendars; at home, the Press were calling for a 'home by Christmas' move. Few could see that a call to action would lie not in the now intermittent negotiations, but with an entirely new set of circumstances reaching a crisis.

[1] In September the G.O.C. Malta issued a letter forbidding official entertainment on the grounds of the political situation. A fortnight later he issued another, couched in sterner tones, saying that his instructions were being flagrantly disregarded.

CHAPTER 3

The Egyptian Scene

In Egypt the Army is the most powerful of that country's three services and it is still the greatest stabilizing influence in the state. Twice a year, in January and July, it parades in Cairo's Republic Square to remind the populace that the existence of the present régime is a legacy of its actions in 1952. Though he rarely appears in uniform nowadays, President Nasser still retains his rank of *bimbashi* (Lieut.-Colonel) and derives his power from control of the Army; it was his able direction and propaganda that were largely responsible for re-equipping it and for the improvement in morale which took place during the years which followed the *coup d'état*.

In 1948 when the Egyptians had undertaken to smash the newly formed state of Israel they had had the utmost difficulty in mustering an expeditionary force capable of doing more than advance to an area where the Israelis were prepared to resist. Its equipment was in poor shape, the officers—mainly town-bred—had little stomach for desert campaigning, and the poorly educated fellaheen conscripts lacked initiative as well as any of the stubborn traits one normally associates with men of the land. Few of the officers had any confidence in their men, the troops had no faith in their leaders and the position was exacerbated by the lack of the middle-link of both reliable N.C.O's and trained technicians. Following a series of defeats, the Army was left smarting and Colonel Nasser, who had taken part in the campaign himself and appreciated the problems, resolved to inject a new spirit when once Farouk was out of the way. German instructors were brought to Egypt, the Army was reorganized; together with a propaganda campaign that attributed the cause of the defeats to the corruption of the deposed régime, every effort was made to develop a new '*esprit de corps*'. The cap badge was changed to a revolutionary eagle; pay and service conditions were improved, new equipment was ordered from Soviet bloc countries—since it was not possible to get arms from the West—and gradually the public image of the Egyptian Army began to change.

With a population of something like 20 millions, reputedly increasing at the rate of half a million a year, it might be supposed that there would be little problem in raising the strength, if not the standards of the troops. Yet despite an improved status the army found it difficult to expand. With no tradition of service, an inherent distrust of all soldiers coupled with a firm desire to stay at home, the fellaheen displayed considerable inertia to any ideas of gaining prestige and glory in Nasser's new model army. The distrust that existed between the fellah and his officers was traditional and even Nasser's methods were unable to imbue his troops with a new respect for the profession of arms quite so quickly. Socially and economically the officers came from a class which had exploited the peasants for generations and it is not easy to overcome an in-bred distrust of this nature. The truth of this was to be apparent in 1956; there were many instances of bravery in both Sinai and the environs of Port Said but the basic distrust was shown to be still there.

Before considering the organization and deployment of the army, something must be said of the other two services in the context of their role and worth at the time of the crisis. To the Anglo-French fleets the Egyptian Navy presented only a negligible hazard but, with the exception of Turkey, Egypt was regarded as having by far the strongest Air Force of all the Middle East countries. By October she had about 200 fighters and 70 bombers—a formidable force. The fighters included British-built Vampire and Meteor jets but the greatest menace derived from Soviet MIG-15s and a small number of the more modern MIG-17s which had recently flown in from Czecho-Slovakia. Of the bombers, two service squadrons, each of some twelve Ilyushin-28 light twin-jets were based at Cairo West airfield; more of these very modern aircraft were known to be at Inchas, another airfield in the Delta; still more were held in reserve at Luxor. Two squadrons of Halifax and Lancaster heavy bombers had also been bequeathed by the British. Besides the fighters and bombers, other aircraft included a squadron of Ilyushin-14 transports, about forty old DC2 and DC3 Dakotas and various odd training machines.

When the Canal was nationalized there was good reasons to suppose that only about half the available aircraft could be used operationally since it was known that the Egyptian air and ground crews for the Soviet MIG's and Ilyushins had not yet completed their training. By October the picture was not quite so rosy. The Egyptian training was being supervised by a large number of Russian technicians and so-called advisers and their role in the event of hostilities was not clear; they might well become volunteers, though in the event most of them retired to Khartoum during the period of the hostilities. Pilots for the British machines who had attended courses in England had not distinguished themselves during their training but it was always possible that the new *esprit de corps*, Soviet training methods and the new machines might produce pilots who were more capable than British experience suggested. If it came to an invasion there was always the possibility that the Egyptian Air Force would be able to assert a considerable measure of air superiority over the battlefield. For the sort of invasion that was being envisaged such a possibility could not be countenanced.

The Egyptian airfields were all well known; those in the Canal Zone itself had been Royal Air Force stations in the days of the British occupation and quite a number of the British pilots subsequently engaged on their neutralization had actually flown from some of them. Egyptian fighter and ground-attack squadrons whose role was to support the Egyptian Army, now occupied these airfields at Abu Sueir, Kabrit, Kasfareet and Fayid. These squadrons represented the bulk of the Egyptian fighter strength since most of the Egyptian Army lay across the Canal in Sinai, deployed then—as now —to face Israel. Forward landing strips in Sinai promised quick reaction to any move by the Israeli Air Force and the powerful build-up of Soviet planes was intended to ensure complete and absolute air superiority over the Israeli front. Clearly this concentration which looked east towards Israel could operate just as well against an enemy approaching from the north, whilst Cyprus was well within the range of the bombers.

Egypt's Navy was small. It possessed no vessel larger than a destroyer and of the four of these that she did have, two—the *Al Qaher* and the *Al Fatteh*—were both in Britain undergoing a refit when the crisis broke in July.[1] Of the other vessels, which included six frigates,

---

[1] The sale of these two former R.N. 'Z' Class destroyers, of 1,700 tons each, had only recently been completed. On the 30th July, when the Prime Minister announced a British ban on the supply of war material to Egypt, the *Al Qaher* was at Portsmouth preparing to sail, and the *Al Fatteh* was undergoing trials at Thorneycroft's yard in Southampton. Asked about the

a corvette, a number of minesweepers and about thirty motor torpedo boats, only the MTB's seemed likely to constitute a real threat to an invasion convoy. Of these a mere dozen which had been received recently from Russia together with another six to twelve received from Yugoslavia were likely to be in good condition; three of British origin and nine vintage Italian vessels were known to be in no fit condition for war. Egypt possessed no seagoing submarines of her own and were it not for the fact that the Russians were believed to have arranged to make up this deficiency, a submarine threat could have been dismissed.[1] However, in the vicinity of either Port Said or Alexandria there was a distinct possibility that midget submarines and, more probably, frogmen could operate against an invasion fleet; even if the ports surrendered, guerrilla frogmen might still continue their activities. (On this account there were constant alarms and excursions during the occupation of Port Said.) The existence of the minesweepers and a variety of small vessels also suggested that the path of an expedition might well be strewn with mines and the possibility of the destroyers acting as pillboxes if and when they were hemmed into their home ports would also have to be considered.

The morale of the Egyptian navy always seemed to be better than that of the Army. A nucleus of its officers and men had undergone considerable training in Britain and undoubtedly some of the service traditions of the Royal Navy had rubbed off on to the Egyptians; certainly the alacrity with which they had been able to take over and make operational the ships which they had bought from Britain suggested that their training had not been ineffectual. Of the rest: those who manned the 'Skori' class destroyers, T43 ocean-going minesweepers and Soviet MTB's had also undergone intensive training at naval establishments in Poland and Russia and by comparison with the training given by Soviet instructors to army tank crews, the naval training seemed to have been much more efficient. The Egyptian Navy did not represent the menace of the Egyptian Air Force but it could not be dismissed altogether.

To return now to Egypt's regular army, the total mobilized strength

future of these two ships Sir Anthony Eden assured the House that 'The Royal Navy will look after them.' In fact, both ships sailed for Alexandria in late August, but without ammunition or torpedoes.

[1] Two submarines flying the Polish flag, manned by Soviet bloc personnel and carrying Egyptian officers, were said to have sailed from Gdynia during July.

of which was about 100,000. Deployed in four main areas, three centring on Alexandria, Ismailia and Cairo, the biggest force was in Sinai. The deployment was intended to guard against an invasion from Libya, to oppose a sea landing on the coast near Alexandria, to protect the Suez Canal, to defend Egypt from an invasion by Israel or conversely in preparation for an invasion of Israel, and finally to provide a mobile reserve based on Cairo. Of all these roles, those concerned with Israel had priority; only the Anglo-French pronouncements and warlike preparations induced a prudent withdrawal of some of the Sinai army to west of the Canal. Nasser himself could not bring himself to believe that the Allies had any serious military intentions, but the news of the concentration of the 16th Parachute Brigade in Cyprus did suggest the possibility of an airborne invasion. Between the beginning of August and the end of October there was a good deal of movement into and out of Sinai as units were shuffled about. Other precautionary measures in Egypt itself led to the setting up of road blocks and guards being mounted on bridges, crossroads, railway stations and public buildings.

At this time, the regular Army totalled eighteen brigades: ten infantry, one medium machine-gun, three armoured—one of which was a training cadre—a coastal defence brigade and three anti-aircraft brigades. Their basic organizations followed the British pattern and the infantry brigades usually consisted of three battalions, each of four rifle companies with a headquarters and support company, the latter having machine-gun, anti-tank mortar, and carrier platoons together with a flame thrower section mounted in three British 'Wasp' carriers. Seven recruit training battalions, allotted one to each of seven of the infantry brigades, were responsible for the training of recruits for their affiliated brigade; in theory this produced a four battalion brigade in times of war. Artillery support was provided by a battery of either British 25-pounders or Soviet 122 mm. guns attached to each of the infantry brigades and an anti-tank company equipped with 17-pounder or 57 mm. guns, or an anti-tank squadron of 'Archers', was also attached. Other artillery support was provided by independent field regiments armed with Soviet self-propelled SU100 guns, or medium regiments equipped with Soviet 152 mm. guns. Four heavy mortar regiments each equipped with three batteries of 120 mm. mortars were also deployed in the operational areas of Sinai and the Canal Zone.

Three so-called armoured 'brigades' each provided three battle groups from a single armoured regiment of three fighting squadrons, the armoured squadrons combining with three squadrons of mechanized infantry carried in Ford Power wagons, Valentine armoured personnel carriers or Soviet BTR 152 Scout cars—each of which could take up to twelve men. The regiments were variously equipped with Shermans, Soviet T34's, Centurion Mk. 3's, or Soviet JS3 tanks but those regiments that had Shermans were busily converting and re-equipping with Russian tanks. The single machine-gun brigade did not function as an entity, its purpose being to provide detachments for the remainder of the field army. The anti-aircraft brigades were deployed similarly; equipped mostly with 30 mm. Hispano Suiza and 40 mm. Bofors light A.A. guns, they were sited in areas considered to be vulnerable to air attack; some of them, especially those located on the mole at Port Said and at the entrance to the Canal, were to prove particularly troublesome in the days to come. The A.A. gunners themselves were probably the best of the Egyptian troops; certainly none of the British troops who knew anything about the Egyptian Army had much regard for their infantry. During the Second World War the A.A. gunners had been trained by British methods on British guns and had proved apt pupils. Afterwards this branch of the army managed to remain efficient and retain a high state of morale even through the period of the Palestine war; they were to fight well during the first two phases of 'Musketeer', though, mercifully, they did little damage.

To back up the regular army in times of war a number of semi-military bodies also existed; of these, the National Guard[2] was the most important. Comparable with the Territorial Army in Britain and wearing the same khaki-drill battledress as the Egyptian Regular Army, the National Guard was a volunteer part-time organization which had only been raised since the War of Independence. Its volunteers, totalling perhaps 100,000 and equating therefore to the size of the regular army, attended for instruction only in their spare time. Training—necessarily sketchy because of its spare-time nature—was on a platoon or section basis which made the National Guard reasonably well suited to a role of guerrilla and underground activities; arms and equipment were of British pattern, the rifles being early models of the Lee Enfield ·303, whereas the regular army had modern 7·62 mm. Soviet weapons. When they were partially mobilized in late

---

[2] This should not be confused with the National Liberation Army—a volunteer organization on the lines of the Home Guard.

July some of the National Guard units were sent to Sinai to get active service experience with the field army and expand their platoon and section training. This experience was sufficient to convince most of the volunteers that army life was not for them and many, who were serving away from their home stations, deserted when hostilities started.

The Frontier Corps and the Police both deserve a mention—one being a military unit and the other falling into the para-military category. The small 3,000 strong Frontier Force had its origins in the old British-officered Camel Corps and was considered to be the Egyptian Army's *corps d'élite*. Its troops wore a distinctive uniform comprising a shirt-type garment which reached to the knees, khaki shorts, and a khaki turban. Some of them, in the remote areas of Sinai, still worked with camels, but the majority were trained to operate in jeeps and half tracks on reconnaissance missions and as such functioned as the eyes and ears of the Sinai army. The Egyptian police force, despite the connotation of its title, was a body deserving of almost as much military consideration as the Egyptian Army. Smart, disciplined, well trained and armed, they had already shown during the last days of the British occupation of the Canal Zone that they were capable of becoming brave and formidable opponents of those with whom they were not prepared to co-operate. It was known that the majority was wholly loyal in their support of Nasser's régime and to 'combat parachutist attacks' they received special training which started in August.

What would be the reactions of the police, troops and even the general populace to an invasion of Egypt was not altogether easy to gauge. Depending on their loyalty and on the leadership of individual officers it seemed probable that the behaviour of policemen and soldiers would vary; some, undoubtedly, would be prepared to fight on 'underground'. King Farouk's deposal had been engineered by a 'Free Officers' movement composed of reliable soldiers backed up by fanatical civilians, well equipped with arms and ammunition; these men had considerable influence still and would certainly oppose an occupation force. In such a situation, also, the communist organizations could also be expected to be used as underground rallying points even though they had been supposedly suppressed. A good many 'thugs' who would be anxious to seize whatever advantage offered could also be expected to join in. So far as ordinary people were concerned, it seemed likely that poor Egyptians would be much too worried about their day-to-day existence to be concerned about resisting occupation when once it was a fact; if they did anything it would be to steal, though mainly for their own needs. On the other hand a good deal of trouble could be expected from the youth and student element which stemmed from the Egyptian middle classes. These individuals were usually the backbone of any mob; in the Middle East a mob is easily excited and in Egypt its mere existence usually spells trouble. The outlook was somewhat depressing though not impossible. If an invasion was to be undertaken, everything really seemed to depend on a quick operation which would destroy the chances of the formation of a coherent underground movement until the occupation was a *fait accompli*.

As the crisis dragged on, Nasser's own attitude as well as that of most Egyptians towards the foreign members of the Egyptian community remained correct and tolerant. Until the end of October, the lives of foreign residents continued almost normally. Most Egyptians shared Nasser's views regarding Anglo-French military action being only a remote possibility and in the big towns, where they were accustomed to living cheek by jowl with foreigners—Greeks, French, British and the like—there was little general antipathy although the secret police are said to have been more than usually active. No one cared to forecast with any certainty what the attitude would be if an invasion did take place but it was suspected tolerance might well be replaced by something much more ugly. In the early stages it was quite likely that Egyptian mobs would terrorize the wretched expatriates and anyone who co-operated with the compatriots of the occupying powers would certainly risk both their future in Egypt and the possibility of victimization of themselves and their families afterwards. This was a problem because there would be little opportunity to help or safeguard any of the people who would claim British or French nationality in the early stages of a landing; all that could be done would be to try not to antagonize them by an apparent disregard forced on the invaders by their need to get on with their real job of invading. Most of the Egyptian civilians were of the Moslem faith with all the Moslem susceptibilities and they too would not have to be antagonized. Unnecessary trouble could easily be aroused unless scrupulous care were taken to observe religious customs; any false move could certainly be expected to be aided and abetted by the prospective underground terrorist organizations.

'El Rayis' was well aware of all this. He knew that if the British and

French took the decision to invade Egypt there was little chance of stopping them by conventional means; his only hope lay in guerrilla tactics. In consequence he lost no time in getting ready for a battle of this nature. Following Sir Anthony Eden's broadcast denouncing him as 'a plunderer, whose appetite grows with feeding' the formation of the 'Home National Liberation Army' under the command of the Minister of Education was announced. At training centres in the towns and villages, rifles were issued, training started and symbolic targets depicting Imperialism, Israel, Britain and France, were set up for shooting practice.

Meanwhile Nasser was prepared to show the West that he had no intention of giving up the Canal. Timed to synchronize with the opening of the London Conference, which was to discuss its future, the Egyptian Government called a national strike for 16th August. A five-minute silence of mourning when all traffic came to a halt was observed during the day; public utilities were unaffected but shops, banks and cafés remained closed. Two days previously the new Egyptian authority had reduced the daily number of convoys in the Canal from four to three supposedly because of shortage of pilots caused by some of those who were on leave in Europe 'not having returned to duty', but no attempt was made to interfere with the shipping during the day of the strike.

As tension mounted, Egyptian counter-espionage agencies also went into action. On 28th August, Colonel Hatan, the head of the Information Office, announced that two British nationals—James Swinburn, the secretary of the British-owned Arab News Agency, and Charles Pittuck, the assistant manager of the Marconi Telegraph Company of Egypt—had been arrested in connection with a spy ring; announcements of arrests of two other British nationals—James Zarb, a Maltese businessman, and John Thornton Stanley, the Cairo manager of the Prudential Assurance Company—on similar charges, followed. (The accused were eventually tried in May 1957, Zarb being sentenced to ten—and Swinburn to five—years' imprisonment.)[1] Prior to this, several Western newspaper correspondents and a couple of oil officials had been expelled, Sefton Delmer of the *Daily Express* being the first to go.

[1] Swinburn was released under an amnesty signed by President Nasser in September 1959, Zarb in February 1961 on a similar amnesty; Zarb's release followed the resumption of diplomatic relations between Britain and the United Arab Republic.

As August gave way to September, the tension seemed to relax a little. The five members of the Suez Council Committee set up by the London Conference and led by Mr. Menzies, the Prime Minister of Australia, visited Cairo for a series of meetings with Colonel Nasser and it was hoped that he would be persuaded to see reason. It was not to be; although the discussions were reported to be conducted in an atmosphere of courtesy they ended in complete deadlock and after the committee had departed, Cairo Radio turned the full fury of its propaganda machine on to its chairman: 'Menzies . . . spoke as an Australian mule . . . he trampled on all the principles in which we live in the twentieth century' the spokesman declared. 'With the Egyptianization of the Canal . . . which is our right . . . the policy of the Egyptian Government remains the same: freedom of passage through the Canal without discrimination, its development, and the establishment of just and equitable dues.' The refusal to negotiate with the committee now led to Britain and France applying a new sanction. From its Paris headquarters, the original Suez Canal Company announced that its 500 non-Egyptian employees in the Canal Zone would cease work; this measure was expected to create a situation whereby navigation of the Canal would be virtually impossible. Nasser's reaction was surprising; no effort was made to prevent those who wished to leave from going; just the reverse; exit visas were granted and everything was done to facilitate their departure. Nevertheless everyone, including Nasser, expected that this would have a serious effect on the working of the Canal and despite an extensive advertisement campaign, together with the speedy arrival of fifteen Russian pilots, obtained through the offices of M. Tchikov the Soviet Consul, the Canal pilots were reduced to about half their former strength. Those remaining were now ordered to work twelve hours a day instead of the normal six; somehow convoys continued to traverse the Canal.

Throughout September and October the crisis continued to move towards its explosive climax. In the middle of October the capture of the motor yacht *Athos*,[1] carrying a large cargo of Egyptian arms, was seized by units of the French navy off the Algerian coast and further provoked French ire. Following two similar cases of arms running to the Algerian rebels which had occurred in June, this was more than sufficient to convince them that their Algerian problems as well as the

---

[1] The Sudanese owner was sentenced by a military court at Oran to ten years' imprisonment—later reduced to three years—in January 1957.

question of who owned the Suez Canal could best be resolved in Egypt. In a broadcast by M. Mollet, Nasser was labelled an 'apprentice dictator' whilst a vituperous verbal duel had already started up between Cairo Radio and the Anglo-French radio stations broadcasting to the Middle East. To add further fuel to the flames, a number of incidents occurred on the Israeli-Jordanian frontier which provoked two retaliation raids into Jordan.

On Sunday the 28th October the climax came. Israel's Mr. Ben-Gurion stressing the Jordanian situation, announced mobilization; at tea-time the following day, without any offensive gesture against Jordan, Israel attacked Egypt.

CHAPTER 4

Israel—Operation 'Kadesh'

I n a speech to the Knesset on the 5th March 1957, Israel's Prime Minister Mr. Ben-Gurion, said that his country's decision to act against Egypt was 'a condition for our very survival, an action in self-defence', which had successfully brought the facts of Arab hostility towards Israel before world opinion. This was true; a decade of Arab hostility and upheaval had led inexorably to the Israelis decision to force a show-down and the roots of the trouble went back to 1947. Then, in view of the imminent end of the British mandate over Palestine, the United Nations had tried to partition the mandated area between the Arabs and Jews, but as soon as British troops evacuated Palestine in the May of the following year, the armies of Egypt, Syria, Iraq and Jordan attacked the new state of Israel. Within six months, however, to the fury of the Arab states, Israel had beaten them in their own so-called 'War of Independence' and had enlarged the territory originally allotted to her. Although an armistice had been arranged, it was quite obvious that this was not the end of the business as the Arab Governments openly declared that they would not rest until Israel had been wiped out. Constant Arab–Israeli border clashes followed and Egypt began to develop the Gaza Strip as a base for guerrilla raids by detachments of 'Fedayeen'[1] commandos; as

---

[1] 'Fedayeen' means self-sacrifice. The men were recruited mainly from Palestine Arabs, many of whom were pathetically eager for a job which would pay well enough to take them out of their refugee existence, as well as to express their hatred of the Jews; recruitment was undertaken by special units of the Egyptian Army Intelligence Corps. A successful raid was rewarded by a cash bonus as well as military honours; success was often rated by the production of 'trophies' such as an ear or finger. Their bases were located in the Gaza Strip and just across the Jordanian frontier. Mr. Ben-Gurion claimed that there were more than 3,000 raids in the seven years between 1949 and the end of 1956.

69

time passed these raids steadily increased in scope and intensity. Other hostile measures included the exclusion of Israel shipping from the Gulf of Aqaba by the threat of Egyptian guns at the mouth of the Gulf and the barring of the Canal even to non-Israeli ships which carried cargoes to Israel. Instructions to Egypt by the United Nations to end the Suez blockade were stonily rejected.

In the middle of 1954, Britain had agreed to evacuate the Canal Zone and as the troops left trouble broke out behind them as it had done before in Palestine. Fedayeen activities against Israel were stepped up and, as her frontiers were virtually indefensible against such activities, her only solution lay in reprisal raids after the pattern of the British operations on the North West Frontier of India in the days of the Raj. The first sizeable raid of this type which was mounted against Gaza in February 1955 resulted in thirty-eight Arabs being killed; as a result Colonel Nasser decided that he must have more arms. Following a United States refusal to upset the Arab–Israeli balance of strength he turned to Russia and on 27th September 1955 announced to the world that he had concluded an arms deal with the Soviet bloc. The implications of open hostilities were obvious and Israel now began to watch the deliveries of Soviet weapons to their self-professed enemies with growing anxiety. After her appeal to the United States for supplies of modern weapons to counter the threat had been rejected for the same reasons as had been given to Egypt, Israel turned to France who agreed to supply aircraft and tanks to correct the military balance. 'At last', said Mr. Ben-Gurion, 'Israel has found a true ally.'[1]

Britain's position in this situation was complicated by her arrangements with Jordan and Iraq. Iraq was an important member of the Baghdad Pact through which Britain had hoped to maintain Arab friendship and win support for the West; Jordan, despite her increasing leaning towards Egypt, was still dependent on British subsidies. When in October it was feared that Jordan's forthcoming elections would result in a pro-Nasser Government getting into power and there was talk of Iraqi troops entering Jordan to help maintain

---

[1] The question of who supplied arms first, the Iron Curtain countries or France, is not relevant to this account. The arguments are fully discussed by Mr. Erskine B. Childers in his book *The Road to Suez*, and in an article in the *Spectator* dated 30th October 1959. Whether or not the 'collusion' between the French and Israelis that is alluded to stems from these negotiations is also not relevant.

70

law and order, Israel let it be known in no uncertain fashion that if Iraqi troops did move into Jordan she would regard it as an act of war and respond accordingly. Britain, linked to Jordan by a Treaty under which she was obliged to go to Jordan's assistance if that country were attacked, interpreted the aggressive terms of Israel's announcements as an indication that Jordan would be the first objective if war broke out. Consequently, Israel was also told in the most explicit terms that Britain would have no option but to go to Jordan's aid if she were attacked. With planning and preparations for a show-down with Egypt going on at the same time, this posed a ludicrous situation; British troops might well be supporting Jordan against an Israeli army helped by the French. The French could hardly believe it.

Fortunately the situation quickly resolved itself. Almost at the eleventh hour Iraq decided that the conditions which Jordan's King Hussein wished to impose on their troops entering his country were unacceptable, and the Jordani elections were conducted without their presence. The result was practically a foregone conclusion; pro-Egyptian candidates carried the poll and Jordan's new Government largely consisted of a party which was committed to pro-Egyptian anti-Western policies, including a more belligerent attitude towards Israel and union with Egypt and Syria. The very day that the election results were announced—23rd October—General Amer, the Egyptian Commander-in-Chief, arrived in Jordan's capital to exploit the success of the pro-Egyptian Jordanians and the next day a military pact between Egypt, Jordan and Syria was proclaimed; a unified command—an 'Arab Entente Militaire'—with General Amer as Commander-in-Chief, was to be established immediately. Jordan had thrown in her lot with Egypt; when they were ready it seemed that three Arab armies would march against Israel under a combined Egyptian command.

To Israel this was the final straw; no immediate aggression might be contemplated but it was only a matter of time before Egypt would strike. If any advantage was to be gained from the Anglo-French rumblings over the Suez Canal, now was the time to undertake the preventive war that members of the Israeli Government Opposition and indeed some of Mr. Ben-Gurion's Government, had been advocating ever since the announcement of Nasser's arms deal. Anglo-French preparations for an operation of sorts against Egypt obviously were nearing perfection and little military genius was needed to deduce the form which such an operation would take. An Israeli appreciation of the situation concluded that an Anglo-French plan would be to occupy the Canal Zone, splitting Egypt's forces and so cutting communications and isolating her Sinai army. As Nasser had already withdrawn a considerable number of units from Sinai for the defence of the Canal and to supplement the mobile reserve which would operate only on orders from Cairo, Sinai probably now had little more than 30,000 troops to garrison it. The odds would never be better; now was the time to act.

The mobilization order in the early hours of Friday the 26th was conducted with the maximum secrecy that such an event can allow. Israel's standing army is relatively small and relies on conscription, the 11,000 strong regular cadre normally being supplemented by about 40,000 conscripts, who serve for two and a half years before being relegated to the reserve. Her population totals about 1,800,000 however, and in an all-out mobilization it is estimated that in about forty-eight hours the standing army can be expanded to about 250,000 (men and women, since women are also conscripted); on this occasion, probably about 100,000 reservists were called up, so producing a total of about 150,000 men and women under arms. The standing army normally provided a field force of sixteen brigade groups, some of which were considered as 'armoured' formations; the role of the reservists was to bring these brigades up to war establishment, strengthen the line of frontier posts and fortified settlements which are Israel's first line of defence, and form additional brigades. Altogether, it is thought that between fourteen and twenty extra brigades were mobilized. The call-up followed lines which had been well rehearsed. There was no general proclamation but key personnel were summoned by telephone and telegram; the remainder being notified by word of mouth. On the Friday morning, key men were rapping on the doors of those for whom they were responsible; cars were stopped at street corners and their owners given cards which directed them to assembly points; the cars were parked, the men quietly collected their kit and reported for duty. In less than twelve hours, twelve brigades were ready for action and on Israel's airfields fighter aircraft were standing ready. Some of these aircraft were old U.S. piston-engined P.51 Mustangs but the majority were Meteors and French Mystères —considerably more of the latter than the single squadron that France was supposed to have delivered. Even so, numerically, Israel's Air Force was greatly inferior to that of Egypt but the Israelis were better trained, and their pilots were of better quality and knew their machines better than the Egyptians.

The operation which was now launched was called 'Kadesh'—a biblical reference of thanksgiving and prayer deriving from the wanderings of the children of Israel in the Sinai desert. It started with a feint towards Jordan. On the Friday night Colonel Ariel Sharon's airborne brigade, less one battalion, ostentatiously trundled north, away from the Sinai border towards Ein Quesib in the north-east corner of the Negev; at the same time a curfew was imposed on the frontier region bordering Jordan.[1] Like the rest of the operation, the feint worked well and right until four days later when the operation began in earnest the Egyptian High Command appears to have assumed that the threat was directed towards Jordan. In any case Sinai could be assumed to offer little prospect for a successful campaign. Not only were the Egyptians confident that their defences were strong enough to withstand any attack, the country itself was thought to present the biggest obstacle to any sustained offensive. Known as the 'landbridge' between Africa and Asia, Sinai is 24,000 square miles of rugged nothingness. Flanked on the north by the Mediterranean, in the south by the Red Sea, the Canal and Gulf of Suez in the west, and the Gulf of Aqaba to the east, it is mostly barren desert which is virtually economically valueless and almost uninhabited. In the north the wandering Bedouin who are compelled to live there follow the strict code of desert hospitality, which allows the throats of any strangers not under their direct protection to be cut without compunction. Southern Sinai where the rolling seas of sand give way to a more mountainous form of desert is rich in the relics of ancient civilizations but the country is no less forbidding. Communications are poor; there are only two main roads and a railway line running east to west, although over most parts it is feasible for vehicles to move across country and for light aircraft to land on flat stretches of sand. The northern route from Egypt into Sinai is a vehicle track which runs alongside the railway from Qantara on the Canal, to El Arish, connecting there with a metalled road which continues on to Gaza. In the centre the main road between Ismailia and Abu Aweigila

---

[1] There was an unfortunate incident at the little village of Kafr Kassim at the start of the curfew. Arab villagers returning to their homes from working in nearby Tel Aviv, were unaware of the sudden imposition of a curfew and were shot down by the border police. News of the massacre was withheld during the period of Operation 'Kadesh'.

is the best route; its first-class classification may be adduced to its being a relic of British administration. Finally, there is a southern route from Suez to Aqaba. This, which is often referred to as the 'Pilgrims' Way, passes through a number of narrow rocky defiles, of which the Mitla Pass is the most important; the state of going on this route is not so good.

Since the War of Independence the Egyptians had maintained and developed the roads from Egypt into Sinai in order to make the area of eastern Sinai ready to serve as their openly declared 'invasion springboard'. And, as has already been mentioned, there were about 30,000 Egyptian troops in Sinai at the end of October. Force head-quarters were in Ismailia; the 8th Infantry Division occupied the Gaza Strip and the 3rd Infantry Division, of three infantry brigades and one armoured battalion, was deployed between defences in the Rafa, El Arish, Jebel Libni, Abu Aweigila and Kuseima areas. Two battalions of the Desert Frontier Force guarded the southern route and two infantry battalions with various ancillary units known as the Red Sea Force, were stationed near Sharm-El-Sheikh, whose coast defences controlled entry to the Gulf of Aqaba. A single battalion only was responsible for the road from Kuntilla to Mitla and this was split between El Thamed and El Nakhl with but one company at the vital pass. In the Canal Zone, immediate Egyptian reserves comprised the 2nd Infantry Division and an armoured brigade; behind them lay the 1st Infantry Division and the 4th Armoured Division near Cairo. Of the troops actually deployed in Sinai the 3rd Infantry Division was probably the best formation. Its rank and file were conscripts but its officers were regulars and it was organized on British lines. Compared with the 3rd Division, the 8th, which had a National Guard brigade in and around Gaza itself, a Palestinian brigade at Khan Yunis and a reserve brigade in the southern part of the Gaza Strip, subsequently showed that it had much less fire in its belly, despite the fact that its volunteer National Guardsmen were said to have a fanatical fervour and its locally recruited Palestinians might have been expected to exhibit a particularly bitter hatred of the Israelis.

On Sunday, 28th October, Israel's mobilization could no longer be considered secret and the whole country was anxiously waiting for something to happen. In fact, a striking force had formed up in the Negev by this time: vehicles of one of the armoured brigades at Elat on the extreme southern tip of the Israeli border being plainly visible to men of the 10th Hussars in the British base at Aqaba just across the Jordan border. Next day was 'D' day and at about 1600 hours, with an hour and a half to go before darkness fell, the advance guard of Sharon's brigade crossed the frontier into Sinai at Suweilma; an hour later his parachute battalion was dropped about fifteen miles east of the Mitla Pass. The first phase of Operation 'Kadesh' and of the Suez War had begun.

'Kadesh' had been planned to permit the Israeli Government to pause after the opening phase—to enable them to review its scope, and, if necessary, to adjust it. The hope was that some tangible success, which would boost the morale of the Israeli nation and cause the Arabs to reconsider their aims, would result; one suitable prize in this category would be the capture of the Gaza Strip since this would liquidate the main fedayeen base; another would be the capture of Sharm-El-Sheikh as this would enable the Gulf of Aqaba to be opened to Israel's shipping. For real success and an absolute victory the defeat and routing of the Egyptian Army in Sinai was necessary. If, during the operation, the Egyptian Army proved more formidable than had been anticipated, however, or the Great Powers intervened, it might be preferable to call it off and its first phase could then be held to have constituted a reprisal raid. With this background a plan was devised in which a four-phase operation using three main axes of advance was envisaged. In the first phase a parachute battalion would be dropped in the Mitla area; this would be quickly reinforced by an armoured brigade advancing up the Kuntilla road. At the same time another force would cross the frontier and capture the road junction at Kuseima;[1] from Kuseima this force then had a choice of two roads by which, if the worst came to the worst, it could go to the assistance of the parachutists at Mitla. The second phase was the pause; before twenty-four hours had elapsed a decision would be taken as to whether to continue with the two remaining phases or withdraw. Then, if the operation was to become a full-scale campaign, the next phase would be a thrust southward from Elat down the Gulf of Aqaba to capture Sharm-El-Sheikh, whilst the forces from Mitla, advancing along the Gulf of Suez road would converge on the same area. At the same time the force which had taken Kuseima would attack the Abu Aweigila complex of defences where another fresh task force would link up with them after it had captured Rafa.

[1] In the event this column moved up the desert road from Kuntilla and attacked Kuseima from the south.

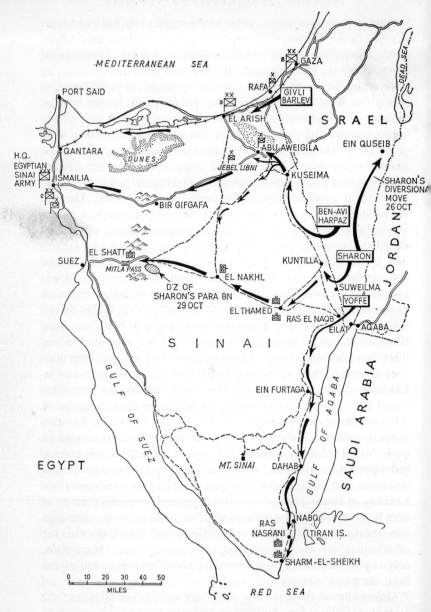

MEDITERRANEAN SEA

PORT SAID

QANTARA

H.Q.
EGYPTIAN
SINAI ARMY

ISMAILIA

2

BIR GIGAFA

SUEZ

EL SHATT

MITLA PASS

EGYPT

GULF OF SUEZ

MT. SINAI

RED SEA

GAZA

8

RAFA

GIVLI
BARLEV

EL ARISH

3

ABU AWEIGILA

JEBEL LIBNI

KUSEIMA

ISRAEL

EIN QUSEIB

DEAD SEA

SHARON'S
DIVERSIONAL
MOVE
26 OCT

BEN-AVI
HARPAZ

KUNTILLA

SHARON

EL NAKHL

DUNES

DZ OF
SHARON'S PARA BN
29 OCT

EL THAMED

RAS EL NAQB

SUWEILMA

YOFFE

JORDAN

SINAI

EIN FURTAGA

EILAT

AQABA

GULF OF AQABA

SAUDI ARABIA

DAHAB

NABQ

RAS
NASRANI

TIRAN IS.

SHARM-EL-SHEIKH

0 10 20 30 40 50
MILES

Operation 'Kadesh'

76

Finally, in the fourth phase, when Abu Aweigila and Rafa had been secured, the key Egyptian defence point at El Arish would be captured. This would seal off the Gaza Strip and make it possible to exploit down the Qantara road, to the Canal.

Returning to the first phase: Sharon's column reached their first objective at Kuntilla about an hour after crossing the border and the garrison of a single infantry platoon was overrun after only about twenty minutes' fighting. Continuing the advance, the column then swept on to Thamed. Here the Egyptians had two companies of infantry in defences on the fortified cliffs overlooking the village, together with a platoon in the village itself. They did not hold out for long; and at a cost of three Israeli dead and six wounded, Thamed was captured shortly after dawn on the 30th. The column now halted to await a re-supply by air of petrol and ammunition and whilst they waited the wounded were evacuated in a Piper Cub which landed close by the village. During this interval, six Egyptian MIG's flew in to strafe and bomb Sharon's men and caused a number of casualties; a similar attack took place about three hours later when four Egyptian Vampires flew in at ground-level and again inflicted casualties on the resting column. By now a message from the parachute battalion fifteen miles east of Mitla in the area of Parker's Memorial to the effect that they were being shelled and also had suffered casualties from air strikes, made it essential that Sharon should press on and he decided to move without any further delay; his decision was reinforced by a Piper Cub reconnaissance which reported an Egyptian column seen to be advancing towards Mitla from Suez. By 1630 hours the advance guard of his force was within small-arms range of the El Nakhl defences. Here, the rest of the Egyptian battalion which had defended Kuntilla and Thamed were expected to put up a spirited resistance. Surprisingly, after only a brief artillery bombardment from a battery of Israeli 25-pounders, the Egyptians evacuated their positions however, leaving Nakhl with all of its wealth of stores, ammunition and food, to Sharon. By nightfall he had linked up with the parachutists and the following day after a stiff battle, Mitla Pass, only twelve miles from Suez, was occupied. The first round of the Sinai campaign was over.

Meanwhile, at dawn on the same day (30th) two brigades, one armoured (Colonel Ben-Avi) and one infantry (Colonel Harpaz), had moved in past Kuntilla and drawn blood at the defences of Kuseima. After less than an hour's fighting, Kuseima fell to Harpaz's infantry

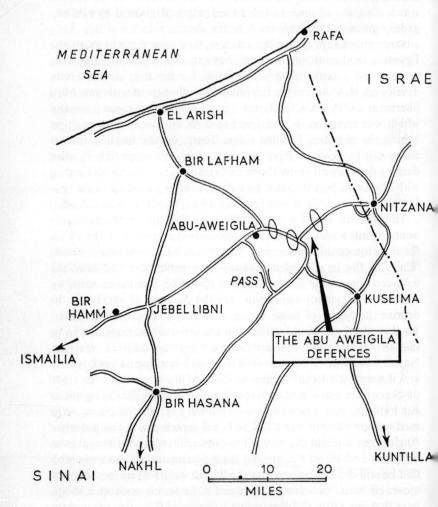

MEDITERRANEAN
SEA

RAFA

ISRAE

EL ARISH

BIR LAFHAM

ABU-AWEIGILA

NITZANA

PASS

KUSEIMA

BIR
HAMM

JEBEL LIBNI

THE ABU AWEIGILA
DEFENCES

ISMAILIA

BIR HASANA

SINAI

NAKHL

KUNTILLA

0   10   20

MILES

The Abu Aweigila Defences

and Ben-Avi's tanks took the lead in the advance on Abu Aweigila, the key position of the Egyptians' Sinai defence system—a complex which consisted of three fortified sand ridges garrisoned by two brigades, one armoured and one infantry. As the vehicles of Ben-Avi's advance guard approached the defences, they fanned out to locate the Egyptian flanks; at this moment they ran into a force of Egyptian armour and a tank battle which lasted for the next sixteen hours developed. However, as the Egyptian T34's shot it out with Ben-Avi's Shermans and AMX's, the Israeli brigades' reconnaissance company which was mounted in jeeps, managed to slip round to a position behind the rearmost fortified ridge. There, on the Ismailia road it effectively blocked all Egyptian rear communications. Then, after dark, a detachment from Harpaz's brigade succeeded in linking up with Sharon at Nakhl so that by dawn on the Wednesday morning— D plus 2—the whole of southern Sinai had, in effect, been cut off.

This was the time for the Israeli pause and their first official announcements were couched in the planned cautionary terms by which the invasion could, if necessary, be interpreted as a retaliatory raid. 'Units of the Israeli defence forces have penetrated and attacked fedayeen commando bases. . . . This operation was necessitated by continuous Egyptian aggression . . . the purpose of which was to deprive the people of Israel of the possibility of peaceful existence.' To this, the Egyptians replied with an airy communiqué implying that all was well: 'We have annihilated the invasion forces'; Colonel Nasser was aware of the success of the Israeli opening moves however and it seems somewhat surprising that Egyptian reactions were not quicker off the mark. Not until the Tuesday morning did the Egyptian Air Force go into action; then only a limited number of planes were used and no attempt was made to bomb Israeli cities. The potential Anglo-French threat can hardly have been the reason for keeping the Egyptian aircraft on the ground since Nasser himself had declared that he still did not believe that the British would make any military move. His miscalculation on this score was to come as another shock later that day (30th October) when he received the cable telling him of the joint British–French ultimatum requiring both Egypt and Israel to stop all military operations and withdraw to lines ten miles from the Canal. When, eventually the Egyptian Air Force did go into action it was not particularly successful; in dog fights over Sinai the Israelis claim to have shot down four MIG's and three Vampires for the loss of only two Mustangs.

Meanwhile, at sea, Nasser's Navy had attempted to show its worth. The destroyer *Ibrahim el Awal*[1] made a single attempt to shell Haifa, although most of her 160 shots fell well short of the target as she opened fire beyond the maximum range of her guns. Chased by an Israeli destroyer of the same vintage as herself and attacked by rocket-firing aircraft the crew attempted to scuttle her after their ship had received several direct hits. Their efforts were abortive as they were unable to find keys to fit many of the seacocks and it was not long before a white flag was run up. An Israeli boarding party quickly went to work on the pumps and by keeping them at full pressure were able to tow the *Ibrahim* into Haifa harbour. There, she was proudly exhibited as war booty.

To return to the land battles. At first light on the morning of the 31st, Colonel Yoffe's 9th Motorized Infantry Brigade[2] crossed into Sinai at Ras el Nagb and set off down the long difficult coastal track which runs along the Gulf of Aqaba towards the southern tip of the peninsula. It took the brigade four days to reach the outer defences of Yoffe's objective—Sharm-El-Sheikh—and during the march it was supplied by sea from Elat, the landing craft performing this service having been transported overland from Haifa. In the north the fighting continued for Abu Aweigila. This was the most promising area for the Egyptians to defend and to reinforce their position there, an infantry brigade with an armoured regiment was despatched from Ismailia. Most of these reinforcements got no farther than Bir Gifgafa, twenty miles up the road. Spotted by Israeli Mystères soon after leaving Ismailia the Israeli Air Force successfully put in a number of damaging air strikes which scattered the column, despite the air cover which was provided by MIG's and Egyptian Vampires. Those vehicles which did get beyond Bir Gifgafa and try to get through to Abu Aweigila were held up by troops from Ben-Avi's force, who by now had infiltrated round Abu Aweigila and were across the road in some strength. Meantime, another column of Egyptian reinforcements comprising a weak armoured brigade which half-heartedly

---

[1] The *Ibrahim el Awal*, armed with 4-4-inch guns, was the ex-British 'Hunt' class destroyer *Cottesmore* launched in 1940 and transferred to Egypt in July 1941. Since this action she has been recommissioned into the Israeli Navy as the *Haifa*.

[2] A reserve brigade, newly mobilized. Yoffe was nicknamed 'Gideon' in the War of Independence and the brigade motto was: 'The Sword for God and Gideon'.

attempted to recapture the Mitla Pass position was repulsed; after a short time it withdrew, being followed up by Israeli patrols which probed almost as far as the Canal banks. By now, Abu Aweigila was virtually surrounded, although the Egyptians were still fighting back hard—certainly with considerably more skill and courage than they had shown in 1948. And, when the Israelis attempted to tighten the encirclement, the Egyptians launched a strong armoured counter-attack—their one major counter stroke of the campaign. The Israeli infantry was pinned down by artillery fire and at dusk (as the first Anglo-French bombers were striking Egypt's airfields) the battle was still raging with the battlefield littered with the wrecks of burning tanks. Ignoring this battle next day (Thursday, 1st November) a fresh task force of an infantry brigade (Colonel Givli) and an armoured brigade (Colonel Barlev), under Brigadier Laskov, the Israeli Armoured Corps commander, bypassed Abu Aweigila by driving west-ward round the defences to strike at Rafa, near the southern end of the Gaza Strip. Rafa had been heavily bombarded during the night by French naval units and its defences were soon overrun by Laskov's men who now turned west down the coast road towards the next important Egyptian post at El Arish.

Meantime, the Abu Aweigila battle was still raging, the Israelis finding that they were unable to make little progress, although by now they were using captured T-34's to supplement their losses in armour. That the position in this sector was causing the Israeli High Command some alarm may be deduced from the fact that their Chief of Staff, General Moshe Dayan, flew to the scene and assumed com-mand. Under his direction a fresh assault was launched and by dusk the Egyptian defences had been breached although the two main defended ridges were still held. When dawn broke the following morning, it was realized that most of the Egyptian garrison had evacuated the area during the night and the rest of that day was spent by Harpaz's troops mopping up the few remaining pockets of resist-ance; by nightfall the whole of Abu Aweigila had been captured. Few prisoners were taken by the Israelis as a result of this action, most of the Egyptians being allowed to escape to make their own way back to the Canal across the inhospitable desert. Meanwhile, while Har-paz's men mopped up what remained of the Abu Aweigila garrison, Ben-Avi collected his brigade and advanced towards Ismailia. Brush-ing aside a weak resistance at Bir Gifgafa he raced down the road, halting only about ten miles from Ismailia.

On the northern coast route, Brigadier Laskov had closed in on the remaining stronghold of El Arish. Garrisoned by an Egyptian brigade, the El Arish area contained an airfield, huge petrol dumps, stores and supplies—a rich prize indeed for the Israelis. As many of the Egyptian garrison had fled during the preceding night it was occupied with little difficulty and a large number of prisoners were taken here despite Israeli preference otherwise, since those who escaped relieved them of the embarrassment and problems in feeding and guarding prisoners. With El Arish in their hands, units of Laskov's column were soon speeding westwards to Qantara and by dusk they too had occupied positions about ten miles from the Canal. Thus, by Friday evening, Israeli troops were occupying positions at three separate strategic points astride the roads into Sinai and well within striking distance of the Canal. That night an army spokesman in Tel Aviv proudly announced: 'We have conquered the bulk of Sinai.' But for the restriction imposed by the Anglo-French ultimatum he might well have been able to say that Israeli troops were fighting in the town of Ismailia.

Operation 'Kadesh' may be said to have ended with the fall of the ancient city of Gaza, although the southern operations at the mouth of the Gulf of Aqaba continued for another two days after this. Supposedly garrisoned by two brigades, the Gaza Strip which was crammed with Palestinian refugees was doomed when Laskov occupied El Arish. Gaza itself had been left to the last and the decision to occupy it was not taken until after the capture of Rafa. A fresh infantry brigade was moved into position opposite the town and at dawn on the Friday morning the Israelis forced their way through its defences and the town was formally surrendered at 1000 hours. The surrender document was signed by an unhappy Governor-General who now handed over the responsibility for 325 square miles of land and a quarter of a million ragged, ill-fed, ill-housed and ill-fated refugees whose very presence obviously had helped to bring about the surrender.

To complete the story, mention must be made of the exploits of Yoffe's brigade which had started out for Sharm-El-Sheikh on the Wednesday. The state of the road which he was compelled to follow was such that it was Friday before they had arrived at Ras Nasrani; this was the site of the Egyptian outpost opposite the island of Tiran from which coast guns prevented entry of Israeli ships into the Gulf of Aqaba. After a brisk action the garrison withdrew south on to their main defences of Sharm-El-Sheikh and Yoffe paused to take stock of the situation. His brigade was tired, the Egyptians at Sharm-El-Sheikh were expecting him and the campaign having gone as it had, there was now less urgency to complete his mission. He was opposed by an infantry battalion which occupied well-prepared defences, including a number of anti-aircraft guns and the garrison could be expected to put up a spirited resistance. Nevertheless after a short respite the offensive was resumed on the 3rd; by which time his men were refreshed and two AMX tanks, which Yoffe had considered would be necessary to break the outer defences, were on their way from Elat in the landing craft. (They arrived too late to take part in the action.) Preceded by an air strike, the Israelis attacked the Sharm-El-Sheikh perimeter and opened up a route to the main positions; the battle continued until the position had been completely overrun and most of the garrison taken prisoner—those who managed to get away escaping across the water to Saudi Arabia. Then, on Sunday morning (4th November) the island of Tiran surrendered and the final action of the Sinai campaign took place on the Monday with an amphibious landing on the neighbouring fortified island of Sinafar. With its capture the entrance to the Gulf of Aqaba was at last open to Israeli shipping and Yoffe signalled to General Dayan: 'It is finished. . . .'

It was. On 5th November, in less than a week, a third of Egypt's army had been defeated, the Egyptian Air Force had been destroyed, Sinai was in the hands of its most hated enemies, and its capacity to resist the Anglo-French invasion was crippled. At midnight on Tuesday the Israeli official communiqué announced: 'The Campaign in Sinai is over . . . and there is no more fighting.'

At that moment, the main Anglo-French assault force was on its way to Port Said.

The Sinai operation may be compared with Wavell's first Western Desert campaign in 1940. At a cost of less than two hundred killed and only four taken prisoner—one of whom was the pilot of a Piper Cub which crash landed behind the Egyptian lines—in four days the Israelis routed at least 50,000 Egyptians, occupied the whole of the Sinai peninsula and captured much rich and welcome military booty. The Egyptian Army defeat was even more humiliating than that of 1948 and at this time there was no King Farouk or corrupt Pashas to blame. Its failure may be attributed to the poor morale of the troops and the poor qualities of leadership shown by the officers;

certainly there was no lack of equipment, it was well organized and the Egyptian fieldworks, which followed German patterns, had been well prepared. There were many reports—particularly from the Abu Aweigila battles—of Egyptian soldiers standing fast to fight bravely and well in small groups or as individuals, but it seems that Colonel Nasser's new *esprit de corps* had not yet penetrated sufficiently to inspire the young officers—many of whom were reported to have deserted their men quite blatantly.

Nothing like this can be said of the Israelis. Unlike any army in Western Europe since the Spanish Civil War, the Israeli Army retains much of the ideological background which was provided by the Haganah in 1948. Despite its increasing professionalism it remains a peoples' army and the people know that so far as the Arabs are concerned they still face the problem of survival. Not that such an outlook necessarily makes them good soldiers. Leadership in Operation 'Kadesh' was characterized by 'speed and risk' and such a theme does not always pay off. If Egyptian morale had been better, so enabling more determined and sustained resistance to be offered, the Israeli attack might well have collapsed. Their vehicles were so unsuitable that about half of them needed base workshop repair by the end of the five days' fighting, and the pace which Moshe Dayan set his commanders strained the logistical support to its absolute limit. For a campaign of short duration 'speed and risk' worked; it is doubtful if it could do so in a prolonged war with long lines of communication. A bold and aggressive plan so often succeeds and this is particularly true of mobile operations, but once such a plan starts to go awry, the advantages often go to the other side, particularly if they have greater resources. No doubt the Israelis are acutely aware of all this and have worked to perfect their tactical doctrine; if the current arms race between Israel and Egypt triggers off another explosion they may well be capable of again giving the Arabs a further trouncing.

Colonel Nasser had always affirmed that Egypt had 'a rod in pickle' for the Israelis—indeed he continues to do so. What happened in 1956 must have been a humiliating experience which as a soldier he would try to see should never happen again. The losses of millions of dollars' worth of Czech and Soviet equipment is still not admitted in public and so far as the Army's defeats are concerned he has managed to put over the idea that the real cause was the need to redeploy and hold back against the imminent Anglo-French assault.

84

Being a master of Middle East propaganda, he has done so extremely well and Arabs ignore the fact that the Egyptian Army was beaten in the field. What matters is that Nasser engaged not only Israel but Britain and France also and yet still managed to survive. But whilst the facts concerning the military breakdown in Sinai have been generally obscured, the Army itself is well aware of the shortcomings of its officers and, like the Israelis, the Egyptians have been working hard to correct their shortcomings. Curiously enough, Nasser's predecessor General Neguib, had suggested that an army which dabbles in politics loses its efficiency and should 'stick to its barracks'. Probably a root cause of the officer weakness of the Egyptian Sinai Army was that so many of the best officers were no longer serving as army officers but were working in quasi-civilian jobs, running ministries, functioning as administrators or policemen. Yet there is little doubt that the cream of Nasser's troops were in Sinai in 1956. The division at Abu Aweigila was the best in the Army and the two brigades in the Gaza Strip were held to be better than other brigades in Egypt. When it came to the crunch they proved to be inferior to the Israelis.

Finally there is one other issue that stands out as a lesson from Operation 'Kadesh'. None of Egypt's Arab allies showed any signs of rushing forward to help out in Sinai—not even to the extent of making threatening moves on their own borders with Israel. Whether or not this would be the same again is difficult to assess. Colonel Nasser's personality stands above everyone else in the Arab world; 1956 has enhanced his reputation and his name strikes fire in the Middle East. But if the Arabs do a lot of talking they remain cautionary by nature: 'Keep your tents separate but bring your hearts together' is an Arab proverb which might provide encouragement to the Israelis if it ever comes to another Operation'.

CHAPTER 5

The Convoys Sail

T he Israeli Operation 'Kadesh', launched on 29th October, was almost completed by 5th November, when the British and French parachutists dropped on Port Said, and it was not until the following day that the seaborne forces started to land in Egypt. In any analysis of the Suez operation, the question is bound to be asked eventually, why the Anglo-French assault did not take place sooner: the answer must be a review of the time and space factors involved. Understandably, the main force could not put to sea before 31st October (the date when the political decision to intervene in the Israeli–Egyptian dispute was finally taken) and, because of the length of the sea journey, 6th November became the earliest possible date for the seaborne assault. Although the Israeli mobilization was a clear indication of the trend of events, the Allied High Command could only take precautionary measures until the British and French politicians had approved the initiation of military action. These precautions started as soon as the news of Israel's mobilization became known.

According to the Brombergers,[1] the French were alerted on the 19th October and units of the French Mediterranean fleet sailed from Toulon, bound ostensibly for Bizerta but in reality for a rendezvous off Cyrenaica; troops of the 7th Mécanique Rapide Division embarked at Algiers on the Saturday and Sunday, 27th and 28th October. Meanwhile, ships of the British Mediterranean Fleet had started assembling in the Central Mediterranean for a combined naval exercise 'Boathook', and on the 26th, the two aircraft carriers H.M.S. *Bulwark* and H.M.S. *Eagle*, had just arrived at Malta, whilst H.M.S. *Albion* was close by. After only a brief halt, the three carriers, together with the French *Arromanches* sailed with all speed for the

[1] *Secrets of Suez.*

Eastern Mediterranean. They arrived at an area approximately fifty miles off the coast of Port Said on the night of the 31st and their role in the first phase of 'Musketeer' will be described in the next chapter.

To revert momentarily to the time and space factor governing the date of the seaborne assault on Port Said: if the French battle fleet left Toulon on the 19th/20th October, it could reasonably be expected to arrive in the Eastern Mediterranean within four days—say by the 26th, the date that 'Kadesh' was launched. And the convoy which carried the French troops from Algiers, leaving on the evening of the 29th October and steaming at an average of 10 knots, could be expected to be off the coast of Egypt within seven days, i.e. by 4th November. H.M.S. *Bulwark*, H.M.S. *Eagle* and the *Arromanches* left Malta on the 26th and arrived off Port Said on the 31st, whilst the main British assault force sailed from Malta on 1st November, and presumably made an average speed of almost 10 knots. H.M.S. *Theseus* and H.M.S. *Ocean*, unencumbered by slow LCT's and merchant shipping, sailed 'with all speed' from Malta on the afternoon of 3rd November, and to meet up with the main convoy, which had preceded them they presumably travelled at over 20 knots. The relevance of these details will be apparent; attempts to analyse the political background and show that there was evidence or not of collusion with Israel over the launching of her operation has been a popular gambit.[1] If these dates are correct, it is clear that the French fleet was in a position to support Israel any time after the 26th, and that French troops could possibly have been used in a seaborne assault on Port Said on the afternoon of 4th November—perhaps even earlier.

Back in Malta, the first indication that something was afoot came on Saturday evening (27th October) when the decision to call an urgent co-ordinating conference for the Sunday morning necessitated a number of officers being 'paged' at the pubs and clubs where they were enjoying the customary Saturday night round. At the conference, orders were issued for a large-scale loading exercise 'as for war' and although it was explained that the exercise was to be regarded as training routine, many of those present realized that this was going to be more than just another exercise. Of the troops who were to take part, the Royal Marine Commandos were obviously destined for a key role even if it were only an exercise. They were not

[1] The reader who wishes to pursue this aspect is referred to an article 'The Ultimatum,' by Erskine B. Childers, in the *Spectator* of 30th October 1959.

unduly perturbed by what promised to be a few days' hectic activity and that afternoon 45 Commando trooped their Colour, to celebrate the anniversary of the raising of the Royal Marines. Those on parade, who were to embark in forty-eight hours time and land on the beaches of Port Said in just over a week gave a magnificent display of faultless turn-out and precision drill.

Whilst the 'exercise' was officially supposed to be regarded as secret, the preparations which were necessary could hardly go unobserved, and some of the Maltese tradesmen went out of their way to say good-bye to their service customers and express fervent hopes for a safe return. In Algiers, the French had the same problem, with the local population watching the harbour to see if the troopships had sailed.

Preparations continued throughout the Monday as news of the Israeli operations began to filter through; on Tuesday the troops in Malta started to embark and by the following morning the main assault force was all on board, ready to sail. The spearhead of 40 and 42 Commandos together with 6th Royal Tanks, were all embarked in ships of the Amphibious Warfare Squadron which had been expanded to a total of eight LST's and nine LCT's; 45 Commando, which was scheduled to play such a unique and unorthodox role, did not embark until 2nd November, two days later. In the early hours of Wednesday morning the main force sailed, escorted by warships of the Mediterranean Fleet, under the command of Rear-Admiral D. E. Holland-Martin. Once at sea, the exercise illusion was dispelled; the ships' crews and troops were told that Britain and France were at war with Egypt and that they were the task force charged with the capture of Port Said. The news was enthusiastically received; it signalled an end to the tedium of training and most of the men regarded the prospect of an action with excited anticipation.

Back in the United Kingdom, men of General Churcher's 3rd Division also were embarking; they would be at sea when the assault on Egypt was launched but when they started to arrive five days later, the assault troops could be relieved and the campaign pressed quickly to its conclusion. Behind the brigades of the 3rd Division would follow the supporting troops, stores and reinforcements, which would ensure that the operation was a success.

The enthusiasm of the men taking part in the initial assault was maintained throughout the voyage and the speeches and political wranglings which came over the ships' wireless produced surprisingly

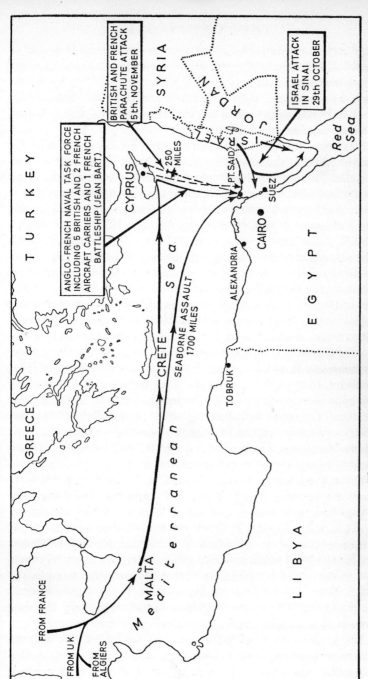

BRITISH AND FRENCH PARACHUTE ATTACK 5th. NOVEMBER

ISRAEL ATTACK IN SINAI 29th OCTOBER

ANGLO - FRENCH NAVAL TASK FORCE INCLUDING 5 BRITISH AND 2 FRENCH AIRCRAFT CARRIERS AND 1 FRENCH BATTLESHIP (JEAN BART)

TURKEY

SYRIA

JORDAN

ISRAEL

Red Sea

CYPRUS

250 MILES

PT. SAID

SUEZ

CAIRO

ALEXANDRIA

EGYPT

CRETE

Sea

SEABORNE ASSAULT 1700 MILES

TOBRUK

GREECE

Mediterranean

MALTA

LIBYA

FROM FRANCE

FROM UK

FROM ALGIERS

The Operations Against Egypt, November 1956

little reaction; the only concern was whether the operation would be cancelled. Morale was of a very high order even with those reservists whose voices had been loudest in protestations that they should be home by Christmas. A similar attitude prevailed with those sailing from England; only when it became apparent that their role had changed, were any doubts expressed.

Meantime, the rest of the Mediterranean Fleet was hurriedly assembling behind the assault force. The change of plan which had cancelled Exercise 'Boathook' meant that there was little opportunity for the final collective briefings of ships' captains, but the Royal Navy went about its task with traditional efficiency undisturbed by the flurry of army activity. On the 30th October, H.M.S. *Theseus* and H.M.S. *Ocean*, who were *en route* to Malta from Gibraltar, received a laconic signal to the effect that their next job would be 'trooping'; no mention was made of the operational aspects which were to be involved. The two ships arrived at Valetta on the Wednesday morning, as the tail of the assault force steamed out towards Port Said. Thursday they spent waiting for something to happen; on Friday it did. Troops, ammunition and stores were embarked, and by the evening they were loaded and ready to sail. *Ocean*, which already had the Army and R.A.F. Joint Experimental Helicopter Unit—J.E.H.U. —aboard, took on 600 men of 215 Wing and the R.A.F. Regiment and approximately half of 45 Commando; *Theseus*, who already had 845 Naval Helicopter Squadron, embarked the remainder of 45 Commando, various small ancillary units including engineers and individuals who would be urgently required in Port Said to get the town back to normal life when the assault was over.

The convoy, which included *Theseus* and *Ocean*, sailed at 1700 hours the following day, Saturday, 3rd November. The start of the voyage had been delayed until dusk, in order to give the convoy twelve hours' steaming in the dark, but by the following afternoon it was under close observation from all the august might of the United States Sixth Fleet which appeared to be steaming on a parallel course and shadowing the British ships. From the American flagship, the U.S.S. *Salem*—reputedly the heaviest cruiser in the world—a signal lamp flickered: 'What ship? Whither bound?' The reply signalled from H.M.S. *Ocean*, '*Ocean*. What fleet?' evoked no response.

The main assault force had also had a brief interchange with the Americans that might have been more serious. The presence of a submarine was detected by one of the destroyer escorts which promptly moved in to attack. As it did so the submarine surfaced and hastily hoisted a large United States flag before sailing on the surface down the middle of the convoy. Its presence was queried by the headquarter ship H.M.S. *Meon*, who signalled: 'Why don't you come and join us,' to which the reply came: 'No thanks, we're holding your coat this time.' An apparent attempt to deter the activities of the French cruiser *Georges Leygues* is also said to have taken place about the same time. A number of dummy attacks on the cruiser were made by a group of jet fighters and the French had to exercise considerable restraint not to open fire. Neither the British nor the French knew what instructions had been given to the Sixth Fleet; the American political attitude suggested that it might even take hostile action to prevent the expedition reaching its objectives. Vice-Admiral Brown, commanding the Sixth Fleet, later denied that any of his ships had 'deliberately manœuvred on the route of the British and French units sailing in Egyptian waters'.[1] His task, he said, was solely one of evacuating United States nationals from the combat area and to do so he had deployed his forces 'in such a way as to best defend the ships and aircraft from attack'. To avoid the possibility of any confusion, his submarines were ordered to stay on the surface and be floodlit at night. And it was absurd to suggest 'that any minor interference of formations passing at sea should have delayed the Allied landings'. With all due respect to Admiral Brown it does seem unlikely that the landings were delayed or that such delay would have made any difference, but even the presence of American warships on the horizon let alone the incidents referred to, with the uncertainty attached to their mission, undoubtedly did cause some embarrassment. Admiral Brown was compelled to evacuate Americans from Egypt by sea, since the Egyptian airfields came under Anglo-French attack. To do this and to protect the ships involved he would have to take some precautionary measures, but it is difficult to understand why he had to shadow the Allied task force right through to the operation, with the display of force that was apparent at the time.

A wartime routine was adopted for the voyage and the ships were darkened at night. With the lack of ventilation and overcrowding in many of the vessels, this was probably the most unpleasant feature of an otherwise almost uneventful journey. The Royal Marine Commandos spent their time in an orgy of briefings, rehearsals and pre-

[1] At an interview reported in the U.S. News and World Report of 14th December 1956.

parations, 45 Commando being fully occupied with developing drills for use with the helicopters of which more will be said later. Everyone was busy studying maps and photographs, checking weapons, ammunition and stores to ensure that no detail had been forgotten or overlooked. And right up to the time when the Egyptian coast came into sight the troops were making bets as to whether the operation would come off or not; the political wranglings broadcast over the B.B.C. and relayed over the ships' wireless sets only added spice to the uncertainty and there was a complete lack of reaction to the news. Very few who took part ever wished to have the operation called off at any stage. Only the crew of the cruiser H.M.N.Z.S. *Royalist* (5,900 tons) were to be disappointed; their ship was recalled from the operation as the fleet approached the Eastern Mediterranean on the orders of the New Zealand Prime Minister. Her withdrawal had been anticipated however and the 8,800 ton cruiser H.M.S. *Ceylon* was speeding out from England to replace her; she arrived in ample time to take part.[1]

The hurried embarkation had not allowed sufficient time for all the details of the assault plan to be finalized before the convoy sailed and the basis of the plan underwent some radical changes during the course of the voyage. Passing the amended orders resultant on these changes to the commandos, who were distributed between twenty ships of the Amphibious Warfare Squadron, *Theseus* and *Ocean* was no simple task in itself; right up to the time when the assault actually got under way a constant stream of messages passed between H.M.S. *Meon*, Brigadier Madoc's headquarter ship, and the vessels carrying the various Royal Marine units. Meanwhile, the men of 45 Commando, split between *Theseus* and *Ocean*, had novel and quite different problems from the rest of the brigade. These arose from the proposal to put them into the battle in helicopters and the fact that they had had no opportunity till then either to practise their role or develop the necessary techniques. Their first problem centred on the fact that there were clearly too few helicopters available to move the entire Commando in one lift and those that were available were of different makes and types which meant differences in the loads they could carry and their speeds of operation. Two alternatives were possible:

[1] H.M.S. *Ceylon* supported the parachutists who landed at Gamil airfield. A Royal Artillery Observation Party, which was provided by the 33rd Parachute Regiment R.A. to direct the fire of H.M.S. *Ceylon*, parachuted in with the 3rd Parachute Battalion.

the first was to operate the helicopters in a stream or 'chain' system, with helicopters taking off, flying and dumping their loads individually, returning individually to repeat the process. By this means the maximum numbers of men and stores could be ferried ashore in the most economical fashion and the marshalling problems of the carriers' flight decks and refuelling simplified; unfortunately this method does not cater for the tactical move of units who might have to face opposition on the ground after their arrival. The alternative was to operate in 'waves'. By this method groups of helicopters, tactically loaded, form up in the air, descend on the agreed landing zone and discharge their cargoes as one entity and this is obviously the only way to assault a defended area.

Then there were other considerations: the time taken to reinforce the first lift, how near the helicopters could get to the enemy defences without sustaining casualties, how many casualties could be expected —either as a result of enemy action or mechanical failure. In this instance the latter consideration was of great significance since it is of little value working out an elaborate loading table based on a precise programme where the helicopters' payloads varied. Payloads themselves vary with weather conditions since wind, temperature and humidity all affect the helicopter lift and allowances have to be made for these factors; refuelling is also a slow business and the amount of fuel carried in the helicopter's tanks controls its available payload since one with full tanks can lift less than one with half-empty tanks. Furthermore, the deck space available for refuelling aircraft whilst others are still operating is strictly limited in carriers of the size of *Theseus* and *Ocean* (each of which, in fact, could operate and refuel only six at a time).

In the event, the problem was to land as many fighting men as possible in the first wave, and the eventual plan allowed for nearly 200 men to land in this first wave and for three further waves to land another 170, with all their support weapons—mortars, machine-guns, anti-tank guns—and ammunition. After the initial landings it could be expected that the operation could proceed at a more leisurely pace and the aim was to put ashore a total of 415 men with 24 tons of stores in two and a half hours. The actual emplaning drill all had to be evolved; obviously it is not feasible for men to wait about on the flight deck during the period that the helicopters are landing and taking-off and this was overcome by detailing men in 'sticks'—analogous to parachutist 'sticks'—to await the call to emplane. The

93

planned timings envisaged waves of twenty-two helicopters taking about five minutes to load and take-off and nine minutes to refuel; on the morning of the 6th November they took less.

The convoy from Cyprus did not sail until Sunday the 4th November. From here, where a large and essential proportion of the invasion force had been assembled, it took only twenty-four hours to reach Port Said. Embarkation started on the Friday night and from then on for the next few days the little port of Limassol and the harbour of Famagusta were scenes of intense overcrowded confusion as French and British warships, assault landing craft, troopships and tugs, ocean-going merchantmen and coastal tramps all endeavoured to equip, embark and put to sea in the correct order. Brigadier Butler's 16th Parachute Brigade Group, less those who would be making the airborne assault on Gamil airfield, had priority. They started to embark in tank landing ships (LST's) and the troopship *Empire Parkeston* early on Saturday, and by Sunday morning their vessels steamed slowly into open waters to form up off Limassol. Now that the operation was finally on the move speed was essential and units with their piles of stores had to be loaded on a strict schedule. Once aboard their respective ships, preparations for the battle ahead began in earnest. Two days' rations, for use after landing, were issued, personal equipment stacked below, heavy equipment was lashed down to the decks. And even as the ships lay at anchor, officers began to give their men a little of the psychological preparation for what they were about to face. Maps were unfurled, air photographs were produced and the detailed plan was gone over again and again. Last-minute changes in the plan led to the inevitable confusion; pontoons, taken against the risk that the bridge out of Port Said would be demolished before it could be captured, replaced a battery of field guns. On the quayside gunner and sapper officers argued vehemently on the efficiency of this change.

The actual process of loading equipment was itself complicated by need to use 'Z' craft to ferry vehicles and stores out to the ships which could not be accommodated at the limited quay space of the Famagusta docks, the limitations of which have already been discussed. This fact was not clear to many of those concerned with loading their units' stores and the delay was variously attributed to the internal security position, inefficiency on the part of the harbour master and the unsuitability of the hired merchantmen, many of which were in a decrepit state and of a type unsuited to a military function. Despite the crews of the Army's 'Z' craft working non-stop, progress was slow. No effort was spared to load the assault troops with their first-line equipment but after that the loading of the second-line equipment which was to follow the troops into Port Said began to flag. The usual complications caused by senior officers overruling the movements of staff in order to ensure the loading of some particular vehicle which to them was essential, produced a complete breakdown in the system on the Sunday afternoon and with dusk approaching it was not possible to reorganize the schedule until the following morning. So far as the Parachute Brigade were concerned, the result of this breakdown combined with delays in entering Port Said harbour was that their stores arrived in Egypt to be delivered to their respective units less than four hours before the brigade was due to re-embark for Cyprus.

On Sunday evening the ships which had formed up off Limassol sailed to join the Malta convoy 100 miles south of Cyprus. With their equipment stowed and the briefing over, this was a time for the troops to relax; some lounged in the well decks and read, some dozed, some played cards, some stared over the rails to watch the ships to port and starboard, like the large white hospital ship with its great scarlet cross painted on its flanks, or the grey anti-radiation painted destroyers that careered through the lines of slower ships, flashing signals to keep them in position. Until at nine o'clock the news came over the ships' tannoy system and everyone stopped to listen. The news was followed by a broadcast by Sir Anthony Eden.

'All my life I have been a man of peace, striving for peace and negotiating for peace. I have been a League of Nations man and a United Nations man. And I am still the same man with the same convictions and the same devotion to peace. I could not be other even if I wished, but I am utterly convinced that the action we have taken is right.' He went on to say: 'Our passionate love of peace and our intense loathing of war have often held us back from using force, even at times when we knew in our heads, if not in our hearts, that its use was in the interests of peace. And I believe with all my heart and my head that this is a time for action effective and swift.'

These were cheering words: soldiers find it easier to go to war with an assurance from the Government that sends them there, that what they do is in the highest interest.

The ships from Cyprus steamed on in four lines, each line four cables apart, each ship four cables astern of the next one, the course:

two, two, one degrees magnetic, speed: one zero three revolutions. On Monday morning the ships from Malta could be seen on the horizon, their masts resembling a growing company of archers as the two convoys converged; later, in the afternoon, the combined convoy joined up with that of the French and from any of the ships it was a truly magnificent sight. Vessels, from battleships to minesweepers, could be seen as far as the eye could see; on the radar screens it was equally impressive. With the blackout that night the troops settled down to await the nine o'clock news which was again relayed over the ships' tannoys. The news was followed by a broadcast by the Leader of the Opposition in Parliament. Of the Prime Minister he said:

'His policy this week has been disastrous, and he is utterly discredited in the eyes of the world. Only one thing now can save the reputation and honour of our country. Parliament must repudiate the Government's policy. The Prime Minister must resign.'

This was sour encouragement to those who were about to risk their lives in defence of the policy which was now being repudiated. Whether it was right or not, at this late hour, the troops were committed to it. Many of them, with a disgust bred of fury, now argued late into the night about the speech they had just heard and its implications of a divided and disillusioned British public. Whatever the wisdom of its substance, no speech could have been more calculatingly ill-timed.

1c. Colonel Haim Bar Lev

1b. Colonel Abraham Yoffe.

1a. General Moshe Dayan, the Israeli Chief of Staff.

2*a*. Egyptian prisoners in the Sinai desert near Kantara. In their flight, many of the Egyptians discarded their boots.

2*b*. The captured Egyptian destroyer *Ibrahim el Awal* off Haifa.

CHAPTER 6

'Musketeer'—The First Phase

After Colonel Nasser's categorical rejection of the joint Anglo-French ultimatum, Sir Anthony Eden announced that Egypt could now be considered 'to be in a state of armed conflict with Britain and France'; his words implied that a 'real' war was not intended. Quasi-war, 'limited' war or 'police action'—whatever it was—the stage was now set and in the last hours of October, following the Prime Minister's announcement, a signal was flashed to Cyprus ordering General Keightley to go ahead with the first phase of the agreed plan. Air Marshal Barnett's task force, composed of aircraft of the Royal Air Force and French Air Force operating from shore bases, with aircraft of the Royal Navy and French Navy operating from the five aircraft carriers of the combined fleets, had been awaiting the order for some time.

With the first air strikes on the evening of the 31st October, the air offensive majestically started to unfold. It was first phase of a combined operation which followed orthodox lines; first the air fight would be won, then the air threat still existing on the ground would be destroyed, then other military installations; finally, by a process of interdiction, the battlefield would be isolated from its sources of supply. The method closely resembled the pattern of the massive air attacks which preceded the Mediterranean landings of the Second World War when careful preparations were of more importance than time. For this operation time was a vital factor which appears to have been given too little heed. Presumably the hope still lingered in the politicians' minds that the Egyptian people would turn against Colonel Nasser before troops actually landed on Egyptian soil; if so, the effect was the exact reverse—they rallied to him. More important still was the fact that as this slow methodical bombing and strafing phase continued like a nagging toothache, world opinion began to crystallize. The General Assembly met in an emergency session and its ultimate resolution followed Mr. Dulles's lead in urging an immediate ceasefire. India's Mr. Nehru, after dashing off a message of sympathy to Colonel Nasser, sent a telegram to the Secretary-General of the United Nations in which he vigorously condemned the Anglo-French action. Russia's M. Bulganin, who saw the chance to muffle current savage Soviet conduct in Hungary, joined in the general outcry in condemnations of aggression; even talking of joining the United States in fighting the British and French. All this took place whilst the bombing continued.

The initial strikes were directed against those airfields which were the known bases of the Egyptian Air Force. That night, as an Arab voice, broadcasting on Egyptian frequencies from Limassol,[1] warned Egyptians to keep away from the targets to be attacked, R.A.F. Valiants and Canberras roared in from Malta and Cyprus to drop bombs on the runways and hangars at Almaza, Kabrit, Abu Sueir and Inchas. Their runways were left pitted and buildings blazing. The same night other bombers, in a mission not popular with the air crews, flew over Cairo and dropped leaflets advising the populace to revolt and oust the tyrant Nasser; meantime Cyprus radio interspersed the advance warnings of places to be attacked and messages urging people to escape death or injury by seeking shelter and keeping away from military installations with similar advice to revolt. No revolt followed despite these appeals and Nasser's own propaganda machine quickly organized a counterblast. After advising everyone to remain calm, Cairo Radio blandly announced that little damage had been done: Egyptian planes had already flown to safety in Saudi Arabia, dummy replicas of the aircraft had been left behind and it was these that were now blazing and smoking on the airfields. Meanwhile, the announcer said, Egyptian anti-aircraft gunners had already taken a heavy toll of the Allied planes.

[1] This was the Near East Arabic Broadcasting Station of Sharq-el-Adna requisitioned by the Government of Cairo on the 3rd October, and under the orders of Brigadier Bernard Fergusson, D.S.O., O.B.E., who had been appointed as Director of Psychological Warfare on General Keightley's staff. It was virtually out of action by 1st November as the Arabic programme staff resigned in protest against the Anglo-French action directed against their 'brothers' in Egypt.

The availability at the start of the first phase of propaganda leaflets printed in Arabic has been the subject of much controversy concerning the question as to whether or not the Allies knew of the impending Israeli attack.

British crews returning from the raids had a different story to tell; little anti-aircraft fire had been encountered and most of it had been of doubtful accuracy. Light anti-aircraft fire, bursting many thousands of feet below the bombers had produced a magnificent firework display, the fire of the heavy guns had been easily evaded and, in spite of the broadcast warnings of the targets to be attacked, navigation had been made easy by the innumerable lights which were blazing in the Nile Delta. Not until the first bombs began to fall on Almaza and a blackout was imposed below, did the lights in the towns begin to disappear. Only one bomber crew reported that they had been intercepted by an Egyptian night fighter and the pilot had opened his throttles and climbed away, leaving the fighter vainly trying to follow. Another crew had sighted a fighter which might have been trying to attack them but it too had been easily evaded, the fighter disappearing into the blackness below.

The raids continued through the night until finally, just before dawn, the last bomber winged effortlessly away, leaving the shaken Egyptian airmen to emerge from their shelters and discover their runways blocked, buildings gutted and aircraft burning. Their inspection of the damage could not be prolonged, however, and there was certainly no question of repair. Fifty miles off the coast of Port Said the aircraft carriers of the invasion fleet had already armed their Seahawks, Sea Venoms and Corsairs, and R.A.F. Venoms and French Thunderstreaks from Cyprus were in the air. An hour before sunrise the aircraft from Cyprus were climbing into the darkness heading south, whilst the carriers had already turned into wind preparing to launch their first sorties. At precisely ten minutes before sunrise—0403 hours G.M.T.—on the 1st November, simultaneous attacks were made on the airfields of Cairo West, Inchas, Almaza, Dekheila near Alexandria and the Canal Zone airfields of Abu Sueir, Kabrit, Fayid and Kasfareet. Again, the Egyptian Air Force was taken completely by surprise. Their aircraft were still parked by the runways, and when the Allied planes dived to attack with rockets and cannon, the Egyptians paid dearly for their unpreparedness. This time the only opposition was confined to light anti-aircraft and small arms fire. As the Allied aircraft broke away from their attack, weaving low to avoid the flak, they left more fires burning in hangars and fuel dumps, and many more Egyptian aircraft smouldering in broken heaps at the dispersal areas.

For the next seventy-two hours the course of the offensive followed this pattern, Allied aircraft being almost constantly over the Egyptian airfields. As soon as the Egyptian ground crews were able to get back to their planes to repair the damage following one raid, another attack took place and they had to run for shelter once more. With every raid the amount of damage increased and the chances of repair and recovery diminished. Off Alexandria, French Corsairs found time to attack an Egyptian destroyer which they left burning, and aircraft of the Royal Navy, whilst continuing to attack the airfields of Cairo West, Inchas, Almaza and Dekheila, also raided the Egyptian Air Training School at Bilbeis and the Air Force installations at Helwan and Heliopolis. The cement-filled blockship *Akka* was attacked on two occasions; first at its mooring in Lake Timsah and later when the Egyptians were seen to be towing it into position in the Canal on the south side of the lake, but both attacks failed to achieve their purpose since the *Akka* was eventually sunk across the channel. Elsewhere, the land-based R.A.F. and French Air Force aircraft, as well as reconnoitring the airfields at El Firdan, Deversoir and Shaffufa to make certain that they were not being used as dispersal areas for the now damaged bases, battered Abu Sueir, Kabrit, Fayid and Kasfareet in a round-the-clock series of attacks.

During this hectic period there was little rest for either the crews of the carriers or the R.A.F. and French Air Force units in Cyprus and R.A.F. in Malta. With the fleet, crews of the ships' anti-aircraft guns stood by and Seahawks high overhead provided an air umbrella ready to repulse any Egyptian counter blow, and Skyraiders and Avengers, with R.A.F. Shackletons, scanned the sea, screening the carriers from submarine or surface vessels. Crews of the ground attack aircraft, who averaged no less than four sorties per day, alternated their offensive missions with spells of 'combat air patrol' as part of the air umbrella above the fleet. Operating in a strict cycle, the carriers with their destroyer escorts, steamed at 30 knots in a fixed pattern, presenting their decks to the wind every twenty minutes, to allow aircraft to be launched or to land throughout the hours of daylight. The *Lafayette* and *Arromanche*, whose Corsairs had a longer range than the British naval aircraft, operated farther out to sea than *Eagle*, *Albion* and *Bulwark*, but both British and French programmes were broadly co-ordinated. The actual battle drills employed by the naval aircraft were all very similar: after taking-off from their respective carriers, squadrons would form up and fly to their targets at about 20,000 feet with their flights culminating in a long shallow dive on to the target; this was usually made from out of the sun in an east to west direction. Cannon were loaded with alternate incendiary and armour-piercing ammunition—a lethal combination indeed, as the evidence of the burning Ilyushins testified. The range of the naval aircraft set Cairo as the limit of their offensive operations but the airfields farther afield were well within the range of the Valiants and Canberras.

In Cyprus, radar stations and anti-aircraft gun crews waited for retaliatory raids by Nasser's air force. On the airfields of Nicosia and Akrotiri, fighter pilots sat sweating in the cockpits of Hunters and Mystères ready to take-off at a moment's notice and engage hostile aircraft which, fortunately, never appeared. It was just as well. Measures to cater for a visit of the Egyptian Air Force were a sensible precaution; Cyprus was easily within the range of Egyptian bombers, and there can be little doubt that a raid on Famagusta would have created untold dislocation. One attempt to try out a simple air-raid drill at Famagusta produced a near panic when the siren was sounded in the dock area. Once the dock gates were closed, in accordance with the drill that was being practised, they were assailed by a frantic mob of Cypriot dock workers who feared for their lives; only troops and police remained in occupation of the dock area when the mob broke through the gates.

Flying high over the battle area, photographic reconnaissance Canberras and French Thunderstreaks photographed the airfields as the offensive continued to provide detailed information for the continuance of the bombing programme and for the landings, whilst Seahawks made other low-level photographic sorties to obtain more detailed information for the latter. Despite considerable reinforcements from the United Kingdom, the intelligence staff was unable to cope with the flood of material which came in and to extract tactical information for the aircrews in time for all the subsequent attacks. The aircraft carriers, for example, had to begin with only a shadow of the efficient air intelligence and photographic interpretation system that had been developed in the Second World War and used again in Korea. Once the system had been revived the effectiveness of naval aircraft attacks on ground targets increased considerably. Opposition to the Allied aircraft was reported early on the Thursday morning when two of the reconnaissance Canberras were intercepted by MIG-15's—proof that the Egyptian Air Force still had a sting. One of the Canberras was damaged but the crew managed to nurse it back to

101

Cyprus and the other got away without being hit. As soon as the reconnaissance aircraft landed, their films were rushed to printing sections and thence to the waiting photographic interpretation experts; from their reports Air Marshal Barnett's staff were able, in theory at least, to adjust ('orchestrate' the French called it) the offensive programme. Yet, despite this orchestration it seems that many strikes were made on the wrecks of aircraft already destroyed on previous raids, particularly as the offensive reached its peak. Much of this frustrated effort may be attributed to the weakness in the air intelligence system, which has been mentioned.

For Nasser, this first day of November had been perhaps the most worrying day of his régime. In three nights he had had little sleep; on Monday the 29th he had learned that the Israeli attack was something more than another retaliatory raid and that the situation of his army in Sinai was rapidly worsening. Late on Tuesday, following other depressing reports from the Sinai front, he had received the news of the Anglo-French ultimatum; on Wednesday he had waited for the heavens to drop on him. Indeed, it looked as if this was about to happen when Cairo's air-raid sirens started to wail to be followed by the deafening noise of exploding bombs from not far away. Another shock that day had been the news of the undignified action and the capture of the destroyer *Ibrahim el Awal*. As the President was suffering from a bad attack of laryngitis, his doctor had prescribed less smoking and little talking. Talking was just about his only way out of this situation and luckily he was well skilled in the art of what to say. On Thursday (1st November) he addressed the Egyptian people over Cairo Radio and in a grim and subdued voice, but in defiant terms, he appealed to the 22 million Egyptians and an enormous Arab audience, stretching from the Atlantic to the Persian Gulf. There was a faded Churchillian echo about these words as he prepared the Egyptians for a guerrilla war: 'Today we face British cunning . . . we shall fight a bitter battle. We shall fight from village to village, from house to house, from place to place . . . we shall fight, fight, fight and never surrender, I promise you, my brethren. . . .' He did not tell his audience that the Army in Sinai had been badly mauled, or that the Air Force was well on the way to annihilation, indeed, his handling of the whole situation was just about as astute as anything ever carried out in the psychological warfare field. When he got back to his office he was so hoarse he could hardly speak but he had set the pattern for retaliation and the same day, from Cairo's

Al Azahar Mosque, a holy war was proclaimed against Britain and France.

By dusk that night, when all the Allied aircraft had returned safely from their missions, the extent of the damage and the build-up of the Egyptian Army round Alexandria and Port Said was becoming clear to the Anglo-French High Command. It was obvious that a high percentage of Nasser's modern aircraft had been totally destroyed and many others damaged, but some aircraft were still intact and some airfields had not yet been put out of action. And so, as darkness fell on the second night, the Valiants and Canberras took off once more from Malta and Cyprus, and set off for the airfields of Cairo West, Luxor, Fayid and Kasfareet. Again the crews reported a poor blackout over the Nile, but this time there were no night fighters, and there was only desultory and ineffective anti-aircraft fire. No untoward difficulty was experienced in completing the missions, the success of which was measured by the number of fires and explosions that had rocked the airfields. Photographic reconnaissances the following morning confirmed their efforts and showed that most of the unobstructed runways had now been blocked.

This offensive air phase was now really getting into its stride. An hour before dawn, as the last Valiants and Canberras were landing back at their bases with R.A.F. Hunters and R.N. Seahawks once more standing by to guard against the now more remote possibility of an Egyptian air attack, Venoms and Thunderstreaks were taking-off from Nicosia, Akrotiri and Tymbou and Seahawks, Sea Venoms and Corsairs from the carriers. Once in the air they were all heading for the Egyptian coast. By now the cumulative effects of so many attacks on the Egyptian airfields was readily apparent to the pilots of the ground attack planes. Runways were strewn with the burnt-out hulks of aircraft irreparably damaged and those few machines which did appear to be serviceable were the subject of fierce competition among the pilots who came in to attack. By 0800 hours that day it had been decided that the Egyptian Air Force no longer existed as an effective fighting force; this meant that in thirty-six hours of concentrated attacks it had been destroyed. Air Marshal Barnett, whilst keeping a wary eye on the runways to make sure that any planes which had been hidden away would not be able to take-off, was now free to seek new targets to ease the path of the assault landing force.

Meanwhile as the Egyptian Air Force was being systematically blasted out of existence, there had been some naval activity in the

Gulf of Suez, where a combined Anglo-French naval force[1] was patrolling to protect Allied shipping. Merchant vessels were warned by Admiralty broadcasts to keep away from Egyptian waters but as they had received only one day's warning of hostilities it was the duty of the Gulf of Suez task force to protect any such shipping from retaliatory Egyptian action. In the critical area where the Gulf of Suez joins the Red Sea, the cruiser H.M.S. *Newfoundland* in company with the destroyer H.M.S. *Diana* spotted a darkened ship following a group of merchant men moving north. The British warships closed in to investigate and in the light of the *Newfoundland*'s searchlights the darkened vessel was seen to be an Egyptian frigate, later identified as the *Domiat*—the former British River class frigate H.M.S. *Nith*. *Newfoundland* ordered: 'Stop or I fire', but after acknowledging this signal, the *Domiat* increased speed and was seen to be training her guns on the British cruiser. At 1,500 yards the *Newfoundland* opened up with her main armament just before the *Domiat* began firing with all her guns. The action was short and sharp; the frigate turned in what appeared to be an attempt to ram the *Newfoundland* but in nine broadsides from the cruiser's six-inch guns the *Domiat* was finished. Both ships stopped firing and the badly damaged *Domiat* capsized and sank within five minutes. The two British ships stopped to pick up survivors and a South African merchant ship also stood by for two hours. In all, six officers and sixty Egyptian ratings, some of whom had been trained in England, were picked up; these men were taken later to Djibouti for repatriation, in the *Diana*.

Despite the fact that she had been hit by two four-inch shells, the damage to the *Newfoundland* was negligible; casualties fortunately were light—one killed, five injured. And after this action, which had taken them well up into the Gulf of Suez, the British ships turned south and steamed at full speed in order to be well clear of the area before dawn when an air attack could be expected.

Two days later, as they continued their patrol at the entrance to the Gulf a radar plot suggested that Egyptian 'E' boats were making a sortie against the same two ships; fortunately nothing came of it and it is possible that the radar gave a false indication. On the same day,

---

[1] Comprising the cruiser H.M.S. *Newfoundland* (8,800 tons) supported by the Daring class destroyer H.M.S. *Diana* (2,610 tons) and the frigates H.M.S. *Crane* and H.M.S. *Modeste* (both of 1,490 tons), together with the French minesweeper *Jasmine* (232 tons); Escort vessels *Gazelle* (647 tons) and *La Perouse* (1,372 tons) with the R.F.A. tanker *Wave-Sovereign*.

however, H.M.S. *Crane*, patrolling off the Straits of Tiran, was attacked and rocketed by five jet aircraft. *Crane* was only slightly damaged and managed to shoot one of the planes down in the course of the action; there was no positive identification of their origin but it seems most likely that they were Israeli machines.

In Cairo, as the bombing spread from airfields to military installations, there were fifty-five separate air-raid alerts during the course of Friday the 2nd November. For Nasser most of the news was bad; the Israelis had sealed off the Gaza Strip, the defence at Abu Aweigila had collapsed and an Israeli army spokesman in Tel Aviv had announced: 'We have conquered the bulk of Sinai,' claiming that 30,000 Egyptian soldiers had been either killed, captured or had fled. In the afternoon Canberras bombed the transmitting station of Cairo Radio and temporarily silenced Nasser's propaganda. (A less efficient stand-by transmitter was back on the air within an hour, however.) This left the air open to the British station at Limassol, which was now calling itself 'Free Egypt' Radio and, on a frequency very close to that of Cairo Radio, was broadcasting messages exhorting the Egyptians to rid themselves of 'that traitor Nasser'. Not that this worried El Rayis; his own psychological warfare executive were much more adept at Arab propaganda than the British, and already had more than a head start on Brigadier Fergusson. Before it went off the air one of the last messages broadcast by Cairo's 'Voice of the Arabs' had been an appeal to Arab workers throughout the Middle East to blow up Western oil installations—'even if it means blowing up all the pipelines in the Arab world'. In Bahrein, the British Oil Company's office buildings had already been set on fire and shortly afterwards three big explosions were reported from along the Iraq Company's 500-mile pipeline to the Mediterranean. The saboteurs presumably acted on their own, since none of the oil-producing nations officially ordered the oil installations to be sabotaged—they were too concerned with the harm such action would do to themselves.

Despite these sympathetic gestures, Colonel Nasser's Arab friends and allies did not exactly appear to be rushing to his aid. Morocco, Tunisia and Saudi Arabia all proclaimed that they were on his side and Iraq, secretly pleased to see her rival Egypt in trouble, also denounced Britain's 'aggression'. Syria—thought to be Egypt's finest ally—broke off diplomatic relations with Britain and France; nothing more. Jordan broke only with France. None of them did much else other than talk, and at this hour Nasser would have appreciated some more positive gestures, yet when 'Free Egypt' Radio announced that landings would soon take place in the Canal Zone he is said to have remained calm. Realizing that the remnants of his air force would be facing hopeless odds, he ordered it to remain on the ground; at the same time he directed that seven cement-filled ships prepared for just such an emergency, should be sunk in the Canal. If Egypt was going to have to submit again to a European occupation then he was determined that the Canal should be kept closed and that no oil should flow. As for fighting, his troops might not be able to stand up to Anglo-French superiority in arms and equipment but there was one way in which he knew that Egyptians could stand and he ordered several hundred thousand rifles to be issued to civilians, in preparation for a grim guerrilla campaign.

The Allied aim now was to reduce the Egyptian capability to oppose the proposed assault landings. The attacks on the Egyptian Air Force and its installations continued on a reduced scale but the main effort was now directed towards the destruction of military equipment and the prevention of its movement. Photographic reconnaissance had shown that there was relatively little Egyptian armour in Port Said and even though the Cyprus Radio had announced the intention of securing the Canal Zone it seemed that the Egyptians were still uncertain of where the landings would take place. There were some indications of troops concentrating round Cairo, however, and if Air Marshal Barnett could destroy the Egyptian armour, prevent the Port Said garrison being reinforced and stop the Egyptian Air Force from recovering then the landings would be comparatively easy.

Early on Friday morning Allied aircraft attacked a large concentration of armoured fighting vehicles at Huckstep Barracks near Cairo—the sort of target that is the ground-attack pilot's dream. Over a thousand tanks, armoured cars, and lorries were parked in lines in a large camp clearly distinguishable from the air, and the Royal Navy Seahawks and Wyverns returned again and again to create havoc and destruction. Guns and vehicles had also been discovered at the Al Maya artillery barracks where Venoms and Corsairs were directed on to them. The radar station at Abu Sultan was destroyed by French Thunderstreaks and periodic attacks continued to be made on the Egyptian airfields to prevent the runways being repaired. And, once again, before dark, Canberras were over Egypt, this time to attack Luxor in the south. One point must be mentioned at this stage, since it proved to be a humane limitation which some, in the belief that the end justifies the means, have criticized. Throughout the whole period of the operation, scrupulous care was exercised in order to preserve civilian lives and restrict damage to military installations.

On Saturday, as more and more Egyptian troops concentrated in the Cairo area, the weight of the daylight offensive was directed at the roads, railways and the canal leading to Port Said. The roads from the west became blocked with burnt-out lorries, the bridge across Lake Manzala was rocketed and collapsed and before long the wrecks of armoured cars and army trucks served as a warning to the Egyptian Army. The roads from the Canal Zone were now crowded with traffic fleeing from the area and Allied pilots had to exercise great care to avoid strafing the wretched refugees. Egyptian military traffic virtually disappeared from the roads and it was suspected that troops were travelling in civilian vehicles for safety; it was impossible to do anything about this. Almost every conceivable military centre was blitzed, the railway marshalling yards at Nefisha near Ismailia on the Cairo to Port Said line were attacked and disrupted as rolling stock was derailed and lines blown up. During these attacks one R.A.F. pilot was lost with his aircraft, although the loss was not attributed to enemy action; a Wyvern was also hit by anti-aircraft fire and the pilot was compelled to bale out over the sea but he was not long in the water before being rescued by a helicopter from H.M.S. *Eagle* over seventy miles away. He returned safely despite the efforts of the Port Said garrison who shelled him with field artillery whilst he floated in the water two miles off the coast.

The accuracy of the Egyptian anti-aircraft fire was now improving; over Port Said it was particularly heavy. (Originally the failure of the gun crews could be attributed to attempting to cope with an aircraft flying speed of 300 m.p.h. whilst the actual speeds approximated to something like 100 m.p.h. faster than this.) To deal with this encroaching menace, since it was imperative that those in and around Port Said should be put out of action if the slow flying and cumbersome transport aircraft carrying the parachutists for the next phase of the operation were to have a safe passage. R.A.F. Venoms from Cyprus and naval aircraft from the carriers attacked and silenced many of the more active guns.

On Sunday morning H.M.S. *Eagle* temporarily withdrew from the operation to refuel, steaming back into the Mediterranean to a rendezvous with one of the fleet auxiliaries operating in support of the fleet south of Crete. During the whole period of the operation her starboard launching catapult had been out of action and her crew took the opportunity to repair it before she returned to the operations that night. Meantime, the opportunity to participate in a naval action had presented itself to H.M.S. *Bulwark*. Three Egyptian motor torpedo-boats were reported by a reconnaissance aircraft to have been seen leaving the shelter of Alexandria. *Bulwark*'s air umbrella struck first, to be followed by a succession of attacks by other aircraft hastily scrambled. Two of the MTB's were sunk, the third was allowed to pick up survivors and return to Alexandria.

These activities made little difference to the pace of the offensive. During the day the defences of Port Said were repeatedly attacked to prepare the way for the airborne assault the following day[1] and a concentration of Soviet tanks and self-propelled artillery near the Pyramids also received the frequent attentions of shore-based aircraft. Other planes patrolled the roads and railways into Port Said to prevent any movement; but by now targets were becoming rare. The final operations were two attacks carried out by Valiants and Canberras, one against coastal guns and radar installations at El Agami Island near Alexandria, intended to draw Egyptian attention away from the Port Said area and the other—the last attack of the day—against the now familiar Huckstep Barracks. Both attacks were completely successful.

In Cyprus, excitement was mounting as Sunday drew to a close. Preparations for the airborne assault were almost complete. R.A.F. ground crews had serviced the Hastings and Valettas; aircrews had been briefed, men of the 16th Parachute Brigade Group had studied aerial photographs and were ready to go. The Egyptian Air Force had been defeated and so would be unable to interfere with the operation. Port Said had been isolated and the Egyptian Army had been prevented from reinforcing the garrison, many of the Egyptian tanks had been destroyed; the stage was now set.

The first phase was over, the role of the Allied Air Force now was to support the parachutists in the hazardous hours ahead of them.

[1] Although Admiral Power, commanding the carrier task force, had no knowledge of the proposed airborne assault until that night (2100 hours).

CHAPTER 7

The Airborne Assault

O
n the 23rd October, when the Arab Entente Militaire was triumphantly announced in Cairo, the men of the 16th Parachute Brigade were moving into position for another drive against the Cypriot terrorists. During the next six days, patrols of paratroopers combed the Troodos mountains or laid up in the thickly wooded valleys in the hope of ambushing members of E.O.K.A. Ninety per cent of their efforts were frustrated but, just as the operation was beginning to show some signs of success, it was abruptly terminated and units were ordered to return to their base to take part in a 'training exercise'. Those at brigade headquarters knew that this phase covered the preparation for an operation outside Cyprus; only the Brigadier and his Brigade Major knew that they were destined for Port Said.

Only one battalion of the 'Red Devils' could be used in an airborne role since the number of aircraft which could operate from the restricted airfields in Cyprus limited the size of the force for the initial assault; the remainder of the brigade would have to be ferried in by air later, or by sea. This battalion which would parachute into Egypt was the spearhead of the Allied expedition; its objective was Port Said's airport, the airfield at Gamil on the outskirts of the town.

For the jump, Colonel Paul Crook's 3rd Battalion was chosen. Whilst his men were fit and eager to go, the same could not be said of the equipment. Not only was the number of aircraft inadequate but the actual types available were hopelessly out of date. Almost every other country possessing airborne troops—the United States, Canada, France, Italy, Belgium and even India—used modern rear-loading aircraft. Britain's airborne strategic reserve of a single parachute brigade, ridiculously small for her world-wide commitments, had to rely on the old Hastings and Valetta side-loading freighters, the latter, a military conversion of the Viking airliner, being known in the R.A.F. as 'The Pig', not only from its appearance but by virtue of its flying capabilities. This shortage of suitable aircraft was despite the fact that for years it had been urged that the strategic reserve should be completely air-transportable and that sufficient air transport should be built up to carry at least a division quickly to any danger spot overseas. The old aircraft not only limited the type of heavy equipment—guns, transport, and the like—which could be dropped; such heavy equipment demanded special subsidiary aerial delivery systems and these were largely obsolescent. The parachutists, following the latest trends, had developed and trained in more modern methods and they had adapted their equipment for the modern transports which had been promised but which existed only in prototype or development stage. Having to fly in Hastings and Valettas meant that aged wartime jeeps hastily had to be brought back into service to take the place of the champs by which they had been replaced. Instead of ammunition and supplies being loaded on to platforms which could be ejected simply from the tail door of the more modern plane they had to be made up into small packages for loading into the containers (CLE) which were slung below the bellies of the Hastings and Valettas. Smaller packages increased the total quantity of aerial delivery equipment, packaging the equipment in smaller loads meant more time and more men to prepare these loads for the operation. For the assault on Port Said less space inside the aircraft precluded the landing of any artillery and necessitated overloading the individual parachutists. As only a few vehicles could be dropped, men carried loads of up to a hundred pounds over and above their personal equipment and parachutes. Such methods result in men, tired by the loads they have to carry to the aircraft, being restricted up to and during the period of their jump.

The inadequacies of the aircraft will be even more apparent later but something must now be said about the replacement aircraft of the future—the Beverley—which, at the time of writing, is now in service. To begin with it had taken far too long to develop, and advances in techniques had outstripped its usefulness. Maintenance problems, which made its flying performance unreliable, primarily precluded its use in this operation although its other defects such as being too big, being awkward to load without special equipment, and needing an excessively long dropping zone, all contributed towards the decision to rely on the obsolescent Hastings and Valettas. As has been re-

Operation 'Musketeer'

PHASE 1: THE AIR BOMBARDMENT

PHASE 2: THE AIRBORNE ASSAULT

PHASE 3: THE SEABORNE ASSAULT

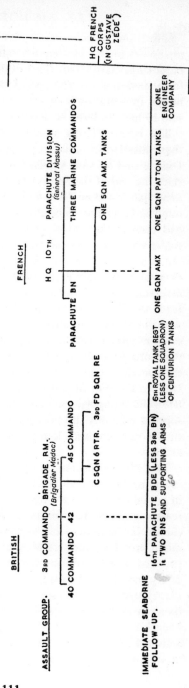

The Development of the Assault on Port Said and the Chain of Command

counted, this decision meant that obsolete gear had to be found and repaired and the parachutists had had to retrain in obsolete techniques associated with the methods of dropping jeeps and trailers from such aircraft. The undesirability of making such changes just before an operation is obvious; luckily the operation cannot fairly be said to have suffered because of them.

The French 'Paras' were more experienced and better equipped than their British colleagues. Many of them who were veterans of Dien Bien Phu and Algeria had been fighting almost continuously since the end of the Second World War and hardly a man amongst them had less than 160 jumps, whereas the last British operational jump had been the Rhine crossing in 1945 and few of the 16th Brigade had been in that. Most of the Frenchmen were long-term regular soldiers and they were on an average some five or six years older than the British 'Red Devils'. As regards training, the men of the 16th Brigade could only expect to take part in a single annual exercise involving a brigade jump—and then only if the brigade was in England; the French reckoned on a Regimental (Battalion equivalent, seven companies totalling 1,300 men) drop as a matter of course every month. Their standard parachuting and re-supply aircraft was the Nord Atlas 2501, a twin-boom boxcar which closely resembled the American C119 Fairchild, familiar as a training machine in the U.K. to the 16th Brigade. The Nord Atlas could either carry thirty-five fully equipped parachutists complete with their wireless sets, support weapons and personal impedimenta, or, with its rear clamshell doors removed, it could carry parachute loads of vehicles or artillery.

The 'Red Devils' mostly used standard British infantry equipment, including weapons, and this meant that much of it had to be dropped in containers separately from the men. Those weapons which were readily available to them in the air, such as the Sten, could not be carried in the harness of the parachute since it was feared that they might protrude, interfere with the static line of the parachute and so cause an accident during the actual jump. 'Les Paras' were not so safety conscious: their weapons were designed specifically for use by parachutists; rifles and sub-machine-guns had folding butts to enable them to be carried across the chest during a descent and when a French parachutist landed on the ground he could go straight into action. In the drop on Port Said, this was invaluable. Both British and French were parachuted directly on to the top of Egyptian-held

112

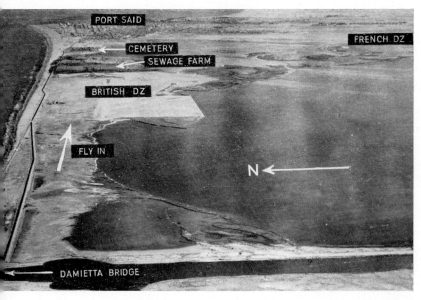

3a. The British Dropping Zone at Gamil.

3b. The French Dropping Zone.

4. These photographs were taken during the actual assault. The figure in the centre of the top picture is that of Lt.-Col. P. Crook.

slit trenches and, as the parachute canopies opened, the Egyptians directed a heavy volume of small arms fire up at them. As they sat in their lift webs, swinging hundreds of feet up in the air, many of the Frenchmen were able to return the fire and captured Egyptians later admitted that they had been discouraged by the prophylactic effect of such shooting. Then, without further ado, when they landed, they were able to put down covering fire for their comrades still in the air. Brigadier Butler's men descended in grim silence, some of them landing perilously close to manned trenches where, as they lay flat on their stomachs they often had to slash at container cords to get at their equipment. One was reduced to hurling his container at the Egyptian occupant of a foxhole before following feet first with his jack-knife as weapon.

French parachuting methods also were less rigid than those of the British—though the exponents of British methods would say more happy-go-lucky. Constant training with regular jumping practice and familiarity derived from recent experience of mounting operations under active service conditions had bred in the French a contempt for formal drills and parachute packing standards like those of the British. Any day in late October, near a disused garage outside the walls of the old city of Nicosia, brown and white parachutes could be seen hanging by their apex cords thirty feet in the air from the trees in the moat, drying out before another training jump. Following the jump they were then bundled into zip bags and returned for hanging again. No elaborate testing for the porosity of the panels was done as at the parachute centre at Abingdon; the French parachutes remained serviceable until they showed signs of wear or until they failed to open— a routine which could be commended for its economy and speed although it was more risky. It was rumoured that two parachutes failed to open over Port Said; in fact, the only accident was one man who made a faulty exit from his aircraft and fell into the Canal.

French aircraft drills reflected the same easy confidence. There was no 'prepare for action' and inspection drill by the parachutist 'stick' commander immediately prior to a drop. The men, most of whom read or dozed during the flight, would be alerted by a red light signal only five minutes before they were required to jump. During the ensuing five minutes they would be expected to collect their gear and do an impromptu check of each other's lift webs, safety-pins and strops, on which the safe opening of their parachutes depended. Then, when the aircraft turned into the dropping zone a green light would replace the red warning, a klaxon horn would sound, and men would jump in two streams from port and starboard, on the heels of each other. There was no question of an individual steadying himself in the doorway to leap out at right-angles; there was no time. The resultant exit speed meant that a 'stick' of seventeen men could be clear of their aircraft in ten seconds, with a consequent lesser dispersion of men on the ground.[1]

'Les Paras' had been in Cyprus since the end of August, and their drab, mottled, but business-like uniforms contrasted sharply with the appearance of the coloured hosetops and pressed drill of the British garrison troops. The red beret is a famous and familiar badge of any who serve with the British airborne forces; French headgear is somewhat more varied since they use three different coloured berets to distinguish their three groups of parachutists—green for the Foreign Legion, red for Colonial troops and blue for the men of Metropolitan France. All these colours were to be seen worn by those assembling at 'Camp X' near Tymbou, where, as November approached and the number of French troops increased, French impatience for action also grew. By Thursday, 1st November, the day that Brigadier Butler was authorized to brief the battalion commander of the British parachute force, General Massu's men were literally seething with restlessness.

The plan that was adopted eventually was of French extraction. From the very beginning, the French had pressed for sufficient troops to be located in Cyprus to make possible a sudden descent on Egypt by air and sea, if and when a favourable political situation presented itself. With the limited facilities that the Cyprus base could provide, the point has already been made that it was not possible to stage any sizeable seaborne force there. And, as has also been described, the amphibious echelon was back in Malta.

On the 31st October, the French Government, via the medium of Admiral Barjot, suggested that the Israeli advance and the Allied air programme now proposed might make it desirable to move much more quickly than the existing plan provided for. If Egyptian resistance suddenly collapsed, the occupation of vulnerable points along

---

[1] Under favourable conditions such a drop meant that the 'stick' will be spaced out over half a mile; hesitation in the air multiplies the distance on the ground. The Nord Atlas drops a 'stick' of seventeen men, the Hastings one of fifteen; this latter 'stick' takes twenty seconds to jump and is spread over a pattern of one mile.

the Canal was vital if it were to be safeguarded. In these circumstances it was essential that there should be no delay in capturing Port Said. And so, on the initiative of Generals Stockwell and Beaufré, a new plan was conceived within the framework of the old 'Musketeer'. A British parachute battalion would drop on Gamil, Royal Marine Commandos would make a helicopter assault on the bridges south of the town, and a French parachute force would seize Port Fuad. Then, as soon as their initial objectives had been consolidated, the three assault forces would turn on the town and with the support of the guns of the combined fleets, Port Said would quickly succumb. Sequential parachute drops would then be made along the Canal at El Kantara, Ismailia and Suez and, as little shooting was expected, it was hoped that the Canal could be occupied within twenty-four hours—before the Egyptians had recovered or regrouped sufficiently to be able to do anything about it. This plan was called 'Omelette'—an apt name perhaps, because Port Said might well have suffered considerable damage in the action.

Although preparations went ahead for the 'Omelette' plan to be put into effect, nothing came of it, and on 2nd November, Admiral Barjot sought out General Beaufré. Pressed by his Government to get the Allied operation under way, the Admiral told his compatriot at about 1600 hours that day, that 'Paris' were of the opinion that the political situation warranted troops being landed in Egypt 'within two hours'! A meeting with the task force commanders followed, during which Admiral Durnford-Slater and General Stockwell refused to commit the 'Omelette' plan. They had concluded that the situation at Port Said had worsened; Egyptian units not committed to the Sinai battles, and even men who had fled before the Israeli columns were now collecting in the Canal Zone to reinforce the defences there. With the Soviet tanks already known to be in Port Said the situation was fraught with danger for a weak airborne force which must rely on the Fleet Air Arm for its artillery support. At the same time the feasibility and wisdom of the untried and novel helicopter assault needed a careful reappraisal.

Barjot's reaction to his failure to get the operation under way was to tell Beaufré to devise some plan which would get the troops moving. And that night (2nd November) Beaufré put forward the idea of a British parachute drop on Gamil, a French drop to replace the helicopter assault on the bridges, and a second French drop to the south of Port Fuad. The time factor was now such that the seaborne element, *en route* from Malta, would only be about twenty-four hours behind the parachute landings, and the French force at the bridges, with water on three sides of their position, ought to be able to hold out until the amphibious support arrived. If this revised 'Omelette' plan—later referred to as 'Telescope'—was agreed, it ought to be possible for the action to start by the morning of the 4th. By 1100 hours the next day, Saturday, 3rd November, the plan had been approved, with the exception of the second French drop south of Port Fuad, and Monday (5th) was fixed as 'D' day for the assault. Subsequently, on Monday afternoon the operation was going so well that it was decided to include the only feature of Beaufré's plan which had been omitted, and French 'Paras' were dropped just outside Port Fuad.

Returning now to the problems of the troops who were to take part in the airborne attack. The point has already been made that airfield space limited the numbers of aircraft[1] available for the operation, and meant that the size of the parachute task force had to be restricted. Only about 600 men of the 3rd Parachute Battalion and 500 from the 2nd Regiment de Parachutistes Coloniaux, together with a few engineers, signallers, a medical detachment and a skeleton brigade headquarters to co-ordinate the attack, could be utilized in the first assault. The time of the assault, still necessarily linked with the arrival of the seaborne assault group coming mainly from Malta, meant that the parachutists would have to jump well after first light. And, since the dropping zones were expected to be defended, in the original 'Musketeer' plan the intention had been to parachute into Port Said half an hour after the start of the seaborne assault on the harbour, after concentrated air strikes on the dropping zones. The effect of Beaufré's 'Telescope' plan was to advance the parachute attack by twenty-four hours. This meant that the preliminary 'softening-up' of the landing zone defences were to miss the Allied air attacks that could have been staged in the extra twenty-four hours, and that the parachutists were deprived of the artillery support which would have been provided by the guns of the combined fleets. In the event, neither of these facts seems to have been relevant. Gamil airfield and the French dropping zone were struck repeatedly before the drop took place, and the squadrons of Seahawks and Corsairs which were over the dropping zones to await the arrival of the airborne assault

[1] Eighteen Valettas and fourteen Hastings for the British Force, twenty-two Nord Atlas for the French.

force provided a capable and formidable substitute for the naval guns.

The long narrow airfield of El Gamil, about a mile and a half long and half a mile wide, which was to function as the 'Red Devils'' dropping zone, is bounded on both the north and south sides by the sea. This permitted the invasion aircraft to approach from only two directions: north-west or south-east. Approaching from the north-west meant flying directly into the sun, an approach from the opposite direction had the disadvantage of having to fly through the anti-aircraft defences of Port Said. So far as the airfield itself was concerned, it had been apparent for some time that the Egyptians were going to defend it in the event of an attack, and only a few days before the operation, a photographic reconnaissance revealed that hundreds of oil drums had been put as obstacles to hamper landing; subsequently these sand-filled drums were to provide useful cover behind which the parachutists' containers could be unpacked and the men could rally.

The first objective of Colonel Pierre Chateau-Jobert's 2nd Colonial Regiment was the twin Raswa bridges near the waterworks—the bridges which cross the Interior Basin waterway and form a vital link in the Port Said–Suez route. The French dropping zone was only 150 yards across and bounded by the sea, roads, the Canal and trees; fortunately the French jumping techniques were suited to a small area and Chateau-Jobert was not unduly perturbed. After the bridges had been secured, 'Les Paras' were scheduled to attack the Port Fuad area on the other bank of the Canal a mile or so away opposite Port Said. This provided simply defined objectives in the capture of which the French were not expected to take very long.

For those not familiar with the mechanics of a parachutist assault, something must be said now about the tactics involved. In planning an operation of this nature the more usual procedure is to select a convenient dropping zone, not too far distant from the eventual objectives, on which 'pathfinders' can precede the main force by about an hour. Then they mark the line of run into the dropping zone by means of flares, and locate the exact point at which the aircraft are to start debouching parachutists, with a cloth 'T'. Quite obviously this procedure was completely out of the question for any daylight attack on the densely populated and restricted area of Port Said. The alternatives were for pathfinders to make a night drop, dig in, and hope to hold out until some time the following morning when the main assault was to be launched, or for a new marking technique to

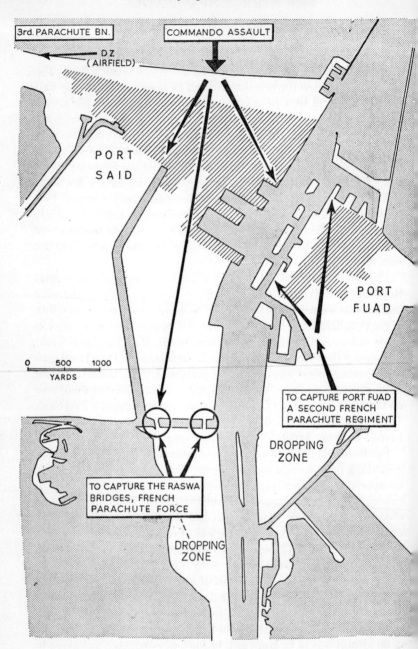

3rd. PARACHUTE BN.

COMMANDO ASSAULT

DZ (AIRFIELD)

PORT SAID

PORT FUAD

0   500   1000
YARDS

TO CAPTURE PORT FUAD
A SECOND FRENCH
PARACHUTE REGIMENT

DROPPING
ZONE

TO CAPTURE THE RASWA
BRIDGES, FRENCH
PARACHUTE FORCE

DROPPING
ZONE

The Objectives of the Airborne Assault
118

be evolved; the latter seemed to be more practical. A Canberra bomber was briefed to drop a flare five miles from the dropping zones to mark the run-in for the transports, and for the Gamil airfield a prominent sea wall marked the start of the dropping zone and equated to the pathfinders 'T' as the release point; the beach immediately west of their zone provided a similar mark for the French drop.

As the drop was to take place well after first light and the direction of fly-in to Gamil was already decided by the shape and location of the dropping zones, it became apparent now that it was going to be difficult for the pilots of the transport aircraft to fly directly into a strong morning sun and be able to see well enough to be able to make an accurate drop. The solution seemed to be to fit sun-vizors which would protect the pilots' vision and one Valetta squadron in fact was specially trained with improvised vizors. The main transport force was being held in the U.K. until the last possible minute, however, and time did not allow for vizors to be fitted; in consequence they went into the action without them. Despite the question of possible sun-blindness at a crucial moment it was still considered that a north-westerly approach to avoid the flak over Port Said was the lesser evil and the pilots concerned regarded the authorities' failure to provide the vizors with considerable disgust—almost equalled by their disgust at an issue of armoured vests which were too hot for comfort. In the event, none of the aircraft deviated from its run into the dropping zone; even without the vizors the pilots managed to place the parachutists accurately over their targets.

One difference in British and French parachuting techniques should be mentioned. In training, the 'Red Devils' wore both a main and a reserve parachute, the latter for emergency use in the unlikely event of the main 'chute failing to open. The French, most of whose recent jumps were on actual operations, did not consider that a reserve was ever necessary. For a reserve parachute to function with any certainty, the jump must be made from an altitude of at least 1,000 feet so that if the main parachute fails to open there is still time to rip the reserve. However, the effect of a cross wind increases with altitude and in the proposed drop on Port Said, the question of cross winds was particularly important. The greater the altitude the greater the likelihood of drifting away from the dropping zone and even a light wind over the restricted area of Port Said could mean the possibility of missing the narrow dropping zones. If this happened the alternatives were of either drowning or landing on the beach, where Cairo Radio had said that mines would produce 'a volcano beneath the feet of the invader'. In the light of these considerations, Brigadier Butler decided to discard the reserve and have his men jump from 600 feet; this had the added advantage that the individual could carry more ammunition in lieu of the extra parachute.

The Valettas were scheduled to lead the flight into Gamil and most of the heavy equipment was slung beneath the Hastings, which would bring up the rear of the aerial convoy. The convoy itself comprised a double column of pairs of aircraft; these pairs flew in blocks of six, with the first two at 600 feet and those following stepped up, at 100-foot intervals, fifteen seconds behind. This formation was intended to provide a safety measure in the actual drop; by the time the second two planes reached the release point, it was estimated that the men from the first pair would be floating 400 feet below them. The blocks of six were then separated by one-minute intervals—about two miles in distance—after which the order was the same, with the first pair again at an altitude of 600 feet. With Egyptians expected to do everything in their power to oppose the landing of the parachutists it is superfluous to add that the dropping operation had to be completed as quickly as possible; and by the method which has just been described it was reckoned that the entire British force would be delivered on to Gamil in eight minutes. (In practice it took longer but 85 per cent of the assault force was down within ten minutes.) Some of the heavier equipment—anti-tank guns, wireless sets to contact the aircraft and warships for artillery support, and the like—would also have to be got into action quickly. This meant dropping troops and heavy loads together, which is generally regarded as an undesirable business if accidents are to be avoided; to overcome it the Hastings aircraft with the heavy equipment flew about 400 feet above the aircraft carrying the men. This arrangement was to prove entirely satisfactory, since no one was hurt by any of the heavy equipment crashing down on them, even though the order of flight subsequently had to be changed.

To turn now to Chateau-Jobert's French. It was because of the restrictions associated with their narrow dropping zone near Raswa that the idea of seizing the bridge with a Commando force landed close by, from helicopters, had been included in the earlier plan. When Barjot pressed for action, those who reconsidered the plan had decided such a move was practicable only if heavy casualties in men and machines were acceptable—which they were not. The experience of the French parachutists showed subsequently that the decision not to use helicopters was a wise one: the area near the bridges was a mass of field defences occupied by Egyptian troops who were prepared to stay and fight and their anti-aircraft guns would have made short work of helicopters hovering to discharge the commandos. Helicopters may be of considerable value as reinforcement lift vehicles and are now regarded less vulnerable to small arms fire than was thought prior to this operation but unarmoured machines of this ilk are not suitable replacements for a parachute force. When it was decided that the French should conduct this part of the operation it was proposed to overcome the disadvantages of the narrow occupied dropping zone by their making an unusually low jump— from 400 feet. In a somewhat similar arrangement to the British, their aircraft were briefed to fly-in in pairs, with sixty yards between each plane of the pair, and a gap of 120 yards separating the pairs. By these tactics it was estimated that the drop would be completed in four minutes. And it was.

The British battalion had had less time to prepare for the operation than their French colleagues. The days between the 29th October, when the battalion returned from their operation in the Troodos mountains, and the 5th November were spent in precipitate preparation. All the stores, ammunition and equipment needed for the operation had to be loaded either into airborne containers or on to the ships of the seaborne follow-up, whilst the men had to be rehearsed in aircraft drills and refreshed with details of parachuting techniques. Right up to the last minute there was anxiety about some of the pieces of R.A.F. equipment. Originally it had been intended that such items as parachutes[1] and roller conveyors—vital for the ejection of heavy loads such as vehicles—should be flown into Cyprus with the task force, four to five days before they were needed. As the days slipped by and tension mounted, there was concern not only for the safe arrival of these essentials but also the order in which some of them would arrive. Fortunately the last bits finally showed up on the

[1] There was no Mobile Parachute Packing Section (MPSU) available, so that all the parachutes had to be obtained direct from the United Kingdom where they were packed. Despite the fact that the 16th Parachute Brigade was part of the strategic reserve—with a role that required them to be prepared to operate anywhere in the world—no provision had been made for packing equipment or repacking parachutes. The French had such facilities, albeit their methods were somewhat different: the British had not.

Friday and it would have been just possible to launch the operation on the Sunday (4th November), for which Barjot and Beaufré were pressing.

On Friday their orders, so far as the men themselves were concerned, were that the assault would take place the following Tuesday —the airborne attack coinciding with the simultaneous naval bombardment and the amphibious assault. On Saturday they were told that the attack would be on the Monday and that the parachutists were scheduled to precede the seaborne invasion by a day; and they realized that this meant they could have no tank or artillery support for that period. The 'Red Devils', locked in their camp since they had been told they were off, were not unduly worried about the time being advanced even though it did mean their having to stand alone in hostile territory; apart from the fact that many did not think they would have to stand for long against the Egyptians, they all had confidence in the support they would be getting from the 'cab rank' of fighters and ground attack aircraft provided by the British and French Air Forces. Nevertheless, since it was known that the Egyptians had over a hundred armoured fighting vehicles in the Port Said area, the decision to launch the assault a day before the seaborne landings was still a calculated risk, one which reflected the degree of confidence in the air arm. If it had not succeeded there could have been organized piecemeal slaughter.

Everything went more or less as planned. A drumhead service on the Sunday morning was followed by a final check of the equipment and men were searched to make sure that they were not carrying personal documents into battle. At 0300 hours on the Monday morning the battalion were driven from their camp to emplane at Nicosia airfield, on the first stage of the journey to Port Said; at Tymbou, Colonel Chateau-Jobert's men were doing the same. The troops emplaned without fuss or difficulty, earlier rehearsals having made sure of this, and on a clear and starlit night drivers parked their vehicles without supervision and parachutist 'stick' commanders quietly settled their men into the aircraft. When the first Valetta taxied out on to Nicosia airfield at 4.15 a.m. it was dawn.[1] Followed by the

[1] At this point it should be noted that all timings were based on Greenwich Mean Time; this meant that dawn in the Eastern Mediterranean was about 4 a.m. and darkness fell about 3.30 p.m. Most of the troops taking part thought that G.M.T. references were ridiculous, but they do help to keep the times of U.K. political decisions in the correct context.

THE AIRBORNE ASSAULT

heavily loaded Hastings, the Valettas led the way to a point over the
south coast of Cyprus where the aerial convoy formed up. From here
the Egyptian coast was some two hours' flying time distant. A last-
minute change of plan in the order of flight due to difficulties with the
Hastings resulted in a different dropping sequence to that which has
been described as the original plan. The latest Hastings (Mk. 2)
aircraft were carrying the heaviest loads of equipment. Since it had
been expected that the older Hastings (Mk. 1), carrying parachutists,
would be able to overtake the heavily laden Mk. 2's, the Mk. 1's were
the last to take-off. However, once they were in the air it was found
that the parachute containers slung below the Mk. 1's produced a
much greater drag than had been anticipated. No earlier trials which
could have revealed this situation had been possible, and coupled
with a delayed take-off and unpredicted head wind, it soon became
clear that the original order of drop could only be adhered to by the
consumption of fuel required for the return journey. Consequently
some of the heavy equipment had to be dropped before the men had
all jumped; fortunately this did not cause any difficulty. The last
Hastings which came in much later had struggled along on an over-
heated engine and only just made the objective.

As has been explained, the fly-in to Gamil airfield was directly into
the sun and as the transports lumbered in towards Port Said the
R.A.F. Canberra, watched by a squadron of Fleet Air Arm Seahawks
awaiting the arrival of the parachutists, dropped a marker flare three
miles from the dropping zone. From here the pilots of the Valettas
and Hastings could see Gamil airfield quite clearly, and the fly-in now
was routine.

Inside the aircraft during the flight, the parachutists had sat opposite each other with their equipment containers between their legs,
their harness tightly adjusted. Most of their faces registered that set
stern look of strain; some slept, some fidgeted, others chewed gum,
all checked and rechecked their equipment several times. The first
order came with ten minutes yet to go: 'Prepare for Action.' Quickly
they hooked their strops to the static lines and rechecked their parachuting equipment once again. Then, having clipped on the containers containing their personal weapons they stood up and pushed
the flap seats back against the fuselage wall. As they waited, the stick
commander struggled up the aircraft between the cables and static
lines of the parachutes. Above the roar of the aircraft's four engines
came the second order, 'Tell off the equipment check'; '15 O.K., 14

123

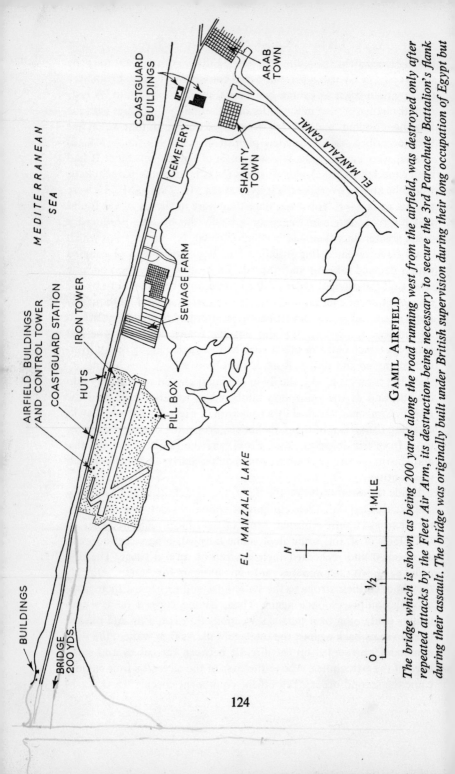

MEDITERRANEAN SEA

BUILDINGS

BRIDGE 200 YDS.

AIRFIELD BUILDINGS AND CONTROL TOWER

COASTGUARD STATION

IRON TOWER

HUTS

COASTGUARD BUILDINGS

CEMETERY

PILL BOX

SEWAGE FARM

SHANTY TOWN

ARAB TOWN

EL MANZALA CANAL

EL MANZALA LAKE

N

0   ½   1 MILE

GAMIL AIRFIELD

The bridge which is shown as being 200 yards along the road running west from the airfield, was destroyed only after repeated attacks by the Fleet Air Arm, its destruction being necessary to secure the 3rd Parachute Battalion's flank during their assault. The bridge was originally built under British supervision during their long occupation of Egypt but

O.K., . . . 2 O.K., 1 O.K., Port Stick O.K.'. The routine was repeated for the starboard stick before the commander turned and nodded to the despatcher at the open door. There was but a short wait now; nerves were forgotten as the aircraft swung on to course south-east into the sun, for the fly-in. One minute to go, and the penultimate order 'Action Stations'. The troops shuffled forward into position for the jump and the stick commander in the doors now had an oblique view of the concrete landing strip of Gamil airfield.

Beyond Gamil, in the line of flight, there was the golf-course; beyond that lay the Raswa bridges and the tiny triangular dropping zone of Chateau-Jobert's 'Paras'. (The Nord Atlas planes were following the Hastings and Valettas and the French jump took place about fifteen minutes after that of the British.)

On Gamil itself the dispersed oil drums appeared as menacing black objects; some still had the fear that such black objects might be mines but a glimpse beyond the mile-long dropping zone gave a boost to the confidence of those waiting to jump as below, the transport aircraft planes of the Fleet Air Arm could be seen striking at targets close by the dropping zone. Then a light flashed over the open doorways; the order 'Red on, stand to the door' was followed by a two-pace shuffle by the waiting sticks and the aircraft finally banked into line. Suddenly the engines quietened and a voice shouting 'Green on . . . GO' was lost in the clouds as the men followed each other in quick succession. A tearing rush of nylon then a series of jerks, a buffeting and a gentle silent oscillation was a prelude to the noise which followed, as the air was rent with the noise of bullets and exploding mortar bombs. Shooting seemed to come from positions well removed from the actual dropping zone as well as from directly below.

Of the actual dispositions of the Egyptian defenders, surprisingly little was known—surprisingly only because a good deal of information might have been expected from an area well suited to intelligence penetration. The garrison of Port Said was known to include a regular infantry battalion, two national guard battalions and a coast artillery regiment and in the area of Gamil one of the infantry battalions was deployed in defences designed to counter both airborne and seaborne attacks. Men from an infantry company specifically deployed for the defence of the airfield manned machine-guns in two pillboxes covering the dropping zone, the remainder of the company being disposed between the beach, the edge of the sewage-farm, and towards the Coast Guard Barracks. Another company position was sited in the neighbouring cemetery from which medium (81 mm.) mortars were also able to fire on to the airfield. Behind them from positions in Port Said proper, heavier weapons, including Soviet SU 100 guns and rockets were also able to shoot on to the airfield. Beyond this, not much was known.

Most of the 'Red Devils' and their equipment had landed inside ten minutes; there were but four major casualties in the drop. Two unfortunates who drifted out to sea beyond the dropping zone floundered about until they managed to rid themselves of their parachutes and swim ashore; one man dropped into a minefield and was killed, and one who landed directly on the airfield control tower was injured. Several others received minor wounds from small arms fire as they descended, otherwise the drop had been accomplished as planned, and the oil barrels now provided welcome cover. Most of the heavy equipment—jeeps, trailers and guns—landed well, only two parachutes failed to open but some of the aircraft had to make more than one run in order to ensure their loads got away safely. Their second approach was only possible because the Egyptian anti-aircraft flak umbrella over Gamil turned out to be less accurate than had been anticipated; even so, nine aircraft were damaged. Mercifully, none were shot down.

As the empty aircraft turned to fly back to Cyprus for a second lift of reinforcements and supplies, Crook's men were busy preparing their next move. The assault force had been organized into three companies each of which had been given a specific task on landing. 'A' Company which had dropped nearest to the release point was ordered to secure the north-west corner of the airfield; 'B' Company, which had jumped last so as to land on the Port Said end of the field, were responsible for sealing off that area; the third company which, with battalion headquarters, the skeleton brigade headquarters and the various supporting units, had been dropped in the middle, were to be utilized where they were needed most. 'A' and 'B' companies quickly went into action. The control tower, still blazing from an attack by Royal Navy Seahawks, was occupied and 'A' Company started to move out towards the north-west, clearing the Egyptian positions as they advanced. *En route* a troublesome pillbox was silenced by the first shot from a rocket launcher which went straight through the firing slit, the explosion killing two and wounding the remaining eight Egyptian occupants. These latter promptly surrendered.

'B' Company, at the Port Said end of the airfield, did not get off to quite such a good start. To what one described as a 'bloody good reception committee' they had landed literally on the heads of Egyptian soldiers and it took a little time for them to sort out friend and foe, but once organized they rapidly set about clearing the Coast Guard buildings. Then in about thirty minutes they were ready to move on. Meanwhile the battalion mortar platoon, which was amongst those in the middle of the airfield, had assembled its three undamaged mortars (four had been dropped) and was engaging enemy posts in the sewage-farm, about a mile away to the south-east. Elsewhere, an Egyptian anti-tank gun which was firing with unexpected precision from the beach was silenced by a 106-mm. recoilless rifle shell. Some of the wireless equipment had been damaged in the drop and it was only after some difficulty that contact was made with the cab-rank of Seahawks constantly circling overhead. As shortage of fuel compelled these aircraft from *Bulwark* to return to their ship their places were taken by others, so that the parachutists never lacked support. As things turned out, rarely were there sufficient targets to utilize all the devastating destructive power that the Seahawks could command. During the battle, aircraft about to return to refuel which had not been summoned to a target by a call for ground attack—'Belly dance'—from one of the ground 'air contact' teams were obliged to see their own targets at which they could dispose of their rockets and ammunition. Because of this the Coast Guard Barracks and various installations[1] in the sewage-farm area received a high proportion of unexpected missiles during the early stages of the battle.

For nine hours, until the garrison of Port Said sued for a cease-fire, the cab-rank of Fleet Air Arm fighter bombers faithfully answered all calls for fire support; as an example of the complementary use of aircraft carriers and shore-based aircraft it was excellent. Whilst the R.A.F. in Cyprus provided the transport force and its escorts, and continued the attacks on the military installations deep in Egypt, the aircraft carriers, close to the coast and assault area, were able to maintain direct radio contact with their own aircraft and the parachutists, and this enabled them to provide the intimate fire support which was

[1] One of these was an air compressor plant designed to pressurize the sewage system of Port Said and so force the rate of effluent flow. Its destruction resulted in Port Said's sewers overflowing into the streets—a distasteful problem which had to be rectified by British sappers.

needed as a substitute for the field artillery the parachutists lacked. In half an hour Gamil airfield had been cleared of all formal opposition; by midday it was capable of accepting such aircraft as could land on its restricted runways and it might now be supposed that having captured an airfield so early in the operation other transports standing ready loaded in Cyprus would soon arrive with reinforcements and artillery. None was available, none came. Hastings and Valettas required longer runways and reinforcements and supplies had to be parachuted down; Gamil was built to receive Dakotas, and none of these was available.

Meantime the French at Raswa were having a lively time. Miraculously, Chateau-Jobert's men had all landed in their dropping zone although this was not a particularly healthy area. Not only was their dropping zone found to be occupied by Egyptian infantry well dug-in in slit trenches, it was also swept with fire from machine-guns sited near the bridge whilst the Bofors anti-aircraft guns protecting the bridge were also able to fire straight across the area. Corsairs from the carrier *Lafayette* and Thunderstreaks from Cyprus were soon effectively directed against these guns by the French Commandant de l'Opération Aéroportée, General Gilles. Gilles, who was circling above the battle area in a Nord Atlas aerial command post, 1,000 feet up in the air, was able to exercise finger-tip control of the battle; his quick and effective deployments of the cab-rank of Corsairs were invaluable that day and proved the worth of this French innovation, of which there was no British equivalent. Throughout the battle Gilles flew round and over Port Said directing his troops, controlling air support, and reporting progress back to General Beaufré at sea in the *Gustave Zède* and to Force Headquarters in Cyprus. Frequently his aircraft was rocked by near bursts of Egyptian flak and his command plane technique is not one which is likely to survive in a battle where nuclear exchanges are made, or even in limited war unless there is air superiority. On this occasion the French Commander was able to provide his superiors with the equivalent of a television eye and his troops with a direction and control which could not have been so effective if it had been exercised on the ground.

Before the French had cleared the immediate area of their dropping zone there was some brisk close-quarter fighting, but once organized resistance had been eliminated 'Les Paras' reorganized and one company advanced on the objective. The eastern road bridge—a pontoon bridge—across the Interior Basin had already been demolished but the western bridge, carrying both the road and railway, was still intact. Egyptian tanks opened up from the golf-course beyond the bridge as they advanced but with a quick dash the bridge was in their hands and to the surprise of the French its piles were found to be clear of demolitions. Within an hour of landing, the sandbagged Egyptian emplacements were empty, the road to the south was open, and the waterworks on the southern bank was cleared, undamaged, with the French securely established in the surrounding area and Chateau-Jobert's headquarters established in one of the waterworks buildings. By 1130 hours the first phase of the French operation was complete; their task had been accomplished at the cost of only ten French casualties for whom over sixty of Nasser's men had paid with their lives. Capture of the Raswa bridge now ensured the breakout from Port Said; securing the undamaged waterworks was an assurance that it could continue to supply the local population and partially resolved a major administrative headache since it will be remembered plans had had to cater for the possibility of supplying the town by water tanker and facing a period of strict water rationing.

With a firm bridge head in Port Said, the way now seemed clear for the tempo of the invasion to increase; this was not to be. Apart from the political outcry which was now rising to a crescendo in America, Britain and elsewhere, neither the resources available nor their deployment were sufficient for a quick military success.

CHAPTER 8

Airborne Aftermath

For the benefit of those who do not know the Canal Zone and to understand better the events which followed the airborne assault, a brief description of Port Said and its environs is now necessary. The town itself is about 145 miles from Cairo and lies on the western side of the Mediterranean entrance to the Canal. Like its residential suburb of Port Fuad on the opposite bank of the Canal, it is situated on a low-lying island and Gamil airfield is located on the long spit of sandy beach to the west. The encroaching sea area joining it is known as Lake Manzala and from here it is about four and a half miles to the Canal mouth from the airfield. The road from Gamil to Port Said runs parallel and close to the sea; south of it the land space gradually widens and near the eastern limits of the airfield the Port Said sewage-farm is sited. From the sewage-farm it is about a mile and a half to the built-up edge of the town. A few farms occupy the first quarter of a mile or so beyond the sewage-farm and then there are the Moslem, Orthodox and Jewish cemeteries; these are followed by a large block of flats and the Isolation Hospital. Beyond this—still on the south side of the road—are the first of the shanty huts at the western limit of Arab town and aptly referred to as Shanty town. As the name implies, Arab town is the poorer native residential area, mostly comprising tightly packed wooden houses several storeys high, squalid and densely populated. Beyond this area the rest of Port Said may be divided into three: the northern seafront where the beach is lined with rows of wooden beach huts, overlooked by some modern blocks of flats and brick or stone built villas; the business section of the town with its shops and offices in the eastern sector; and the docks and associated warehouses in the south. In the southern sector there is an impressive and very modern railway station, from which, through a waste area which includes a golf-course, the railway line runs down to the Raswa bridge across the Interior Basin.

Port Fuad, which is also almost an island, is on the eastern side of the Inner Harbour. Prior to 'Musketeer' it was largely Suez Canal Company property and is connected to Port Said only by a ferry service across the Canal. The design and appearance of the buildings of Port Fuad reflect the French influence in the Canal Company; the layout, the names of the streets, and the language that predominated there were all reminiscent of the Provençale. To the 'Paras' the atmosphere was almost nostalgic.

Gamil, as has already been described, lies on a long narrow spit of sand and is about 5,000 yards from Port Said town. North of the airfield is the surf-ridden seashore; in the south there is salt marsh and a lake. On Monday morning the 5th November the progress of Crook's men along the straight open road running eastwards towards the town could be clearly observed from the tall buildings which lie along the route. To get to the middle of Port Said from here their route lay first over ditches and through the thick reeds and half-drained marshland of the sewage-farm, then across the cemetery with its numerous graves into the shanties of Arab town, and finally through the built-up area. The narrowness of the approach with the sea or lake on both sides allowed no room for manœuvre or outflanking moves; it meant a straightforward advance up the axis of the road.

The huts and bungalows along the beach adjoining the airfield were cleared first and the 'Red Devils' then rushed up the long narrow neck of open sand to the high line of reeds which marked the edge of the sewage-farm. As they did so the Egyptian troops, hidden in the reeds, put down intense fire from rifles and machine-guns with little apparent regard for the amount of ammunition they were expending. From farther back, mortars and the guns of what were either tanks or Soviet SU100 self-propelled artillery pieces were supporting them and thickening up the small arms fire; from still farther back near the docks the fire of some multiple rocket launchers also contributed. These latter pieces were subsequently silenced by air strikes of the Fleet Air Arm. The task of clearing the 500-yard square of reeds which bounded the sewage-farm was a slow drawn-out process somewhat analogous to a jungle warfare operation which took the parachutists almost an hour; during this process an anti-tank gun, manned by an Egyptian crew and firing with unexpected precision, was knocked out by one of the recently issued 106-mm. recoilless anti-tank rifles. Following the laborious clearance operation, they were almost thankful to emerge on the open banks and beds of the sewage-farm proper. Worse was ahead. As they emerged from the reeds on the right of the sewage-farm they came under heavy fire from the edge of the cemetery about 400 yards away, across an open stretch of sand dunes. To make matters worse, they were also spotted by a vigilant French aircraft and strafed as they came into the open. Fortunately there were no casualties and this was the only air recognition mistake made throughout the day—a day which could not have been carried without the air forces' invaluable support provided by the Seahawks, Sea Venoms and Corsairs guided by the Anglo-French air contact teams. Their guns and rockets were the only substitute for the tanks and artillery which both Crook and Chateau-Jobert needed that morning.

Having reached the edge of the sewage-farm there was a lull in the ground fighting whilst plans were being made for a concerted attack against the cemetery but air strikes on the hostile area ahead of them continued relentlessly during the lull. The blocks of flats behind the sewage-farm were clearly being used as observation posts and machine-gun fire was coming from the Coast Guard Barracks on the other side of the road. These were struck repeatedly by rocket-firing Seahawks. At 1028 hours an air strike directly in front of the forward parachutists was the prelude to the attack. The aircraft screamed down on the cemetery with their cannon blazing and the troops left the cover of the reeds and doubled across the open sand to the cemetery wall; there then followed what the training manuals call the 'dog-fight' in which men fought singly or in small groups at a range of only a few yards.

The attack was completely successful. Having killed thirty of the enemy and captured an old ex-British Bren-gun carrier at no cost to themselves, Crook's men now found themselves in complete control of the cemetery area. Their patrols, probing forward, quickly reached the vicinity of the flats and the Coast Guard Barracks, and the way now seemed open for a further advance into the town. By this time ammunition was running short however. Less than fifty mortar bombs remained for the support of any further offensive or as a safeguard against the anticipated counter-attack and even though a further supply of ammunition was known to be on its way from Cyprus there seemed little point in advancing into an area which was due to be bombarded by the guns of the combined Anglo-French fleet in just over twelve hours' time. It seemed more prudent to dig in and hold firmly on to what had been gained. In retrospect this decision may be questioned since it may now seem reasonable to suppose that once the ammunition problems had been overcome by the afternoon re-supply, the advance could have been continued and the docks captured. The cease-fire which came into effect during the afternoon lent weight to the argument that it was best to dig in and wait, and it is improbable that Crook's men could have got through Arab town unless they had been reinforced. Having taken the decision to halt and consolidate, a defensive position, based on the sewage-farm and airfield, was eventually taken up by last light (1530 hours G.M.T.) and the parachutists settled down to a night which was disturbed occasionally by some inaccurate mortaring of their positions and once by the chatter of the engine of a mysterious and unseen motor-boat moving close inshore.

As soon as Egyptian resistance at Gamil had been suppressed, Brigadier Butler, prompted by a surgeon, signalled to H.M.S. *Tyne* for the services of helicopters to evacuate the casualties which had been incurred at both dropping zones. From *Bulwark* and *Albion*, which at this juncture were about 150 miles off the coast, naval helicopters flew in to Gamil to pick up the wounded and return them to the hospital ships of the invasion convoy. The first with a welcome gift to the parachutists of cigarettes and beer from the two carriers ships' companies touched down at Gamil at 9.30 a.m. and from then on there was a steady stream flying between the fleet and the two dropping zones. At 1030 hours, as the attack on the cemetery was going in, an unexpected French Dakota touched down on the runway which was still partially obstructed with the oil drums; Colonel de Fouquieres, one of Admiral Barjot's staff officers, was seeking first-hand information on the possibility of flying in French reinforcements to Gamil. He left after about ten minutes with a full load of casualties that had congregated at the Dressing Station on the airfield perimeter. His Dakota was not allowed to return and other French aircraft were reputedly banned.[1] It should also be mentioned here that the British admiral in command of the Allied carrier force, Vice-Admiral Power, had also appreciated the vital necessity for speed in capturing Port Said and had offered to land by helicopter all

[1] *Secrets of Suez*—Bromberger:
'The British [*sic*] . . . anxiously saw some impetuous performances from Admiral Barjot who was grinding his teeth at the deliberate slowness of the operation. . . .'

the Royal Marines borne in the carriers, so as to reinforce the para-chutists. This offer was refused by the Joint Command in H.M.S. *Tyne* whose faith apparently lay in the seaborne assault which was planned to follow the next day.

Returning to the battle, this seems a suitable point to describe the medical arrangements. Army doctors with the airborne troops had parachuted into both Gamil and Raswa. The French were less fortunate than their British colleagues as they lost most of their surgical kit in the drop and consequently were unable to treat any of the serious cases which were among the thirty-three wounded sus-tained by Chateau-Jobert's men during the course of the fighting that day. Those of 'Les Paras' who needed treatment were patched up and sent across to Gamil where the hard-worked British team did what was necessary prior to including them in the helicopter evacuation. In the 'Musketeer' master plan there was certainly no general lack of medical facilities. Two field ambulances, from one of which the Field Surgical Team operating with the 'Red Devils' had been detached, were scheduled to land directly behind the seaborne assault. (One of these field ambulances was attached to the Commando Brigade, whose organization—unlike that of an ordinary infantry brigade group—does not include a unit of this type.) Behind them two Casualty Clearing Stations and one of the General Hospitals located in Cyprus were to follow; another General Hospital in the United Kingdom was also packed and ready to follow, if it too should be required. For the drop on Gamil, the 3rd Battalion's regimental medical officer, his small staff of orderlies, stretcher bearers and a section of the 23rd Parachute Field Ambulance, were augmented by a Field Surgical Team, made up of a R.A.M.C. surgeon, an anaesthetist and four orderlies. This, it was thought, would provide sufficient medical resources to cater for the expected number of casualties, which, from statistics acquired in Europe over the period of the Second World War, were expected to be about 5 per cent of the troops involved during the anticipated maximum period of eight hours which would elapse before the seaborne force linked up with those at Gamil and proper medical services became available. On the basis of the same statistics, the Field Surgical Team could be expected to have to perform six to eight operations; with the need to treat Egyptian casualties as well as the French already mentioned, the numbers considerably exceeded this estimate.

In July, at the start of the planning, no surgical team existed which had been trained either in parachutist techniques or the sort of task which would face them in an airborne assault as the teams which had served with the airborne division at the end of the war had been disbanded; shortage of surgeons precluded any 'luxury' units of this nature. To the credit of the medical planners however, an immediate effort was made to rectify the deficiency and a surgeon was selected and despatched post-haste to Abingdon to be put through his 're-fresher' parachute training. Once he had completed the requisite num-ber of drops this officer flew out to Cyprus to face the larger problems of training for his ground role following an airborne assault. It is not intended to dwell on the technical issues; many of these will be self-evident. Surgeons are accustomed to working in clean and sterile con-ditions and clearly none of the 'Emergency-Ward 10' facilities were likely to be available in the battle which follows a parachute attack. Nor is it possible for large quantities of medical stores or heavy equip-ment to accompany an assault of this nature; ammunition and specialist weapons have a justifiable priority. Blood for transfusions has to be kept under refrigerated conditions—obviously not possible in these circumstances—so that for the seriously injured 'blood on the hoof' has to be extracted from such men as are available to give it. And with only primitive, light and portable equipment to administer them, even anaesthetics are a problem.

Like those of the French, the arrangements which had been so tediously perfected during the waiting period suffered something of a set-back on landing. Most serious was the disability suffered by the regimental medical officer who was hit in the eye during his descent, although he carried on for about four hours despite intense pain. This left the surgeon, his anaesthetist and section officer to cope with the entire problem of casualties, most of which occurred during the first two or three hours whilst the airfield was being shelled and mortared. The primitive anaesthetizing equipment was damaged in the landing and was found to be useless; the sterilizing apparatus which had accompanied one of the medical orderlies who landed in the no-man's-land between the 'Red Devils' and the Egyptians in the cemetery area, was not available until two hours later in the day when he managed to get back to the British lines under fire.

A garage behind the airfield control tower had been selected from air photographs as a suitable location for the advanced dressing station and as soon as the medical detachment had collected them-selves together they set about establishing their base. Although a considerable amount of Egyptian filth had to be cleared out before it could be used, the garage proved to be adequate. An operating theatre of sorts was set up in the former office block and a cooking-pot, functioning as a sterilizer, was soon boiling away. Casualties began to flow in and out, and the hands of the medical team assisted by the Padre and all others[1] who could be pressed into service were kept busy. Pressure only began to ease when the helicopter evacuation service started and with the first helicopter an R.N. Surgeon-Lieutenant arrived to help out and replace the wounded regimental medical officer who had been evacuated to Cyprus in Gilles's Dakota. His first operation was to assist in removing a bullet from a wounded Egyptian who, in due course, recovered completely.

On this first day, the work of the doctors and all who assisted them was invaluable, and it has not generally been appreciated that their performance was something equivalent to that experienced in the worst days of the fighting in Normandy. The total number of casualties sustained by Crook's force on the 5th November totalled 6 per cent of its strength—a slightly higher rate than had been expected and comparable to the casualties of an average day's fighting in Europe in 1944.

Returning now to the battle: at the Raswa bridgehead, a detachment from the 9th Independent Squadron R.E. and from the Guards Parachute Company which had dropped with Chateau-Jobert's men, had set about finding how far it was possible to get down the Suez road. As has been described already, the peculiar geography of Port Said is such that the routes leading inland from the town are strictly limited, vulnerable and exposed. Excluding the Suez Canal and the railway there are only two routes out of the town and until one reaches firm ground at Kantara twenty-five miles inland, both of the roads and the railway run parallel to each other along a long neck of low-lying land; movement between Port Said and Kantara is confined to this exposed defile. The Sweetwater Canal also runs along this defile, between the railway and the minor—Suez Canal—road. (As the Sweetwater Canal is not navigable between Port Said and Kantara it was not capable of providing an additional emergency route.) At Raswa, the bridges provided the first possible bottleneck in the proposed break-out from Port Said towards Suez and it will be remembered that the French parachutists' objective had been to make

---

[1] Including Peter Woods, then a correspondent of the *Daily Mirror*, who had dropped with the force.

certain that the main Treaty Road bridge was not demolished; once this had been achieved it was necessary to make sure that it was capable of accepting the traffic which was intended for it. As the battle still raged round them, the sappers discovered the first minor snag: the roadway across the bridge was two feet narrower than the official specification had led the planners to believe. This meant working to widen it so that Centurions could traverse it safely.[1] But if this was a snag it was amply offset by the results of their next investigation. When the Egyptian defences in the immediate vicinity of the southern end of the bridge had been silenced, the road reconnaissance party drove off along the Treaty Road towards Suez in two jeeps and enjoyed a drive which was almost without incident. The limit of their reconnaissance had been set as ten kilometres from Raswa, which was the Anglo-French bomb-line; beyond this point their movement on the road was likely to draw the offensive attention of the Allied Air Forces who were still intent on isolating Port Said during the period of the assault. Surprisingly enough, the Treaty Road was clear of mines, although there was a number of wrecked vehicles and some minor craters which later proved to be hazards during the advance towards Suez. At one point the Egyptians had made preparations to crater both the Treaty and Canal roads but the explosive for this was found unguarded in a nearby hut and quietly removed. A chance contact with four civilian Egyptians produced a little information on the defences farther up the road although this seemed likely to be untrue and the reconnaissance party returned to Raswa. The information that they had accrued suggested that the route to Suez was wide open and that an armoured column should quickly be able to traverse the whole length of the Canal; from Raswa to Kantara ought to take less than two hours, from there to Ismailia was another four; with an early start the column could be in Suez by nightfall. Against this assessment the more pessimistic news from civilians interrogated in Port Fuad had to be set. 'Egyptian tanks are all along the beach in Port Said, from De Lesseps's statue out towards the west,' they said. 'Any landing from the sea may expect a lively reception.' If this proved to be so, the Centurions of the British and the AMX tanks of the French would probably be delayed in Port Said and an early advance from Raswa would be unlikely.

The results of the road reconnaissance and the information gleaned

---

[1] In effect this only meant blowing off the handrails to allow a total width of 11 ft. 6 in.

from the Egyptians was radioed back to Brigadier Butler's head-quarters at Gamil; from there it was relayed back to General Stock-well in H.M.S. *Tyne*. This was not so simple as it sounds, there were communication difficulties which have not, as yet, been mentioned. In any operation the need for good communications has always been of prime importance; the last decisive battle fought under the per-sonal command of a Supreme Commander was Waterloo, and since then the development of weapons and changes in tactics have made the problems of command and control increasingly difficult. Nowa-days, reliance is almost entirely on wireless links and the 'Musketeer' wireless equipment, being old and unreliable, fell far short of the requirements of the operation. Of the three long-range wireless sets that were dropped at Gamil, not a single one worked; the parachutes attached to two of them had failed to open and the third apparently landed more heavily than was good for it. In view of the obsolete parachuting equipment which had to be used to deliver the sets none of these mishaps could really be regarded as surprising. Yet even if one of them had arrived on the ground in a working condition it is unlikely that it would have provided a really satisfactory communica-tions link. Fortunately, the geography of Port Said proved advan-tageous in this instance; conditions were ideal for wireless trans-mission and it was possible to get some communication between Gamil and H.M.S. *Tyne* by using a lower-powered set. And, as the distance between the invasion fleet and Port Said lessened and the wireless range decreased, so the reception improved and the com-munication problem eased.

During the afternoon, a second lift, bringing reinforcements and more ammunition, was delivered to the parachutists at both Gamil and Raswa. A large amount of stores and a fourth company—the remainder of the 3rd Battalion Group—were safely parachuted into Gamil, whilst the French took the opportunity to drop another bat-talion on the southern end of Port Fuad. This latter operation drew a considerable amount of fire from the residential area of Port Fuad but there was no real opposition; after taking pot shots at the men swinging down on their parachutes, the Egyptian troops in the area, hoping to escape across the Canal to Port Said before 'Les Paras' arrived, made off towards the ferry stage abandoning their equipment as they ran. Those remaining to form pockets of resistance were quickly silenced as the French closed in on the ferry to isolate Port Fuad and seal in the remaining Egyptian units. The French manœuvres were supported by aircraft from the cab rank still circling overhead and a convoy of vehicles which arrived at the ferry in front of the pursuing Frenchmen was quickly turned into a blazing inferno, adding to the general confusion and making any systematic evacuation impossible. By the evening the resistance was confined to snipers on the roofs and balconies of buildings; Port Fuad had been captured virtually un-damaged. The only real fighting had been in isolated buildings away from the residential area and in the town itself only one strongpoint had resisted. With Port Fuad cleared and in their hands, 'Les Paras' were thoroughly at home in its French environment[1] and now awaited the next stage of the operation; this did not seem to be too far distant since events were moving faster than had been anticipated.

That afternoon, as the troops at Gamil and Raswa sorted out the stores of the re-supply drop, the telephone rang in the main office of the waterworks, which was now Chateau-Jobert's headquarters, and a voice spoke from the Governate of Port Said. It appeared that the Egyptian Commandant, General El Moguy, would be willing to negotiate a cease-fire with the Anglo-French Commander, if a meet-ing could be arranged and the incessant air attacks on Port Said could be stopped. Chateau-Jobert lost no time in contacting Brigadier Butler, who, it so happened, was about to visit the waterworks in one of the naval helicopters. A signal, explaining the position and asking for an immediate cessation of air offensive activities, was sent to H.M.S. *Tyne* whilst Butler and Chateau-Jobert set about hammering out the conditions for a cease-fire. Butler was well aware that these conditions would have to be approved by the Supreme Commander in Cyprus and it was evident that there would be difficulties in formu-lating terms; the basis must be one of unconditional surrender and it was very doubtful if the Egyptian Commandant would be em-powered to agree to such terms. With their eyes on the signpost pointing to Suez, both Butler and Chateau-Jobert were anxious not to become embroiled in a street-fighting battle in Port Said and by 1530 hours, temporary terms had been drawn up and read out to General El Moguy. 'These', said Brigadier Butler, 'are binding only until the Allied Commander arrives in Port Said tomorrow,' and he

[1] During their sojourn in Port Fuad, Gallic instincts apparently got the better of some of them. Following a sharp reproof resultant on complaints that their behaviour towards the ladies of Port Fuad left something to be desired, the Parachute Commander is reputed to have replied with a shrug: 'I am sorry, mes amis, mais c'est la guerre.'

went on to demand an immediate curfew and that El Moguy's troops should lay down their arms and march out of Port Said into concentration areas at Gamil airfield and the salt mills of Port Fuad. It was clear that these conditions went beyond the Egyptians' expectations and El Moguy announced stiffly that he would have to refer them to Cairo and return to his headquarters in Port Said. About 2000 hours he telephoned to say that Cairo had rejected the conditions. This decision had been feared and it was now apparent that the airborne assault had not won the day after all and hostilities recommenced about half an hour later when shooting flared up in the Arab town area.

Meanwhile, away from the battle area, the Soviet Premier Bulganin had sent a note to the British and French Prime Ministers; in it he alluded to the use of rockets in his determination to crush aggression and Cairo had taken heart from this threat and a simultaneous offer of Soviet 'volunteers' to help Egypt. Thus it was when the Egyptian Governor of Port Said had telephoned for endorsement of the surrender terms he had been ordered to fight on. To his amazement he had been told that World War III had begun, Russian aircraft had bombed London and Paris, and Soviet troops were on the way to relieve the gallant defenders of Port Said. Instructed and heartened by this message and ably counselled by M. Tchikov, the Soviet Consul, El Moguy reluctantly accepted that Port Said should become an Egyptian Stalingrad. Tchikov had already determined that the stacks of Czech rifles and machine-guns still in their original crates in Port Said warehouses, should not fall unused into Anglo-French hands and when the parachutists were seen landing on the outskirts of the town the police had been persuaded to distribute weapons and ammunition to anyone who cared to take part in the battle. Children, women, old men, could all take a carbine or automatic from the lorries touring the streets, and some took more than one. With a firearm many of the Egyptians saw an opportunity to pay off old scores or the ideal equipment for shooting off locks in their looting activities, whilst some weapons undoubtedly were hidden for sale at a future date. These were not old worn rifles either, but brand-new modern Czech weapons, the 7·62-mm. rifle being the most common, and hundreds of them, still shrouded in their packing grease, were collected after the cease-fire. In such circumstances every little boy could become a sniper and many did. It was an astute move and the Allied soldiers were to feel the bite of these weapons next day. Inevitably the antics of some young Egyptians with their lethal new toys led to accidents amongst themselves but they were the cause of many pointless casualties in the next phase of the fighting—somewhat appropriately labelled 'the children's war'.

Despite this issue of a plethora of small arms there was little shooting during that night. An occasional magazine was discharged in the direction of the parachutists, other shots in the town were presumably in settlement of old scores or fired in the course of looting sorties. The storm was yet to come and the quiet night enjoyed by Crook's men at Gamil and the French at Port Fuad was the prelude to the shooting which was due to start with the arrival of the seaborne force shortly after first light next day.

Life for the foreign inhabitants of Port Said had not been easy during this period. More than 800 British civilians were still living in the town, some in the blocks of flats which overlooked the invasion beaches, and soon after the Anglo-French intentions had become clear to the Egyptians these individuals were confined to their homes under house arrest. Policemen were stationed outside their quarters and as the frequency of Allied aircraft appearing over Port Said increased, the wretched expatriates pondered on their fate. Since the air strikes started on the 3rd November, they had seen Egyptians streaming out of Port Said in trains packed to capacity, shops closing and normal business grinding to a halt, whilst military activity—particularly that of the anti-aircraft gunners—increased proportionately; some of the foreign consuls, notably those of Italy, U.S.A., and Greece, had made arrangements to look after their nationals during the anticipated crisis but clearly no such arrangements for British and French aliens were acceptable to the Egyptian authorities. Many thought that the parachute landings would be the signal for their own summary execution but in a number of instances the effect of the increased air activity was to induce the police guards to abandon their posts and leave the British civilians, still theoretically under house arrest, to watch and wait on an uncertain future. Following the abortive cease-fire, loudspeaker vans were heard touring the streets, ordering the Egyptian troops to remain at their posts,[1] announcing the attack on London and Paris, and promising early Soviet troop support. And, as the Arabic speakers exhorted the citizens of Port Said to defend their town house by house, the distribution of arms and ammunition continued, under shaded lights in the warehouses or in the pitch darkness of the streets.

[1] Many had already deserted.

AIRBORNE AFTERMATH

At sea little news had filtered through to the men sailing in the combined convoy, ships' wireless sets, released from their normal tasks by a convoy-wide wireless silence, were being used on every available channel in the hope of picking up the wavelength of the airborne task force. Ultimately the B.B.C. news was the main fount of information however, and it was from this source that they were astounded to hear that Port Said had surrendered; poor wireless communication had resulted in Brigadier Butler's original message relayed to Cyprus being expanded into a spurious full-scale newsflash. The troops on board ship greeted the news with mixed feelings, they were glad that it seemed to be all over, with little bloodshed, but sorry that they had come so far to find out what war was about. They need not have worried, their opportunity was still to come.

CHAPTER 9

The Capture of Port Said

At dawn on the morning of 6th November, the situation in Port
Said may be summarized as follows: Port Fuad was quiet and
firmly held by two battalions of French 'Paras'; Crook's
parachutists on the outskirts of Arab town were getting ready to
battle their way into Port Said proper. There were still approximately
three battalions of Egyptian infantry which had not been committed
to the battle of the previous day and there was also a sizeable force
of armed police—equivalent to at least another two battalions of
infantry—that could be expected to put up a fight. The civilian population had been evacuated from the dock areas and the centre of the
town where a number of buildings had been barricaded to form
strongpoints, elsewhere an indeterminate number of civilians equipped
with the weapons issued in the past twenty-four hours could also be
expected to assist the Egyptian troops and wreak havoc and destruction as opportunities were presented. Some of the Soviet tanks and
self-propelled guns were known to be lurking in the southern outskirts of the town and near the golf-course whilst mortars, Czech and
Russian anti-tank and field artillery guns undoubtedly would stiffen
the Egyptian defences. Clearly the seaborne assault force had a grim
task ahead.

The stillness of the dawn was first shattered by the cannon of a
solitary low-flying MIG fighter which swept in to strafe Gamil. As it
banked and turned south, back towards its base, its place was taken
by Allied aircraft from Cyprus and the fleet carriers coming to rocket,
bomb and machine-gun the beach-heads where the Royal Marine
Commandos were to land in less than an hour's time. For ten minutes
they struck repeatedly at the beach defences and then the bombardment was taken up by the guns of the combined fleets. And, as the
first salvoes began to fall, the ships of the amphibious force were

143

clearly visible from Gamil; as far as the eye could see an impressive number of warships with battle ensigns fluttering was converging on the port.

Originally it had been intended that every available warship, from the great 35,000-ton battleship *Jean Bart*[1] down to the most humble escort-destroyer should participate in the preliminary barrage, to produce a devastating concentration of fire which would literally pulverize the town's defences. At the eleventh hour, in the belief that the massive effort originally planned would only result in the loss of many civilian lives and in needless destruction, the bombardment was restricted to guns of not more than 4·5-inch calibre. This eliminated the battleship and cruisers, diminishing the effect to something like a tenth of its potential; at the same time the number of shells to be fired was also reduced and the depth of the target area restricted. The original ammunition allotment had been on a scale of 700 rounds per gun, but each 4·5-inch gun was now restricted to a maximum of 200 rounds and, in the event, not all this ammunition was expended. For three-quarters of an hour shells rained on 3,000 yards of beach and the coast defences, which appeared to be completely devastated as a result. Certain specific targets, like that of the coast batteries on the breakwater at the Canal entrance, were found already to have been amply catered for by the Fleet Air Arm.

As has already been observed, the details of the assault plan had been changed frequently during the voyage of the assault force. The final version of the plan was for two of the Commandos to land from assault craft on the beaches, whilst the third, in its heli-

---

[1] The ships originally available for the bombardment were as follows:

Battleships: *Jean Bart* (8 15-in., 9 6-in., 24 3·9-in. guns).

Cruisers: *Georges Leygues* (9 6-in. guns).

              H.M.S. *Jamaica* (9 6-in., 8 4-in. guns).

              H.M.N.Z.S. *Royalist* (8 5·25-in. guns). (As has been described, for political reasons the *Royalist* was withdrawn after sailing from Malta with the convoy. She was replaced by H.M.S. *Ceylon*.)

Destroyers: 5 Daring class destroyers (*Daring, Duchess, Diamond, Decoy, Delight*, each with 6 4·5-in. guns).

             2 French destroyers *Cassard* and *Bouvet*, each with 6 5-in. guns.

             3 French (ex-U.S.) destroyer escorts *Soudanais, Berbère* and *Touareg* each with 3 3-in. guns and the 2 anti-submarine destroyers H.M.S. *Chieftain* and H.M.S. *Chevron* each with 2 4·5-in. guns.

5*a* and 5*b*.

6. Disembarkation at Casino Quay.

copters, would act as a mobile reserve to exploit the success of the seaborne attack. Lieut.-Colonel D. G. Tweed's 40 Commando would land on the left of the Casino pier and advance down the Canal to link up with the French parachutists at Raswa; Lieut.-Colonel P. L. Norcock's 42 Commando was to land on the right of the pier and go through the town to link up on their left with 40 Commando and on their right with Crook's parachutists battling towards them through Arab town. The mobile reserve of Lieut.-Colonel N. H. Tailyour's 45 Commando, split between *Theseus* and *Ocean*, would be held in reserve to land on the beaches or south of the town, depending on how the battle progressed. (At this point it will be remembered that an earlier intention had been for 45 Commando to make a helicopter descent as part of the first wave assault, to capture the Raswa bridges. The troops had, in fact, trained for just this role. Doubts as to the wisdom of such a daring move followed second thoughts on the expected resistance.) In the second phase, Centurions of the 6th Royal Tanks, specially waterproofed to allow them to wade up the beaches, would follow the Commandos and support the advance through the town. Then, about an hour later the two remaining parachute battalion groups of the 16th Parachute Brigade were scheduled to be landed farther inland and to the west of the western breakwater; they were not concerned with the initial assault and their advance down the Canal is described in the next chapter.

Following channels swept by the minesweepers which preceded it, the huge armada arrived off its destination exactly as planned, having taken six days to cover the trip from Malta. From the ships, Port Said appeared to be covered with a pall of smoke; the first few salvoes of the naval bombardment had set ablaze the rows of huts on the beaches and an oil storage tank south of the town was also belching fire and smoke as burning oil gushed out; it had been struck by the cannon shells of Corsairs attacking an SU100 gun which had been shooting up the French positions near Raswa.

For those on board the ships, reveille had been uncomfortably early. The commandos had been roused at 0230 hours to breakfast and assemble two hours before they were to lower themselves into their landing craft or climb into the helicopters; for many it was to be their longest day. Shortly after 0400 hours they took up their positions in the assault craft or the LVT's[1] inside the LST's; half an

---

[1] An LVT—Landing Vehicle Tracked—is an amphibious vehicle rather like a tank without a turret, which can carry about thirty men through the

hour later the ships' bow doors opened and the LVT's trundled out into the sea. As they ploughed towards the shore, the umbrella of naval gunfire controlled by Royal Artillery officers in the assault craft, was gradually lifted from the beaches. The run-in took about twenty minutes and at 0450 hours the LVT's of the first wave of 40 Commando crawled ashore on the 'Sierra Red' beach and the Marines leapt out. As they ran up the beaches,[1] the parachutists at Gamil, with their machine-guns shooting along the shore line to discourage any of the defenders who had recovered from the bombardment, were able to cover them; this was just as well as some shots were directed at them as they left their vehicles. The second wave which had travelled in LCA's were compelled to wade some thirty yards to get ashore, but they were not shot up during their move. When they reached dry land it seemed from the number of abandoned positions that the beaches had been heavily defended although there was no sign of any Egyptians. That they had been there and had been caught as they were about to have breakfast was evident from the mounds of dates lying near the trenches around the area; they had fled from the barrage, abandoning their weapons and equipment as they ran. Behind the beaches the town remained almost undamaged, the bombardment had drenched the foreshore with explosives but the houses behind were comparatively unharmed and in them, sheltering amongst the civilians, was a substantial proportion of those—Egyptian soldiers and members of the Liberation Army—who had fled before the barrage.

In theory, the guns of the fleet still remained on call to support the manœuvres of the Commandos but shortly after the landings the Royal Artillery observation parties, whose job it was to control this fire, received a message saying that no more naval gunfire was to be used; this was a further effort to minimize civilian casualties and save damage to the town even if it meant jeopardizing the assaulting troops. The result was that none of the ships fired again although the gunner observation parties remained to watch and report back to General Stockwell in H.M.S. *Tyne*—a role which proved to be of the greatest value in the early stages of the battle when the picture was

water at about seven knots. It is manned by men of the Royal Armoured Corps.

[1] Wearing their distinctive green berets; some 'rigged' photographs which appeared in the Press falsely showed the Commandos wearing steel helmets.

obscured by the fog of war and little information was forthcoming from other sources.

By good fortune 42 Commando arrived at their beach—'Sierra Green'—three minutes late; the final air strikes which immediately preceded the assault were some seven minutes behind time and there was a good deal of smoke shrouding the area as the first wave ran up from the shore. When the Commandos scrambled out of their LVT's and doubled for the cover of their first objectives—the buildings on the line of the main road beyond the beach—there was a good deal of sniping and some bursts of automatic fire from the right flank; this did not stop the Marines capturing the buildings. These were the modern multi-storeyed blocks of flats already described, very modern and largely furnished in a pseudo-baroque style with much gilt and brocade. The ones nearest the beach showed clear signs of having been evacuated in a hurry, even dirty dishes on tables had not been cleared. Some had suffered from direct hits by shells but subsequently others were damaged in the clearing process, which involved throwing grenades or firing short bursts into the rooms as the advance progressed. Farther back, the upper-storey flats were occupied by snipers, civilians as well as soldiers, who had discarded their uniforms for the ubiquitous night-shirt *galabiyeh* which is the hallmark of the poorer classes. From windows, balconies and parapets the snipers fired their new weapons; the unrestricted distribution of arms on the previous day coupled with the story of early relief, was now showing Colonel Nasser high dividend and in return the Commandos were to pay a high price in casualties as they pressed forward through the maze of dwellings.

Soon after 0500 hours, the first of the fourteen Centurions of 'C' Squadron of the 6th Royal Tanks rumbled ashore on the beach, west of the breakwater. As they reached firm ground, after wading 150 yards through six feet of water, each tank fired an armour-piercing shell to clear the waterproofing from the barrels of their guns. Their crews had also to get rid of the waterproofing covers and this was not so simple. The explosive bolts which retained the basic material and which had been exposed to wind, surf and sea-water for too long, failed to operate and had to be knocked off with sledge-hammers and the covers prised off with crowbars. As these operations were conducted whilst snipers potted them there was every incentive for the task to be completed quickly.

By 0530 hours the tanks had linked up with the Marines, one troop

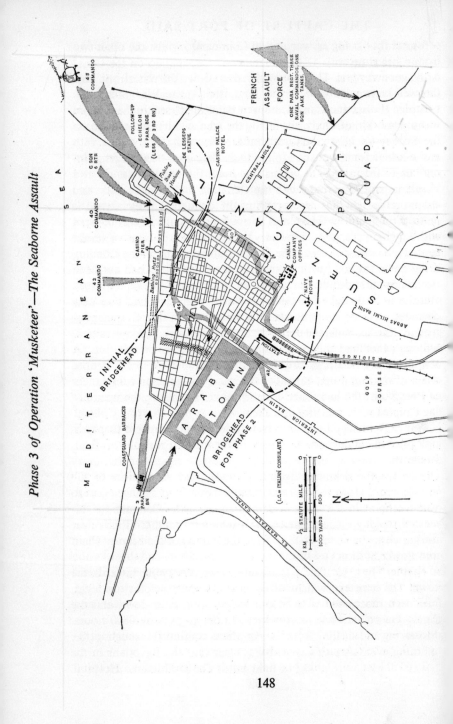

Phase 3 of Operation 'Musketeer'—The Seaborne Assault

—four tanks—being assigned to 40 Commando whilst the other two troops joined up with 42 Commando; 40 Commando on the Canal flank, got away first. Their job was to drive down the waterfront, past the well-known store of Simon Arzt, the Anzac War Memorial, Customs Houses and Canal Company building, to secure the Arsenal Basin, Navy House Quay and finally the Abbas Hilmi Basin opposite the Sacony-Vacuum oil storage tanks, where the rest of the 16th Parachute Brigade were due to land any time after 0630 hours. Slipping eastwards along the waterfront road, the Marines set off at a spanking pace. The road, with the Canal on its left and houses and shops on the right, has streets running off to the right every fifty yards or so throughout its length and as every road junction was covered with Egyptian fire, it was necessary to cross under the cover of smoke from a grenade or else wait for a tank to station itself at the junction, firing down the road with its machine-gun, and then dash across in two stages; first behind the tank, then to the other side of the street. Despite a brisk fight for the Port Police Station which was ably defended by a police detachment it was not until the Commandos reached the Commercial Basin that they met any real opposition, although they had suffered a number of casualties by this time. A few prisoners had also been taken and there was some surprise when it was found that Brigadier Amiralai, the garrison commander of Port Said, who had found himself cut off by the rapid advance of the Commandos, was amongst them.

On the right, 42 Commando had the less spectacular but thankless task of working through the streets of the modern part of Port Said, where the towering buildings flanking narrow streets offered every chance for the defenders to use grenades and small arms to the utmost effect. However, with the tanks moving from vantage point to vantage point in the boulevards and squares, the Commandos advanced steadily through the town, reaching its southern limits near the gasworks by about 0800 hours, capturing the Cold Storage Plant and Power Station *en route*.

Farther west, Crook's parachutists were advancing towards the town. The cemetery, which had evacuated during the previous night, had been reoccupied without opposition soon after dawn and the Coast Guard Barracks were attacked and overrun by 0800 hours. Mortaring and shelling from the Egyptians continued throughout the morning even after this, and it was clear that the Egyptians in the native quarter were going to fight hard. The Ophthalmic Hospital, which borders on this area, was captured without much trouble but a patrol which attempted to advance up to the edge of Shanty town was soon in difficulties. Every man of the patrol was wounded but all except the patrol commander were extricated by the gallant efforts of a medical officer[1] who had come to the hospital looking for surgical equipment. As the air offensive had been called off by this time a 105-mm. anti-tank gun was brought up, manœuvred into position, and fired into the troublesome area; this had the effect of blasting Shanty town, causing a fire. Another conflagration, caused by the exploding shells of a destroyer shooting back at an SU100 gun dug-in near the shanties, was quickly carried into the area by a stiff breeze and the whole insanitary collection of shacks was soon blazing. Following the fire there was no question of further opposition from this quarter, but behind the blazing shanties Egyptian snipers in the more substantial buildings of Arab town were clearly going to provide a major obstruction to further progress. From strongpoints centred round the police station the Egyptians were intent on keeping open the escape route of the Manzala Canal behind them; troops and civilians—almost all in *galabiyehs*—streamed down this one line of retreat throughout the battle and as it was not possible to discriminate between soldier and civilian, and with women, children and old people clearly seen in the escaping feluccas, the majority of the refugees were able to make a clean getaway. This situation continued until dawn the following morning by which time a general cease-fire had come into effect and the battle of Crook's parachutists was over.

Whilst the battle raged in the streets, the local populace, other than those members of it that were shooting at the Marines, hid. There was the expected concern for the safety of all foreign residents and particularly for the fate of the foreign Consuls still living in Port Said. In order to bring back those who wished to return to the safety of the Anglo-French sector, two Centurions were despatched to their Consulate area shortly after landing. And, even as the Commandos worked their way through the town towards the Consulates, the tanks, in a taxi-like shuttle between the Consuls residential area and the beaches, drove through the sniping in still occupied zones. Of all the Consuls, Mr. Mareri, who represented Italy's interests in Port

[1] Captain J. M. Elliott, R.A.M.C., who was awarded a well-earned Military Cross for his efforts. The patrol commander, who was severely wounded, managed to crawl back to the British lines after eight hours alone in the area. Later he recovered completely.

Said, is perhaps most deserving of special mention. He was one of the few who had foreseen that the British and French really did intend business—so many of the other nations' representatives had thought that when it came to a show-down there would be no invasion. Consequently Mareri's preparations were more advanced than those of the others and when the bombing had started on the 5th he had rounded up about 140 Italian nationals and quartered them either within his own Consulate precincts or in the Roman Catholic Cathedral next door. The Consulate itself lay directly in front of one of the landing areas and when he saw how events were moving he took the opportunity to impress his own stamp on the turn of events. Throughout the whole of Monday he laboured ceaselessly to negotiate a cease-fire between the Egyptians and the Allies and although 'his activities subsequently caused him to regard the 6th November as his St. Crispin's Day',[1] it was not his fault that his efforts were frustrated. An attempt by the Allies to negotiate a surrender with the captured Brigadier Amiralai was equally abortive. At the time he was taken prisoner it had been understood that he had wished to agree to a cease-fire on the terms offered the night before by Brigadier Butler. When it came to a formal agreement, however, it turned out that Amiralai needed his authority confirming by a superior who appeared to be the local Commissar and who was hiding in Arab town. The Brigadier had, until recently, been a fellow student on a gunnery course at Larkhill with the senior British artillery observation officer, to whom fell the duty of acting as escort. If he had been prepared to assert himself, Amiralai might have been able to save many Egyptian lives although his dependence on the authority of a Commissar may make it questionable whether he would have been able to exert sufficient influence after the landings for a cease-fire order to have become effective.

Meantime, 45 Commando had been committed to the battle. Soon after 42 Commando had reported the beach area to be clear, there was a multiple roar of engines, and from *Ocean* and *Theseus* helicopter after helicopter—painted British racing-green—circled over the western breakwater, hovered, and settled on the firm ground in front of the Casino Palace Hotel. The point has been made already that this was the first time that such an operation had been attempted and Tailyour's men and the twenty-two R.N. and R.A.F. helicopters were making history. That there had been very little time to develop

[1] Sir Edwin Herbert's report on the damage and casualties in Port Said.

the techniques involved, and their helicopters—Whirlwinds which carried five or seven fully equipped men,[1] and Sycamores only three —were not really suited to such operations, must again be stressed as must some of the practical difficulties not so far mentioned. The men flying in the Sycamores sat on the floor of the helicopter, the one in the middle, with six mortar bombs on his lap holding on to the other two, who were compelled to sit at the door edge with their legs over the side whilst each hugged a three-foot long 106-mm. shell. In the Whirlwinds the passengers were able to get into the body of the helicopter but there were no seats, doors or windows and precious few hand-holds. Communication between the pilot and his passengers, in both cases, was effected by shouts or by one of the Marines tugging at the pilot's legs.

Like their fellows of 40 and 42 Commandos, as soon as the naval bombardment had started, Tailyour's men were ready to emplane; it was not until two hours later (0540 hours) that the first helicopter—a Whirlwind carrying the commanding officer, his staff officer and two signallers with wireless sets—was given permission to land in the beach-head. Arriving over the beach-head to find that the intended landing zone was totally obscured by smoke, the pilot set out to look for a clear area and a landing was made in the sports stadium. Almost as soon as the passengers had jumped clear of the aircraft it became apparent that the stadium was still occupied by the Egyptians as a strongpoint.

The helicopter pilot, who had already taken off, realizing what was happening, landed again; the passengers hastily scrambled back and the machine soared upwards to safety. Fortunately there was little damage to the machine and only the pilot was slightly wounded. A safe landing was then negotiated in the shadow of De Lesseps's statue at the end of the western breakwater. Ten minutes later, six Whirlwinds followed by six Sycamores from *Ocean*, with ten Whirlwinds from *Theseus*, took off for the landing zone. As they approached the area, the helicopters from *Ocean* orbited in a left-hand circuit and those from *Theseus* in a right-handed circuit; then, at three-minute intervals, they came in to hover about a foot above the ground amidst clouds of dust set up by the rotors. As soon as the passengers had scrambled out, the helicopters roared away back to their ships and in four waves the majority of the Commando had been de-

---

[1] The ten Whirlwinds from 845 Squadron each carried seven men, the six Whirlwinds of the J.E.H.U. each carried five.

livered, as originally planned. The helicopters then maintained a ferry service between ship and shore, bringing the Marines' stores ashore and taking wounded back to the ships. In just under an hour and a half the entire fighting echelon of the Commando, with all its stores were delivered safely to the beach and a considerable number of casualties, including quite a number of Egyptians, were evacuated to *Theseus* and *Ocean* to receive expert medical attention. There was only one flying casualty—one machine ran out of fuel and suddenly plummeted into the sea 300 or 400 yards from *Theseus*; within seconds a launch from the ship had reached the sinking helicopter and rescued the pilot and the three casualties he was carrying.

When they were all ashore, the men of 45 Commando set about clearing the town between the other two Commando units. Prior to moving off on this task, however, an unfortunate incident occurred when a Fleet Air Arm Wyvern, with its cannon firing, suddenly dived on to their assembly area near the beach road. One Marine was killed and fifteen others were wounded—the wounded included the Commanding Officer, Tailyour, and his intelligence officer—and almost all the Commando's wireless sets were damaged, albeit temporarily. Before it flew off, accompanied by considerable verbal abuse from the unfortunate troops on the ground, the same aircraft struck at Madoc's brigade headquarters farther along the road and there were more casualties in both 42 Commando and at the headquarters. The subsequent inquiry into the incident showed that the pilot had attacked the map reference which he had been given by the Joint Fire Support Control Committee—a committee, still afloat, which decided on what targets should be subjected to air strikes—but that this reference was erroneous. It was one of those regrettable occurrences which sometimes happen in war; in this case the troops ashore had not been warned that an impending strike was to be made near them, it had not been passed to an Air Contact Team[1] to control, and the sacrosanct bomb line, behind which no offensive air weapons should ever be used, was ignored.

The men of 45 Commando now began to work their way methodically through the same streets that the other two Commandos had fought over but had not remained to clear. Whilst the tanks fired high-explosive shells at the machine-gun nests and pockets of resistance which were encountered, they combed the arcades

[1] An Air Contact Team is a small unit which works with forward troops to demand and control aircraft which are providing intimate air support.

and front gardens of private houses. The Egyptians did not appear to have co-ordinated their defence of the streets but groups of snipers and machine-gunners fought with grim determination and resisted the Marines' advance every inch of the way. It was 1100 hours before the area of the original beach-head could be considered clear and now the commandos turned west to suppress the area which lay between them and Crook's parachutists still battling in Arab town. Fighting continued until it was dark when the link-up with the 'Red Devils' had not yet been effected.

By mid-afternoon, men of 40 Commando had reached the Commercial Basin and had captured the vast series of resplendent buildings which were the Suez Canal Company's offices. The Customs warehouse close by was the next objective and the Marines ran into very stiff opposition here; it was only cleared after tanks had fired shells into it for about ten minutes at point-blank range and even then two officers were killed and three Marines wounded during the assault. Navy House—the Royal Navy's headquarters in Port Said during the British occupation in Egypt—which was a massive stone edifice, standing on its own quay jutting into the water, sandwiched between the Canal Company offices and the Customs warehouse, had to be tackled next. From the beginning it was obvious that this was going to be a tough nut to crack. It was heavily defended by about 130 tough, brave and desperate Egyptians; as events subsequently proved, of all their fighting that day, this was to be the fiercest that the Marines were to experience. As a preliminary, there were more warehouses to be dealt with and each had to be cleared in turn; by midday Navy House was still holding out. By then it was apparent that the Commandos would be unable to take it without strong support and they were ordered to pull back, seal the area and await the results of an air strike. Admiral Power sanctioned the strike with regret, for he was ordering the destruction of a building long associated with the Royal Navy. When the Fleet Air Arm planes attacked at last light, their performance was an impressive and terrifying sight. Plane after plane dived on to the now isolated Navy House and fired rockets into it, shortly afterwards all Egyptian resistance inside ceased and the following morning about twenty men came out of the blazing building to surrender; they left behind them thirty dead.

This was one of the last air strikes on a day which had been a very full one for the Allied Air Force. Not only had the naval aircraft been engaged in providing close support for the parachutists and Marines since dawn, but naval and land based aircraft had also been occupying the Egyptian Air Force by carrying out more raids on the airfields around Cairo, whilst both R.A.F. and French Air Force ground attack aircraft had continued their ceaseless offensive reconnaissances of the roads and railways leading to Port Said. It was during one such reconnaissance that a Wyvern from *Eagle* caught fire over Ismailia and the pilot was compelled to bale out from about 8,000 feet over the Canal. Landing near the Qantara road he set off walking towards Israel whilst French Corsairs, who had witnessed his descent and were now acting as an escort, effectively discouraged Egyptian attempts to pursue him. Ten miles beyond the Canal, the men of an Israeli unit had bivouacked in accordance with the terms of the Anglo-French ultimatum; the antics of the Allied aircraft soon excited their curiosity sufficiently to cause them to try to contact the lone airman, who by now was sitting on the roadside patiently awaiting the turn of events. A burst of cannon fire from one of the aircraft was as effective discouragement to the Israelis as it had been to the Egyptians and the pilot continued to sit and wait until a helicopter arrived from *Bulwark*. Little the worse for his experience he was back in his own ship within two hours of baling out of his blazing machine.

At Gamil, the R.A.F. helicopters of the Joint Experimental Helicopter Unit which, from *Ocean*, had participated in the landing of 45 Commando and subsequently helped to ferry their stores ashore, flew in the advance party of 215 Wing R.A.F. together with a skeleton airfield staff and an advance party of 48 Squadron of the R.A.F. Regiment. As soon as they arrived, work began on the preparation of an R.A.F. Staging Post and a Casualty Air Evacuation Unit and at 1230 hours the first of four R.A.F. Valettas touched down on the airfield. From then on a steady stream of stores were flown in to Gamil from Cyprus, casualties being flown out on the return journey. Later that day the main party of 215 Wing arrived at Port Said, landing from an LST and driving out to Gamil the next morning—dodging sniper bullets along the route. The R.A.F. Regiment then took over the defence of the airfield from the parachutists, garrisoning it until its evacuation, whilst the helicopters from *Ocean* stayed on for use on security and reconnaissance duties—carrying out an unglamourous but vital role.

Over at Port Fuad the French had also landed an assault force, consisting of the 1st Regiment Etranger Parachutistes, three naval commandos and a squadron of light tanks,[1] but as Port Fuad had been occupied during the night, the landing was unopposed; in consequence their planned naval support had been cancelled. Meantime at Raswa, Chateau-Jobert's parachutists had had a hard day. The Raswa bridges offered the Egyptian troops in Port Said the only means of exit if they were to withdraw as a formed body and during the morning and early afternoon, repeated attacks were made on the French positions, by tanks supported by infantry and SU100 guns; time and again these were repelled and the Egyptians again suffered severely from the air strikes that were called in support of 'Les Paras'. There was to be no escape by this route and, eventually, those who sought to get away joined the remainder streaming out through Arab town across the desert to the south-west. As darkness fell it became evident that with the exception of continual sniping and sabotage in the town, organized resistance was at an end.

Port Said had been captured.

---

[1] These light tanks were AMX, weighing only 13 tons apiece and of an exceptionally low silhouette. They are designed on the principle that lack of armour can be offset by speed and tactical mobility. The engine is mounted in front so that the automatic loading 75-mm. gun, with which the AMX is armed, is within the length of the tank; it cruises at nearly 60 m.p.h. For the operation General Stockwell took a number of AMX's under his command to guard his headquarters.

CHAPTER 10

The Break-Out

As the assault craft carrying the Commandos sped towards the beaches, ships of the Royal Navy were working to clear a channel into the inner harbour so that troops and equipment could be discharged directly on to the quays of Port Said. Closely following the group of minesweepers which had swept the first narrow passage to the outer harbour came the two anti-submarine and mine-laying destroyers *Chevron* and *Sallyport*. In *Chevron* was the naval officer who as N.O.I.C. (Naval Officer in Charge) Port Said had been appointed to supervise the clearance operations; his deputy was in *Sallyport*. Under his orders were the coastal minesweepers *Darlaston* and *Letterston*, carrying the Clearance Diving Teams of both the Home and Mediterranean fleets, the survey vessel *Dalrymple*, the tugs *Antic* and *Careful*, and the *Chieftain*—a sister ship of *Chevron*. Leaving *Chieftain* to control the entry of other shipping at the northern end of the western breakwater, *Chevron* and *Sallyport* coasted past the breakwater, through the harbour entrance and cautiously entered the Outer Basin to tie up at the Western Mole. Having negotiated this far, the first task was to remove three small coasters which had been secured at the Central Mole and whose berths would now be required. Landing parties from the two ships, with the assistance of the two tugs, soon completed this. The scene was one of absolute devastation: blockships had been sunk at both the harbour and canal entrances and the masts and superstructures of many other sunken vessels were plainly visible—a survey of the port later showed that there was a total of twenty-four. The harbour itself was expected to have been extensively mined and before any ships, other than those engaged in the clearance operations, could be berthed, the area had to be thoroughly searched by the clearance diving teams. The divers were at work by 0800 hours and were withdrawn four hours later when no mines had been discovered.

During the actual assault phase the LCT's *Bastion* and *Portcullis* had entered the fishing harbour and, even as the search for mines went on, as berths became available, the remaining LCT's were called in and unloaded. This was a slow business at a time when speed was vital. At 0740 hours a reconnaissance team from *Letterston* landed at Casino Wharf opposite the Casino Palace Hotel. Having reported that the area was suitable for LST's they promptly set about breaking down the fence and wall which obstructed the exits from the wharf; this allowed LST's to unload over the wall at the fishing harbour as well as at the wharf opposite the Casino Palace. The N.O.I.C. quickly called forward the LST's and at 0830 hours the first of them, the LST *Ravager*, berthed at the wharf and off-loaded the tanks of 'A' Squadron of the 6th Royal Tanks; within the hour the squadron had formed up and moved off through 40 Commando. The leading tanks arrived at the open ground near the golf-course about 1000 hours and four hours later most of the squadron had collected at the Raswa bridgehead and were ready to advance up the Canal road. Meanwhile the LST's *Puncher* and *Salerno*, carrying the regimental headquarters and 'B' Squadron of the tanks had followed *Ravager* into the harbour and the regiment was now complete, on its proper element, in Port Said. By nightfall a total of fourteen LST's had discharged men, stores and vehicles at either the Casino wharf or in the fishing harbour. Farther on, at the inner harbour, the first troopships were called forward into the harbour as soon as berths were pronounced clear of mines. During the afternoon H.M.S. *Theseus* was unloaded by ferry, LCT's and LCA's—four Army Z craft fulfilling a particularly useful role in the unloading of the troops. H.M.S. *Ocean* and the troopship *Empire Ken* were also berthed but, as General Stockwell did not consider that the units on board could be usefully deployed until the position in the town was more favourable, they remained on board, chafing at the delay. The berths in the inner harbour could not be used yet as the sunken blockships had to be cleared first and this involved a major salvage operation. Salvage work for which an enormous fleet of specialized ships had been assembled, had already started and it went on at high pressure up to the time of evacuation of Port Said but it was not until Friday the 9th November that the first LCT was able to sail down a channel between the blockships into the inner harbour.

At this time the seaborne units of Butler's 16th Parachute Brigade Group which had the task of pushing on to Ismailia had landing priority. (It will be recalled that this brigade, less Crook's 3rd Battalion which had dropped at Gamil, had sailed from Cyprus in LST's and the *Empire Parkeston*,[1] all of which were now standing off Port Said amongst the rest of the invasion convoy.) In the original plan the two seaborne parachute battalions were to land about an hour after the Commandos' assault at somewhere suitable, farther inland from the original Commando beach-heads. With Navy House still holding out and the harbour blocked much nearer the Canal mouth than had been anticipated, landing places now had to be found closer to the beach-heads. The Casino wharf near De Lesseps's statue seemed to offer the best prospects. Shortly before 4 o'clock, the LST's of the parachute brigade swung across the Canal and lined up beside each other under the shadow of what had been the smartest hotel in Port Said. The bow doors opened, the ramps dropped on to the tarmac and the first Champ and trailer of the 2nd Battalion rolled down to land in front of the Casino Palace Hotel, where only two days before, people had been sitting out on the terraces drinking aperitifs. The hotel had been badly battered; 'DEWAR'S WHIS' was all that was left of a sign on its parapet, and the trellised glass front, frosted partitions, Venetian chandeliers and wall mirrors, all lay in heaps on the tiled floor round the coffee tables. In front of the hotel, on the open ground, a Casualty Clearing Post had been set up and stretcher parties were busy loading wounded into helicopters just as fast as the helicopters could ferry them off to the ships at sea.

As the *Empire Parkeston* steamed into the mouth of the Canal to its berth opposite the fishing harbour, the scene was somewhat reminiscent of a painting of the Dieppe raid. Two dredgers lay on the sea bed so that only the top few silt buckets protruded from the water, masts, bridges and funnels of other sunken vessels stood out of the oily water. The first air strike on to Navy House was just going in at this time and four of the aircraft involved flew low over the ship as she berthed. There was a harsh hiss as they released their rockets over De Lesseps's statue followed by a crash as they struck the sandbag emplacements of the target. A pall of smoke from Shanty town and what remained of the beach huts, together with the widening pillar of smoke from the oil refinery spreading until it rose into darkness in the background, all contributed a grim picture of the

---

[1] The *Empire Parkeston*, originally a steamer on the Canadian Great Lakes, had been employed on the Harwich–Hook of Holland channel crossing prior to this.

havoc caused by war. And as the parachutists of the 2nd Battalion disembarked and made their way to a concentration area on a stretch of open ground amongst the blocks of flats on the seafront there was plenty of evidence of the morning's fighting. Close to the beaches, where anti-personnel mines could be seen mounted on sticks, an ammunition lorry which had received a direct hit lay gutted and charred, surrounded by what remained of its contents. Near the ruined bathing chalets an upturned trailer had been ripped from its chassis. Walls of buildings had been spattered by bullets, some had been pierced by shells; a street lamp had been severed near its base and crashed to the ground where it now obstructed the thoroughfare. Many of the cars that had been parked at the kerbside had starred windscreens or flattened tyres: beside some of them troops hopefully tampered with the ignition. Farther on, a lorry lay on its side with its load strewn across the road and petrol from a pierced tank spilling on to the tarmac, its driver dead beside his cab. At the intersection of some of the main roads self-propelled guns stood vigilant and machine-guns manned by Marines covered open spaces from balconies, or from behind low walls. From the direction of the centre of the town the sound of mortars and the fire of the 20-pounder guns of the Centurions could still be heard.

As soon as they could be assembled and their vehicles unloaded, an advance party of the Guards Independent Parachute Company, under command of the 2nd Parachute Battalion, sped to the Water Filtration Plant at the far side of the Raswa bridge, along a route still subjected to sniping. When they arrived, to find the Frenchmen wondering why they had been so late in coming, windscreens had been smashed by snipers' bullets although they had suffered no harm otherwise. Meanwhile the rest of the 2nd Battalion were following them up on foot, moving by platoons in section groups close together, so as to be able to cover each other. The troops hugged the shadows at the sides of the roads and kept well in under the arcades of the shopping centres; roads were crossed at the double. Along their route the occasional sniper's bullet reverberated through the deserted arcades and there were answering bursts of automatic fire: some of this shooting came from frightened men seeking the comfort that the noise of their own guns could afford. A large school in an open square had been turned into a casualty clearing station by the Marines and its main compound was congested with jeeps, Saracens of the 6th Royal Tanks, and requisitioned vans all painted with red

7*a*. Part of the contents of the L.C.T. *Bastion*.
(Photograph taken during the voyage to Port Said)

7*b*. An L.S.T. unloads at the Fishing Harbour.

8a. "Casevac."

8b. View of the Advanced Dressing Station at Gamil during the
morning of 5th November 1956.

crosses. It was dark as the marching column turned left at this square to follow the railway line that led south past the golf-course: the ground here was open and the Centurions which had reached it earlier in the day and some AMX tanks were settling down to lager for the night. A few bodies lay with blood congealing at the side of the road, a dog whimpered beside its dead master, the tank men smoked; in a siding nearby a goods train could be seen by the dim background light of the burning buildings of Port Said; beside the open doors of some of the wagons lay piles of Soviet automatic rifles.

The Cattle Quarantine Park lay next along the route; here the orses had bolted and were wandering about the road; some had shrapnel wounds and were bleeding, one lay dead between afts of a cart. Another with a gaping stomach wound was lying against a wall where—in compassion—one of the parachutists shot it.

At 1900 hours the troops arrived at Raswa and were greeted by the French, as guides from their own advance party led them across the bridge to the previous morning's dropping zone. Here they halted and re-formed for the task which lay ahead. On the information of the reconnaissance party which had already motored up the Treaty Road, meeting nobody on the way, it seemed that they had little to worry about: the road to Ismailia was open.

As has been recounted, 'A' Squadron of the 6th Royal Tanks had moved through 40 Commando to the golf-course earlier in the day, they had then continued to Raswa. There, they had collected a section of French parachutists and rumbled on down as far as the Canal Company's signal station at El Tina, arriving as darkness fell, where they were joined soon afterwards by Lieut.-Colonel T. H. Gibbon and his regimental headquarters. In the absence of any precise orders and in the light of circumstances as they appeared at the time, Gibbon deemed it would be unsafe to proceed any farther down the road without infantry protection. Tanks are particularly vulnerable at night and to support his conclusions it is fair to say that he had supposed that a 'balanced' force of infantry tanks and artillery would continue the advance; there was no real assurance that the advance on Ismailia would be unopposed for the entire forty miles or so that lay ahead and what is more, as yet, he had no reason to believe that there was any undue urgency. The tanks settled down for the night to await the rest of the force and then crews started to brew their evening meal; within the hour the first of Bredin's parachutists started to arrive and they were imbued with a sense of urgency.

L

Although Gibbon was unaware of the need, it was imperative that the column should move quickly now if 'Musketeer' was to attain any real success.

In London, at six o'clock that evening—little more than an hour before—another sort of battle was drawing to a close on the floor of the House of Commons. The Prime Minister had given the British Government's reply to a demand by the United Nations Secretary-General for a cessation of hostilities: 'If the Government received confirmation that Egypt and Israel had accepted an unconditional cease-fire', he said, 'and that the proposed international force would be competent to secure and supervise the objectives out in the General Assembly resolution' . . . he would agree further military operations. 'Pending the confirmation of this, continued, 'Her Majesty's Government are ordering their forces to cease fire at midnight tonight unless they are attacked.' The news was greeted in the House by cheering on both sides—the Labour members cheering in the belief that they had been the main pressure effecting the decision, the Conservatives in the belief that their policy had been fulfilled, without the necessity of fighting on to occupy Ismailia and Suez. The armies of Israel and Egypt had been parted and the Canal had not been fought over although it was firmly blocked by sunken shipping throughout its length and it was to be many months before freedom of trade through it would be established once more.

Most of the troops in Port Said were unaware of the Government's decision; the knowledge would have been sour encouragement in any case; right or wrong these men were committed to the operation and they were only concerned in finishing it quickly and successfully—few thought of anything of the issues beyond its speedy conclusion. Much is written about the maintenance of morale in battle: one of the prime factors of high morale is said to be a just 'cause'. At Suez the majority of the Marines, parachutists and others committed to the fighting, neither knew nor cared about the 'cause' but morale was extremely high. Possibly there were exceptions—some who examined their consciences and doubted—but they were few. Others—including the son of a Labour Member of Parliament who strongly disagreed with the views of his father—felt the 'cause' was more than just; most had no deep feelings either way.

At Raswa, Bredin's men heard the broadcast news of the impending cease-fire over the battalion wireless sets; shortly afterwards they were ordered to push on as fast as possible. It did not look as if this would be very fast: with the few vehicles available, the majority of the infantry faced a ten-mile march to El Tina. However, they set off to march at 1900 hours with their jeeps ferrying troops forward as best they could and it was nearly three hours later before the combined parachutist–tank column was ready to move on. If this force was going to secure a foothold on the open ground beyond the causeway there was no time for any delay; less than two hours remained until the cease-fire. A bridgehead beyond the causeway was vital for any further action which might follow the cease-fire and few really believed that the end of the operation was in sight at midnight: there had been cease-fires already and they had come to nothing. The crews of the Centurions packed up their brew cans, the parachutists picked up their weapons and the column shook out. By 2300 hours it was on the move. One of Bredin's companies had climbed on to the tanks and led by Brigadier Butler who was with Gibbon in the first Centurion, the column started out. Qantara, the village which marked the end of the causeway was twenty-odd miles farther on and Butler, who was determined to see that the force got as far as possible before the sands of the 6th November had run out, was intent on getting as far as this if not farther. (General Stockwell had ordered him to 'make every effort' to reach El Cap by midnight—a more attainable object in fact.)

Behind the first infantry, a small section of engineers, who were on call to lift any mines found along the route, also rode on the tanks; behind them again, the remainder of Bredin's men, their packs stacked in the few jeeps available to them, marched at a brisk pace. Not for long; soon after the resumption of the advance a staff officer[1] drove up from Port Said with a motley collection of commandeered transport—a circus of Coca Cola wagons, cattle trucks, furniture vans, even a pink truck labelled 'Memphis Touring Agency'; anything which would serve to lift the troops. The parachutists scrambled aboard and began to catch up the armour in front.

As no lights were used, progress was slow; craters, resulting from the Air Force's strikes of the previous days, also took their toll and slowed them down. The champ of one of the leading company commanders became the casualty of one such crater and another delay was occasioned by a stores truck of the engineers leaving the road to disgorge its explosive stores and injure some of the occupants.

[1] The Brigade D.A.A. and Q.M.G.—Major (now Lieut.-Colonel) A. N. Farrer-Hockley, D.S.O., M.B.E., M.C.

THE BREAK-OUT

At five minutes to midnight there were still four miles to go to Qantara; the column had passed the Canal Station at El Cap and had searched the deserted shanty village beyond. With the mainland now out of range in the time available the village of El Cap would have to be the limit of the advance and the column halted and deployed among the rotting timbers of the native huts. In the dark and without lights it had come seven miles in about forty-five minutes, stopping to clear the El Tina and El Cap signal stations along the way.

November the 7th was but a few minutes away and the cease-fire was now effective. But the last shot had not been fired.

CHAPTER 11

The Occupation of Port Said

When the cease-fire came into effect the population of Port Said were mostly unaware of it; Cairo Radio was still urging the people to fight, kill, and take revenge. All through that Wednesday night, fires raged throughout the town as buildings, already blazing, spread the conflagration unchecked; on the outskirts, more oil tanks caught fire. One shattering series of explosions, emanating from a warehouse which contained ammunition and which had been set alight earlier, rocked the town causing some of the British troops, who had been warned of the possibility of Soviet bombing attacks, to believe that their so-called police action was now over and that a real war had started. Meanwhile, fighting continued as Crook's parachutists strove to effect a junction with the Commandos who were themselves mopping up through the streets and along the quay.

When dawn broke, the twofold task of smashing the remaining pockets of resistance and restoring the town's administration began in earnest. Crook's battalion had at last got through to the Commandos and together they set about the slow process of clearing those houses in which snipers were still active, and of collecting enemy weapons. The Egyptian soldiery, now clad in the ubiquitous *galabiyeh*, were immune from detection as they mingled with the civilian population and so long as they acted the part of civilians they were safe. Locked in basements or hidden away in cupboards amongst the household linen, the boxes of grenades, belts of machine-gun ammunition, or crates of sub-machine-guns were a potential menace that the occupation troops could not ignore. And recovering this equipment was no sinecure; many of the Egyptian youths were loth to give up their new acquisitions, automatics or rifles, without some show of fight. As the arms were collected, they were taken to a

165

wired-off compound near the beaches where the best of the Czech and Soviet weapons were set aside for examination and trial, the remainder being destined to be dumped in the sea at a later date. Equipment from many countries and of differing ages found its way to this dump; old 1914 Lee-Enfield rifles with their separate long-bladed bayonets, modern Czech semi-automatic rifles whose stubby bayonets folded back along the rifle barrels, wireless sets, and artillery pieces. Most of it was small arms and no less than fifty-seven three-ton lorry loads of this warlike equipment and stores were collected by 45 Commando on 8th November in the area of Arab town. Regrettably, this initial collection of arms did not have the expected success mainly because other arms were ferried in coastal dhows to Arab town throughout the occupation.

The administration of Port Said now began to take up the resources of the supply columns and as these became effective the town gradually began to return to normal. Engineers were among the first of the follow-up troops and soon after first light on the Thursday, they were working at the waterworks at Raswa and the power station to restore two of the town's essential services. Little damage had been done to either of the plants but the distribution systems had suffered considerably as a result of the fighting and it was some days before they were back to normal. Mention has already been made of the major public utility—the Port Said sewage system—and the fact that sewage disposal had to be assisted by compressed air. Its blockage had led to an increase in flies and at one time the medical authorities were most apprehensive regarding dysentery. Even after the compressor plant had been repaired and the sewage was flowing 'normally' again, the system continued to give trouble. This was hardly surprising; even in the best of times the system was inadequate. Its small pipes were intended to cater for the local habits where toilet paper is not used and the influx of a large number of healthy British soldiers, who used complete pages of popular newspapers, soon had a disastrous effect.

Several hospitals were soon running in Consulates, hotels and public buildings and something must be said here about the performance of the R.A.M.C. and to refute the allegation that there was little medical assistance given by the Allies to the Egyptians. The fact that no differentiation was made between British, French or Egyptian casualties and that all received the same treatment during the course of the fighting has already been stressed. As soon as the cease-fire came into effect, medical supplies were rushed to the Egyptian hospitals, all of which had already accumulated a large number of casualties. Without delay and with no considerations other than those dictated by their Hippocratic oath, British and French doctors set themselves to work, operating as fast as they could, with few facilities and grossly in need of trained staff. As other medical units arrived with the follow-up echelon, these too were hurriedly put to work to alleviate the suffering. And, within forty-eight hours of the cease-fire, after representatives of the International Red Cross had negotiated its passage past the cease-fire line at El Cap, an Egyptian train drawn by a new American-built diesel-electric engine pulled into Port Said railway station; it was to be the first of the hospital trains which were to evacuate wounded Egyptians to Cairo under the joint auspices of the Red Cross organization and Red Crescent—the Moslem equivalent of the Red Cross. Two hundred wounded, many of whom were considered by the British doctors to be hardly in a fit state to travel but in whose selection they had no say, were loaded into this train by British medical orderlies, and the second-in-command of the 23rd Field Ambulance accompanied it as senior medical officer, on its journey back to the Egyptian lines.[1] After an uneventful run to El Cap the train was handed over unceremoniously and without incident to an Egyptian deputation in the no-man's-land between the British and Egyptian lines.

The Canal station at El Cap had become Bredin's headquarters and at dawn on Thursday morning the parachutists had started to dig in among the reeds. On each of the roads one of the new anti-tank rifles was set up on the low bank with machine-guns, in pairs, sited to cover the open ground; behind them a troop of Centurions also stood guard. Along the causeway at this point there were more trees than elsewhere and a short distance ahead was an old railway embankment in which empty slit trenches denoted a prepared but un-

[1] Before the train left Port Said, those reporters who had managed to sneak aboard, contrary to the order that none should accompany it, were ejected. Prominent amongst these was the *Life* magazine reporter. Two miles farther on, the same correspondent was seen to be trying to climb aboard; five miles farther on he was again repelled when he attempted to transfer to the train from a jeep. In spite of these vicissitudes, the handover of the train to the Egyptian authorities at El Cap was witnessed and recorded by the same persistent, but now jaded representative of *Life*. In recognition of his persistence he was accorded an official lift back to Port Said.

occupied Egyptian position. With such a narrow front it was not possible to deploy more than two platoons in line and the remainder of the battalion together with the Parachute Field Battery, occupied defences staggered back from the forward company. The front was only 250 yards wide; as such it was most unreal and unmilitary. The crow's-nest on top of the Canal signal station made an excellent observation post and from here, shortly after midday, about fifty Egyptians in civilian clothes carrying rifles were spotted working their way through the trees towards the British lines. The parachutists, who were quickly warned that they should fire only in self-defence, stood to and waited as the patrol came on towards them; the crew of one of the Centurions, who were stripped to the waist and cleaning the tank's 20-pounder gun, continued with their work. At fifty yards the Egyptians stopped and fired a few shots, one of which wounded one of the tank crew. They then fled towards a lorry which was waiting to return them to the safety of distance; as they did so one of the tanks could not be constrained from firing and two of the Egyptians fell dead. They escaped lightly, since the 'Red Devils', who had had the patrol in their sights since the time it was spotted, could have turned the action into a massacre, had they wished to do so.

In the course of the afternoon a helicopter was called up to recon-noitre the area forward of the cease-fire line and a short flight was sufficient to confirm that the Egyptians were beginning to move troops forward and consolidate their positions beyond the forward line. Columns of dust which marked the movement of vehicles amongst the desert scrub and Egyptian transport partially hidden in the copses along the Sweetwater Canal could be seen quite plainly. Anti-aircraft defences were also on the alert. As the helicopter circled at 1,000 feet above no-man's-land a burst of fire directed at it from the Egyptian positions caused the pilot to dive and swing away from the danger area. As he did so it was just possible to see Israeli Army vehicles—identifiable by the white-ringed star painted on their ve-hicles—in the Sinai desert at the limit of their ten-mile zone from the Canal.

Meantime, whilst the men in the forward area were digging in and roofing their dugouts with railway sleepers, Bredin had sent a handful of officers and N.C.O's into Port Said to see if they could requisition some vehicles to supplement the frugal scale with which his battalion had landed and the few he had acquired during the previous night's advance. When the party arrived in Port Said however, they found that most of the vehicles which had been in the streets had either been commandeered already or were broken down and in transport yards and garages; owners, wisely, had deflated their tyres or drained the fuel tanks and walked off with the ignition keys. Only after a considerable search was it possible to requisition sufficient vehicles and those that were taken constituted a very mixed bag.

That night, as the sun went down on the bewildered soldiers at El Cap, tired from their first experience of battle and two days with only a modicum of sleep, it was not clear that their military task was then at an end. Two ideas still predominated: the threat of a Russian air attack and the belief that the cease-fire was a mere diplomatic manœuvre designed to allow Nasser's troops time to re-group in front of Qantara and Ismailia. The positions in front of them were empty that morning, two days later they were occupied by Egyptian infantry and the helicopter reconnaissance had suggested that Egyptian tanks were moving up from towards El Cap. With this knowledge and the evidence developing before their eyes the bewilderment of the parachutists may be understood; like so many others they could only believe that an opportunity had been missed by halting on the stroke of midnight.

Back in Port Said most of the population stayed at home during the first few days after the cease-fire. Some Egyptians did attempt to get away in boats by sailing west along the Manzala Canal, but as this route was known to have been used by a large number of the Egyptian garrison already, the Allies were quick to establish control posts at its terminal area of the Interior Basin and Salt Pans. Boats were diligently searched for weapons and male Egyptians of military age taken off. Within two days the overt traffic had virtually ceased. On the Saturday morning (10th November) some of the shops opened, Egyptians appeared on the streets and fifty or so policemen reported for duty; one or two old gentlemen, with British war medals pinned to their *gallabiyehs*, who claimed previous service with the British forces, even volunteered for further service. There was no apparent hostility towards the Allies and it was hoped that this was a sign that the occupation would be free of internal security problems; by the same night it was clear that such a hope was ill-founded. 'The Voice of the Arabs' continued with the theme that 'The defenders of Port Said, the new Stalingrad, have fought to the death and now lie buried beneath the ruins' and as this propaganda blared out over the radio other more insidious elements were at work in the town. The capable

169

and obstreperous Soviet Consul, M. Tchikov, who had already done more than anyone else towards strengthening Nasser's hand, now set about organizing subversion. Tchikov's worth to Colonel Nasser throughout the period of the Suez activity can be estimated as at least one division; General Stockwell's own recognition of his value to the Egyptians may be judged from the fact that, later on, the machine-gun platoon of the West Yorkshires became Tchikov's escort—a constraint to his activities that he tried to shake off on numerous occasions. It was not long before a campaign of intimidation had begun to threaten the peaceful development of the occupation. The first signs were apparent by Saturday lunchtime when it was learned that an Egyptian telephone operator, who had taken a job with General Stockwell's headquarters, was murdered. Soon afterwards the shop of a newsagent whose proprietor remembered the business pickings that were to be had from British troops, was burned down. From then on things went quickly from bad to worse. The civilian labour force which had been engaged to unload the ships and who had seemed only too willing to work for the cash return, began to fade away; British civilians, who had a difficult enough time already, were threatened and insulted. Gradually, as the political wrangles continued in the United Nations and in London and the Egyptians grew more bold, the situation became increasingly difficult.

In the early days of the occupation there was a certain amount of looting and misappropriation. A stern order from Stockwell's Corps headquarters soon put a stop to any tendencies that the British troops might have had to 'win' things; but the French who had a somewhat different regard for their rights to property were not above extending their activities across the ferry from Port Fuad. In the final evacuation they took with them many vehicles and much equipment which they had liberated from civilian warehouses, some of it being quite blatantly displayed in Cyprus on their way back to Algeria. Their attitude to Egyptian civilians also was different from that of the British and they refused to tolerate any nonsense. In consequence, Port Fuad, under the control of the trigger-happy Légionnaires, proved to be less of a security problem than Port Said.[1]

[1] Civilians who wished to travel into the area occupied by the French troops were required by the French to carry a British authority for their journey from Port Said. This provided a formidable filter on the British side of the ferry, solved by one British officer charged with supervising the issue of passes by writing down 'Abdul bin Hamid' as the name of all applicants.

One of the first tasks which had to be undertaken in the efforts to restore the normal life of Port Said was to clear the streets of the bodies of the Egyptian casualties. Their removal to the cemetery area and burial was done mostly by Egyptian prisoners of war supervised by British military personnel and there were some difficult moments at one stage when some of the Egyptians refused to dig graves for bodies which were rapidly beginning to decompose. Relatives of the deceased eventually accepted the task. One anticipated administrative headache fortunately failed to materialize. The water supply for the town continued to flow from the Sweet Water Canal and it was not until much later that the Egyptians behind the cease-fire line conceived the idea of interfering with it. Priority was given to the landing of food and the stores necessary for civilian rehabilitation and the Commandos experienced some shortage of rations in consequence; tinned mutton stew ('Scotch style', so called!) and Rowntree's wine gums assuming a prominence which the Army dieticians had never intended. The occupation force, whose routine also was beginning to return to something resembling peacetime normality, accepted the hardships imposed by the situation with their customary, cheerful, grumbling grace.

Patrols and curfew enforcement had to continue. These duties were performed mostly by the infantry and the Centurions, whose movement through the streets damaged the drains, were retained in a reserve role. By day they were not allowed to move in the town at all, but at night they moved out to the boundary between the old Shanty town and the still troublesome Arab town area to stop the movement of arms into Port Said proper; like the attempt to control the waterborne traffic, this was largely ineffectual. Attempts to locate the arms caches known to be in Arab town were no more effective. The prime consideration of the Allied Command was to avoid unnecessary casualties or friction with the locals and as this meant restricting the methods of conducting searches the results reflected the advantage taken by the Egyptians of such an attitude.

By now the advance guard of General Churcher's 3rd Division had started to arrive off Port Said. The 19th and 29th Infantry Brigades[1] together with the 1st Royal Tanks, having embarked on the troopships *Empire Fowey*, *New Australia* and *Asturias* on the 1st and 2nd

---

[1] The third brigade of the division (1st Guards Brigade) was in the United Kingdom waiting to follow and it was never committed to the operation.

November, had enjoyed an uneventful journey from the United Kingdom. Their transports arrived to anchor among the vast array of British and French shipping five miles from the Egyptian coast in the early hours of Saturday morning, the 10th November, and the presence of these fresh troops now allowed some redeployment and for the withdrawal of the 'shock troops', which had been agreed in the United Nations General Assembly. Apart from the fact that the shock troops of parachutists and commandos had to be withdrawn in deference to the United Nations resolution, the Middle East situation was still seething and presented such intricate and delicate possibilities that it seemed quite possible that further airborne operations would be necessary. At the time, the Russians' aim appeared to be the elimination of Western influence in the Middle East by every means, short of war. Sustaining Colonel Nasser would be one of the more obvious methods of doing this, fortifying other Arab countries also had advantageous merit and Syria seemed ripe for provocation. From a purely military point of view, the evidence provided by those few Egyptian pilots in Soviet aircraft who had actually been engaged with the Israelis or the Allies, it was likely to be only too painfully apparent to the Russians that releasing aircraft to the Arab countries without 'volunteer' pilots was almost useless. Nevertheless, such aircraft manned by Soviet-bloc pilots and operating either from Damascus or the Egyptian airfields, could resuscitate the same threat that had been the *raison d'être* of phase one of the 'Musketeer' operation and for this reason picket ships of the Allied fleet kept watch in the east, covering with their air warning radar an area which probed deep into Syria. In the light of these uncertainties, getting Brigadier Butler's parachute brigade back into reserve again as soon as possible seemed sensible. There was some confusion as to where it was to go initially. The 1st Parachute Battalion, which had never really been committed to 'Musketeer', had returned to Cyprus on the 8th November; on the 11th, orders were issued for the brigade headquarters and remainder of the parachute brigade group to return direct to the United Kingdom but these orders were cancelled in less than an hour and the brigade was ordered to Cyprus. There, where during the period of the Suez interlude the E.O.K.A. terrorists had caused more casualties than had been experienced by the entire expedition in Egypt, they were to await the final outcome of the Egyptian operation.

Returning to Port Said, where the 29th Brigade was the first formation of the 3rd Division to set foot in Egypt: the troops of this brigade disembarked at the Casino Palace on Sunday, 11th November, amidst the confusion that still reigned at the docks and to the stale smell of death which persisted over the town. Some sniping was still going on as they moved out of the dock area. The 1st Battalion Royal West Kents, for whom 1956 was the bicentenary of the raising of their regiment, had been ordered to take over from Bredin's parachutists at El Cap. Their Commanding Officer, who had been flown up to El Cap from the helicopter field near the Casino Palace, arrived just in time to witness the death of two Press photographers[1] whose jeep, which had driven through the British forward defences, came under Egyptian machine-gun fire and swerved off the road into the Sweet Water Canal. By now Nasser's troops, showing a recovery in their morale, had completely reoccupied the trenches opposite El Cap and closed up to the Allied line. Civilians who lived at El Cap and who had passed through the Egyptian defences on their return home after the cease-fire, said that the Egyptian Army was unaware of any cease-fire; the troops facing Bredin's men firmly believed that they were holding up the British advance.

Soon after dark that evening the advance parties of the Royal West Kents arrived at El Cap and their first impressions of the effectiveness of the cease-fire can hardly have been favourable, with spasmodic bursts of machine-gun fire directed against the parachutists' lines causing one of their number to become a casualty. Bredin was not impressed either. If the hand-over was to go smoothly it was clearly necessary to take some retaliatory action and he ordered two belts of machine-gun fire to be directed against the offending area. This fire effectively silenced the Egyptians and were the last shots that day; nevertheless, after this display the men of Kent were somewhat apprehensive of the method by which they were to conduct the relief. Both sides were in full view of each other during daylight and it seemed possible that the Egyptians could assume that the change-over was really reinforcements being brought up as the prelude to an Allied attack. In the event the Egyptians appeared totally unconcerned and 600 yards away they could be seen walking around, sitting out on top of their defences or digging and improving their trenches.

In the next ten days the Royal West Kents continued to man the

---

[1] An American, Mr. David Seymour, and a Frenchman, M. Jean Roy, who were looking for news, did not slow down and appeared to ignore signals to stop. Their bodies, wrapped in linen, were returned to the British lines about a week later.

positions at El Cap. As has already been remarked, it was an unreal situation. El Cap was in the world news and apart from the fact that their every move was overlooked by the Egyptians as the troops tried to dig new trenches, put up wire set out trip flares, they were beset by hordes of visitors. Everyone wished to see the front and it was easy enough to get there from Port Said. Some were there on very serious business. The staff and air squadron commander of the aircraft carriers came up with the brigade commander to plan the air support which would be necessary if the battle flared up again. Others had less important reasons for venturing up to the 'sharp end'; possibly some were even prompted to make the journey by the rumours that a medal would be awarded only to those who had actually participated in the operation or who could claim to have been in the forward area. Journalists, B.B.C. radio and television technicians, Generals, Admirals, Navy and Army staff officers, French officers, United Nations observers and others averaging a total of sixty visitors per day all descended on the focal point of 15,000 troops. Here, a battalion deployed on a two-platoon front—one platoon being commanded by a newly joined National Service subaltern—held the peace of the world. Behind there was a Corps headquarters, division headquarters and two brigades were in support. The forward troops were trampled on by the visitors, whose cars also raised the dust which covered their weapons; minesweepers brought visiting Admirals on their own element up the Canal, to be piped ashore with all due ceremony; the battalion officers' mess became nothing less than a bar-cum-café. Militarily, as well as internationally, it was a remarkable situation. In it the Egyptians generally behaved very well. Except at night they did very little shooting although they were in the habit of firing off a single shot whenever their troops were relieved, and although this may well have been the method by which they unloaded their weapons it had the effect of keeping the British troops on the alert. As compensations for the visitors and the sleepless nights, however, the troops were able to enjoy wonderful and undisturbed bathing facilities in the Canal and when the time came for their relief and return to more dangerous and certainly less glamorous duties in Port Said many of the men were sorry to go.

The Royal Fusiliers, who had relieved Crook's battalion, took over from the Royal West Kents on the 21st November and they, in turn, were relieved six days later by the remaining battalion of the 29th Brigade—the 1st Battalion of the York and Lancaster Regiment. By this time the activities at El Cap had settled down to a steady routine, largely governed by the United Nations observers who had arrived in advance of the United Nations Expeditionary Force and who were functioning in the manner of umpires. As observers, they were free to visit both sides and they went to great pains to preserve the correct and neutral attitude on which their authority rested. No information on the dispositions of the Egyptians was revealed to the British troops, but explanations which followed 'incidents' invariably eased the concern which the incident had created. A burst of firing from the Egyptians' lines was revealed as a '*feu de joie*' fired at a wedding ceremony near the Egyptian headquarters; another had been directed against a civilian who failed to produce the correct papers; a third was to repel a (mythical) attack by British frogmen who had 'swum down the Canal each night into the Egyptian positions'.

Two companies of Danish troops, wearing the light blue helmets[1] and United Nations armbands, eventually arrived from Abu Sueir in a train which had been held up by the Egyptians for the best part of a day, and took over the forward positions on the 30th November. With their positioning as a buffer it was now clear that the Allied troops' duties at El Cap were almost over and, as camera-men continued to pursue them in the hope of getting a scoop photograph, the men of the York and Lancasters withdrew from the area on the evening of the 7th December. After staging at El Tina, they embarked on H.M.S. *Theseus* on the 8th December to return to the United Kingdom.

Turning briefly now to General Keightley's planning problems: whilst the political arguments regarding the future of the Allied forces in Port Said were raging in New York, the Allied Command were having to make simultaneous provision for three eventualities. First, there was the possibility that the advance would be resumed and that the Canal Zone would be occupied as had been originally intended. Secondly, there might have to be a speedy withdrawal from Port Said; finally, the Allies faced the possibility of an indefinite occupation of Port Said if no political compromise could be arrived at. These conflicting requirements meant that the cargoes of a whole fleet of ships had to be sorted out, stores landed at Cyprus and Malta and yet a reserve still had to remain afloat. And, whilst the aftermath of 'Musketeer' was being dealt with, E.O.K.A. were making full use

[1] As a result of which the United Nations troops were dubbed 'the —— Bluebells'.

of the second wind they had gained during its course. General Keightley, in his role of Commander-in-Chief of the British Middle East Land Forces, found that he might soon have to face pressing problems on the Arabian peninsula. For these provision would also have to be made. It was not until 22nd November when United Nations troops started to arrive in Egypt that it was clear that there could be no question of a resumption of forward operations in Egypt and the following day the administrative plans were recast in the light of this development. The sailing of ships which had been loaded with stores and ammunition for Port Said were postponed indefinitely and some of those at sea were recalled to Malta and Cyprus. Things now began to move quickly as the planners, relieved of the possibility of resumption of belligerent activities, were able to consider what could be withdrawn from Port Said prior to a complete withdrawal of the expeditionary force. Not only was the question of the redeployment of the troops involved to be considered in the light of possible future developments, but the release of reservists and time-expired regular soldiers who had been retained during the period of the emergency, together with their return home and the effect of their withdrawal, had all to be worked out. Very little information as to the future commitments was available and no withdrawal from Port Said was actually specified until the 3rd December. Then, when the evacuation order was given, the two days' notice necessary to preposition the shipping and the fifteen days which had been expected would be needed to complete it were reduced to fourteen days all told.

Back at Port Said, the Royal Fusiliers and the York and Lancaster Regiments—the two other battalions of the 29th Brigade—had followed the Royal West Kents ashore on 11th November, relieving Crook's parachutists who returned to Cyprus. On the 19th Infantry Brigade and these two battalions of the 29th Brigade fell the onerous task of preserving the uneasy peace of Port Said. The 19th Brigade, comprising the Royal Scots, the West Yorkshire Regiment, and the Argyll and Sutherland Highlanders, were not able to disembark until three days after the 10th. The *Empire Fowey*, in which the greater proportion of the brigade had travelled, steamed into the harbour on the 10th; she had to go back to her anchorage off the coast that night, when it was clear that there would be no space for her to unload at the overworked quays. And a landing craft, which came alongside the next day, had to return to the harbour after five hours of pitching and tossing, without having been able to take off any of her troops. In the

9a. The Israeli frigate *Miznoh* passing through the Straits of Tira under the muzzle of a captured Egyptian gun at Ras Nasarahi

9b. Men of the Royal Marines in action in the beach head.

9c The Egyptian Police Station near the Commercial Basin.

10*a*. General Sir Charles Keightley, Admiral D. F. Durnford-Slater, Air Marshal D. H. F. Barnett and General Sir Hugh Stockwell.

10*b*. General A. Beaufré, General Sir Hugh Stockwell and Admiral P. Barjot.

evening when the *Fowey* steamed into the harbour again she had to be ordered back to her anchorage once more. This time the tug which had been sent out to help the troopship rammed and holed her. It was the following evening before she finally made it and it was then so late that it was deemed preferable for the troops to remain on board until the next morning. When the brigade finally disembarked it relieved Madoc's 3rd Commando Brigade, who, like their red-bereted parachutist brothers-in-arms, were also able to revert to a reserve role and return to Malta.

The new arrivals entered the operation—already dubbed a fiasco—at a depressing stage; facing them was an unpleasant and often humiliating task of clearing up the mess and as the time for the Allies to withdraw approached, the Egyptians more boldly showed their resentfulness of the Anglo-French presence. The role of the troops was the usual one associated with internal security duties; law and order had to be maintained—this included the enforcement of a dusk to dawn curfew—and there were still considerable quantities of arms at large which had to be found and collected. The town was divided up into areas of responsibility of individual battalions and to maintain effective control of the land it soon became apparent that it would also be necessary to control the surrounding water. To cope with this the West Yorkshires, who had been allotted the waterfront area, requisitioned boats and raised their own private navy to patrol the harbour from a base in the Arsenal basin.

The Royal Scots' assignment was a particularly thankless task. Their area included the infamous Arab town and the occasional sniping activity which was still fashionable there was hardly calculated to endear the Egyptians to the Jocks. In spite of this, their correct, dignified behaviour and willingness to help Arabs in distress earned them the dubious reputation of being 'saviours of the poor'. One feature of the daily life of the area at this time was the distribution of food, relief money and kerosene, on which most of the inhabitants depended for their cooking. These amenities were handed out by the civilian police who were anything but effective at controlling the unruly mob which gathered, screaming and clamouring for help, whilst fighting to get at the precious food and oil. On one such occasion a civilian policeman was accidentally shot and invariably it fell to the lot of the unfortunate troops to restore order and supervise the distribution.

The Egyptian police themselves were generally co-operative and towards the end of the occupation permission was given for them to be reinforced. The normal police complement of Port Said was declared (by the Governor) to be 1,500 men, of which only 800 were available for duty after the fighting had ceased, the remainder having either become casualties or had deserted. Three hundred and fifty replacements were sent up from Cairo and after these had been checked by the United Nations Military Observers to ensure that they were really policemen and not fedayeen they were allowed into the town; where subsequently they worked with the United Nations Force.

Colonel Nasser's propaganda machine was less co-operative and on 16th November General Stockwell, in an attempt to control the wild statements which were calculated to unsettle the population of Port Said, ordered Cairo's 'Voice of the Arabs' to be jammed. Ever since the cease-fire had come into operation it had been broadcasting anti-British and anti-French propaganda which had exaggerated the damage in Port Said and alleged continued attacks and other horrors on the civilian population. Nor was the unsettling process confined to broadcast messages. Printing presses working in Port Said itself turned out leaflets and posters which underground agents, under the leadership of a mysterious character known as the 'Black Hand', enthusiastically distributed. As a result a proclamation threatening dire penalties on anyone who intimidated civilians had to be issued shortly after the radio-jamming procedure had been put into effect. The entire propaganda programme seems to have been very successful and morale throughout Egypt was extraordinarily high;[1] if hostilities had had to be resumed after the cease-fire there seems little doubt that the Egyptians would have fought hard. Militarily, they had taken the respite of the cease-fire to strengthen their grip on the Canal, particularly round Qantara and Ismailia; they had also re-organized their logistical support, largely by opening up the old British supply depots in the Fayid area and if they were not aware of its advantages previously, the lessons of Port Said had shown them that fighting in built-up areas was far and away preferable to fighting

---

[1] When the 16th Parachute Brigade was sent to Jordan in July 1958, during a crisis largely provoked by continued virulent Egyptian propaganda, the Jordanians found it difficult to believe that the brigade was the same one as that which had been engaged in Port Said eighteen months before. They had been led to believe that a British airborne division had been used and that two-thirds of it had been annihilated.

in the open where they would have little hope of making a stand against the British and French troops. With this in mind they had begun to prepare Ismailia for a battle of street fighting.

The frequency and severity of attacks on Allied patrols increased as the days of December slipped away. The exact date of the evacuation was kept secret; clearly, withdrawal in the face of an enemy who is aware of the intention is likely to be a hazardous business and despite the cease-fire the situation in Port Said was such that every precaution was desirable. About ten days before the Anglo-French last troops embarked the worst incident occurred. On Monday evening, 10th December, a young officer of the West Yorkshires, Lieutenant Moorhouse, took part in a raid on a flat in the Arab town area; this resulted in the arrest of six fedayeen officers. A small guard was left in the flat for the night and early the next morning two individuals who visited the flat were also arrested. Moorhouse, with an escort of four men, had collected the prisoners and then sent his driver and escort off to get breakfast—a laudable and natural action. Apparently he then decided to ascertain that a relief was being provided for the guard at the flat and having dispensed with the services of his driver and escort, drove off alone in the vehicle. At this time in the morning the streets were almost empty. Sometime later, after an Arab youth had reported that there had been a fracas nearby, the vehicle was found abandoned a few hundred yards away from the flat, but there was no sign of Moorhouse. The story of what happened was pieced together later. On his way to the flat Moorhouse is believed to have seen an Egyptian boy putting up a propaganda poster and he stopped to arrest him. In the altercation which ensued a small crowd collected, Moorhouse's pistol was seized and he was hustled into a large black car which was subsequently found abandoned on the edge of Arab town. A cordon was thrown round the area and an intensive house-to-house search was organized but all inquiries were without result and no trace could be found of the missing subaltern. General Stockwell then appealed directly to General Burns, the Commander of the United Nations Force, and through the Governor of Port Said every effort was made to locate his whereabouts and to secure his release. Nothing came of these inquiries, the Egyptian authorities claiming that they had no control over what went on in the town.

From the evidence that became available subsequently, it seems that Moorhouse's captors had intended to hold him for exchange against Egyptians who were then in the hands of the British—possibly those who had been taken on the previous night. Bound and gagged, he had been locked in the cupboard of a house which had had to be abandoned during the house searches which had started when his abduction was known. When his captors were able to return to release him they found he had died of suffocation and he was reported to have been buried in the house where he had died. (Later his body was exhumed and sent back to England.) This tragic affair caused a good deal of attention in the British Press and inquiries continued to be directed to the Egyptian authorities through the United Nations until the middle of January, when the facts became known. One unfortunate side to the whole sad business was the hoax played on a very brave officer of the U.N. Force, who was endeavouring to locate Moorhouse. This officer was led blindfolded from a secret rendezvous to a house, to be shown an individual, dressed in British officer's uniform, whom he assumed was the missing subaltern; the news, which was passed to General Stockwell just before the evacuation, raised hopes that Moorhouse was still alive.

Moorhouse's abduction signalled the start of a whole series of incidents. As soon as the 'Voice of the Arabs' announced that the Anglo-French forces were withdrawing, the Egyptians assumed that they were safe to do as they pleased and as offensive acts against Allied troops increased and tension grew the town again began to assume the appearance of a battlefield. Civilian activity lessened, shops closed, the girls who had started to appear on the streets and the traders with the postcards suddenly disappeared. Grenades were thrown at Allied vehicles, patrols were ambushed, snipers restarted their activity. Finally after a particularly bold attack, as a result of which a Major in the Royal Scots subsequently died of his wounds, 'force was met with force', as General Stockwell had threatened, and the skirmish developed into a regular street battle which involved a troop of Centurions and resulted in at least twenty-seven Egyptian casualties. After that there were no more incidents until the final embarkation.

CHAPTER 12

The Withdrawal

When General Stockwell received the order to evacuate the Anglo-French forces from Port Said, he is reputed to have said to his headquarters staff: 'At last, gentlemen, it seems that we have achieved what I had always believed to be impossible—an operation going on in two directions at the same time.' The movement of shipping, full of ancillary units, reinforcements and stores from the United Kingdom to Port Said at the same time as troops were being withdrawn from Port Said certainly gave that impression. The difficulty was that the political decisions which were taken as a result of the United Nations resolutions did not allow sufficient time for a logistical programme reorganization and military horses of this ilk cannot be changed so easily in mid stream.

Immediately the cease-fire came into effect the declared policy of the British and French Governments was to hold firmly on to the Port Said beach-head until a United Nations Emergency Force was able to take over; to do this the massive armada of land, sea and air forces which had been assembled for 'Musketeer' was obviously no longer necessary. By mid November the Valiants and Canberras had returned to the United Kingdom from Cyprus and Malta, much of the naval armada had dispersed and the build-up of the British 3rd and the French 7th Mécanique Rapide Divisions in Egypt had been halted. The assault force of parachutists and Commandos were withdrawn before the end of the month and, as has been seen already, Port Said was garrisoned by General Churcher's two infantry brigades and the 6th Royal Tanks, with a French brigade supported by a regiment of AMX tanks remaining in Port Fuad. The first United Nations troops, a company of 200 Norwegians, arrived in Port Said on 21st November; they had flown in to Abu Sueir, staged at the hurriedly established U.N.E.F. base near the airfield and travelled up to Port Said by train. By the time that they formed up outside the railway station to march to their tented camp in the park near Government House a vociferous and enthusiastic crowd of Egyptians had gathered to welcome them and for a brief period it looked as if the Norwegians would be enveloped by the crowd. It was not an ugly or hostile crowd but a mêlée ensued, during which General Stockwell's hat was knocked off. Order was eventually restored by a company of the West Yorkshires assisted by men of the Royal Scots and one of the Port Operating Squadrons. The British troops, who had been hastily called out, diverted the crowd into Arab town, where it eventually dispersed.

Other contingents of Danes, Swedes, Colombians and Indians followed the Norwegians into the town as the U.N.E.F. in Egypt was gradually built up to the agreed total of 6,000 men.[1] Most of them had flown from their home countries to Abu Sueir, coming up to Port Said by rail, but the Jugoslav contingent, which were providing an armoured car unit for Sinai, arrived by sea. In their long overcoats and Russian-style boots they looked strangely alien, but they were not unfriendly when once they had overcome their surprise at being dependent to get off their ships on those whom they were supposed to be ushering out of Egypt. Few of the U.N.E.F. troops had anything other than the light equipment which they had been able to bring with them by air and it fell to the Anglo-French authorities to make up the deficiencies of transport, fuel and equipment, before General Burns's force could start to function; all of them wore the light blue helmet—blue because of the colour of the United Nations flag—and United Nations armbands, although their uniforms were those of their own national forces. Which countries should contribute to the U.N.E.F. had itself been a sore point with the Egyptian Government. Some which offered contingents to the U.N.E.F.—notably Australia, New Zealand and Pakistan—Egypt refused to counten-

---

[1] The U.N.E.F. raised for service in Egypt eventually contained about six infantry battalions comprising:

    One Indian battalion (3rd Parachute Regiment (Kumaon)).
    One Danish–Norwegian battalion.
    Two companies (about 450 men) of a Swedish battalion.
    One Finnish company.
    Three companies of an Indonesian battalion, and
    Three companies of a Brazilian battalion.
    (Canada provided some of the important supporting arms; Colombia
      also participated.)

ance; because Canadians looked like, dressed and behaved like the British and were members of the Commonwealth, they too were regarded with the greatest suspicion; even the Danes and Norwegians, because of their N.A.T.O. connections, were barely acceptable. Nations whose contributions to the U.N.E.F. were acceptable had a strong neo-Soviet flavour about them.

General Burns's first task was to interpose United Nations troops between the Egyptians and the British at El Cap. Once the two belligerents had been separated his next step was gradually to assume responsibility for Port Said and its environs, allowing the Allies to conduct a phased and orderly withdrawal; as they left, the Allied perimeter would shrink back along the causeway from Port Said and the buffer zone would increase. So far as the town itself was concerned, the plan which was eventually agreed upon provided for the U.N.E.F. to take over additional areas of responsibility as and when United Nations troops became available. Vital installations and vulnerable points, like the power and water pumping stations, telephone exchanges and food dumps, had to be guarded in order to ensure that the life of the community continued as 'normally' as possible during the withdrawal, since opportunists under the guise of patriotic saboteurs would undoubtedly do their best to cash in on any uncertainty as to responsibility. Then, in the final stage of the evacuation, the Anglo-French troops would retire behind a narrow perimeter defined by a barbed wire fence close to the Canal entrance, the L-shaped British sector including a mile of the north waterfront and the docks, and in Port Fuad the French would have a half-mile strip covering the Workshops Basin. By this time it was hoped that U.N.E.F. would have taken over responsibility for the remainder of the town and that it would be generally quiet. However, for this, the last act, it was proposed to create a special zone beyond the barbed wire barricade, several hundred yards wide and also defined on its far side by a wire fence. From this zone all civilians would be evacuated.

Although it had been all too apparent that there could be no alternative to an Allied withdrawal, the formal intention to do so was not announced until 3rd December; at the same time General Keightley was instructed to work out with General Burns a timetable for the evacuation. Like the assault which had preceded it, this was an operation of considerable magnitude. At the beginning of December it was estimated that there were some 22,000 Allied troops—13,500 being British—with close on 5,000 vehicles and 10,000 tons of stores ashore in Port Said. Even after all the ships had been assembled, at least a fortnight would be needed to get the troops and military stores away and there was also a large number of Allied refugees who would have to be evacuated. During the withdrawal, in spite of the U.N.E.F., the trend of events suggested that there would be internal security problems and that the Allies certainly would have to be prepared to deal with any sudden Egyptian move. As already described, the final phase of the plan was a joint U.N.E.F.–Allied undertaking and it was decided that the last remaining British element in Port Said would comprise the 19th Brigade and a squadron of the 6th Royal Tanks, with a similar French rearguard of two battalions of the French Foreign Legion (about 1,500 men) with their own squadron AMX tanks in Port Fuad. More than 11,000 British troops were evacuated in the second week of December, most of them sailing in the troopships *Dilwara* and *Ascania* and H.M.S. *Theseus*, *en route* for Cyprus, Malta or Britain. So far as possible the principle of 'first in, first out' was followed but most of the reservists were included in the early evacuations in an effort to get them home for Christmas. And as the Allied garrison thinned out, the strength of the U.N.E.F. in Port Said grew.

British, French and Italian nationals were evacuated next. All went according to plan and the Egyptians made no attempt to interfere with their departure. Some of these refugees who had been born in Egypt and had never left it even to visit the country whose nationality they were proud to claim, had odd ideas about the prospects of their homecoming. One little man, very brown, smilingly declared whilst drawing his £5 cash allowance for the journey, that he was 'going home to a merry English Christmas in the snow'.[1] No doubt some were more fortunate than others when they arrived in their native lands but many had to abandon their homes and most of their possessions. To this day many are still trying to re-shape their lives in what, to them, are really alien surroundings.

One of the more satisfactory phases of the withdrawal was the exchange of prisoners of war, which took place, under the code-name, Yo-Yo,[2] on the day before the final embarkation. Between them the

[1] Lieut.-Colonel Edward Fursdon: 'Musketeer' (*The Unquiet Peace*).
[2] This code-name, 'Yo-Yo', was coined by the then D.A.A. and Q.M.G. of the 19th Infantry Brigade, Major (now Lieut.-Colonel) F. W. E. Fursdon. The name was considered to be apt because of the frequency with which the operation was agreed, cancelled, and agreed again.

British and French had 230 Egyptian prisoners in their joint bridge-head, some being true prisoners of war—officers and men of the Egyptian armed forces—but most of whom were civilians. On the other side, the Egyptians had detained all the Britons—about 450 all told—who had been employed prior to the invasion by the contractors in charge of the military bases in the Canal Zone; these men had been taken to Cairo and imprisoned there. A suggestion put forward by one of General Burns's staff officers to the effect that an exchange ought to be possible was received favourably on both sides. After several delays and a number of difficulties, not the least of which was incurred by the French shipping some of their prisoners out of the country and having to fetch them back, the exchange eventually took place on the afternoon of 21st December. The prisoners of the Allies were collected together, medically examined and put aboard a train at Port Said under Finnish guards of the U.N.E.F., whilst at Kantara the Egyptians handed over a train which had come from Cairo carrying 472 British nationals. The actual exchange took place very quickly at El Cap, and although they had had nothing to eat all day the contractors' men were in good spirits and glad to get out. As they drank the tea the troops had prepared for them one question was prevalent: 'Why didn't you take the whole bloody Canal while you were at it?'[1] There was no answer; many of the troops themselves still wondered why the operation had wound up as it did.

'E' Day—Saturday, 22nd December—was a beautiful bright day. What remained of the Anglo-French force had now withdrawn behind the perimeters centred on the Casino Palace Hotel and the landing stage at Port Fuad. Jet fighters still screamed overhead and out to sea there were the naval ships whose fire could be summoned by wireless if the Egyptians were minded to resume hostilities. It was a last great, but sad, show of defiance; the Allies were getting out and it was the end of an epoch—maybe the last time that two empires, in association, would ever try to impose their will on a weaker nation. A mood of defiance coupled with exasperation and wounded pride had descended on many of the last contingent. During the night one man had climbed the flag pole that was sited in the field behind De Lesseps's statue and nailed to it an enormous Union Jack. Before climbing down he had hauled up or severed all the ropes which remained at ground-level and as he slid down the pole he left a thick

[1] 'Musketeer' (*The Unquiet Peace*), Lieut.-Colonel Edward Fursdon.

smear of grease preventing others repeating his climb to remove the flag. Another more ambitious party tackled the statue itself. With considerable ingenuity and display of mountaineering skill two men eventually achieved a sitting position on De Lesseps's right arm, from here they were able to secure in his right hand a pole carrying a large White Ensign and a French Tricolour.

In the early morning sunshine the fluttering flags were a fine sight, though De Lesseps himself—soon to be dynamited and toppled into the Canal—was a forlorn spectacle.

The remaining troops started to embark about 1700 hours and about an hour later the rearguard provided by the West Yorkshire Regiment left the final perimeter positions. As they did so a burst of fire from an Egyptian automatic spattered against the wall a few feet above their heads; luckily no one was hurt. Then the last of the Centurions clattered up the ramp into the waiting landing craft at the Casino quay. At Port Fuad, the French too were leaving; just as it had been an Allied invasion, so too it was an Allied withdrawal. Shortly before 1900 hours, the last of the infantry who had formed a tight cordon round the landing stage, jumped into one of the two remaining landing craft, which took them out to a waiting troopship at the Canal entrance. Now, only Brigadier E. H. W. Grimshaw, the Commander of the 19th Infantry Brigade, together with two of his staff officers, remained on the quay, talking to the U.N.E.F. liaison officer, Captain Ghellinck. It had been rumoured that the Egyptians would hand over Lieutenant Moorhouse during the final embarkation, and the hope still lingered that a vehicle carrying the missing officer would suddenly drive up to the landing stage and Moorhouse would step out. Finally, however, the brigadier ordered the remaining officers to get into the last assault craft, shook hands with Captain Ghellinck and followed them into the boat. And, as the boat was slowly reversed into the main harbour, prior to making for the last troopship waiting in mid stream, the code word LOBSTER was signalled to Allied headquarters on a portable radio set. Other than the destroyer H.M.S. *Duchess* which remained a short while longer, in the hope that Moorhouse might yet be released, and the ships of the salvage fleet which were now under United Nations command, Egypt was clear of Allied troops. Forty-seven days after the start of the operation, the withdrawal of the invaders was complete.

Although it was an operation in its own right, it is fitting that the story of the Suez activities should end with a brief account of what was done by the Anglo-French salvage organization. The efficient clearance of the obstructions in that part of the Canal under their control after the cease-fire, and the rapidity with which the British and French navies performed this task, were in marked contrast to the long period which the United Nations took to clear the rest; as such, it emphasized the high efficiency of the Royal Navy and its salvage department. Port Said harbour alone was littered with the wrecks of no less than twenty-four ships, varying from small craft of about 100 tons to the 368-foot long, 3,600 tons dredger *Paul Solente*. To make salvage more difficult the bottoms had been blown out of some of the vessels. Apart from the 165-foot span El Ferdan railway bridge, which had been expertly dynamited and dumped into the Canal channel half-way down its length and a pontoon bridge at the southern end of Lake Timsah, in an orgy of reprisals, the Egyptians had scuttled another twenty-seven ships, including tugs, dredgers, cement-laden barges, salvage vessels, a tank landing craft and floating cranes between Port Said and Suez. Some of these were totally submerged, others had their superstructure showing above the water; all presented a formidable salvage task and were bottling up sixteen freighters and tankers which had been marooned in the Canal at the start of the hostilities. Until the obstructions were cleared these vessels were unable to leave the Canal either by its northern or southern exit.

As has already been mentioned, the British and French began salvage operations almost as soon as they landed. Fortunately both the Royal Navy and the French had maintained skeleton salvage organizations after 1946 and salvage vessels had been included in the assault force.[1] Within three weeks of the initial landing, i.e. by 25th November, they had opened up Port Said harbour to vessels of 10,000 tons and cleared a twenty-five-foot deep channel as far as El

---

[1] Initially this comprised: 3 Ocean Salvage Vessels
                                    9 Coastal Salvage Vessels
                                    7 Boom Defence Vessels
                                    6 Lifting Craft
                                    4 Lifting Pontoons (6 more in reserve at Malta)
                                    2 Wreck Dispersal Craft.

One other Ocean Salvage Vessel and 4 Boom Defence Vessels were also standing by to go to the Suez entrance.

Cap, the limit of their jurisdiction.[1] To help with the clearance operations two German heavy-lifting vessels (the *Ausdauer* and *Energie*) were chartered by the Admiralty and brought from Hamburg to deal with the larger wrecks, and before the operations were taken over by the United Nations the joint Anglo-French Salvage Command under Rear-Admiral Jean Campion had collected together one of the largest salvage fleets ever assembled. By mid December it comprised nineteen ships at work with another twenty-one held ready to go to either Port Said or Suez. If this fleet had been allowed to continue work beyond El Cap it is reasonable to suppose that a passage would have been cleared through the Canal by the end of January; only Egypt's insistence on 'all neutral' crews and that the work should be conducted by the United Nations precluded this eventuality.

On 24th November, following discussions in Cairo conducted by the Secretary General, the United Nations took on not only the responsibility for getting the wrecks up but also for raising the $40 million then estimated necessary to pay for the operation, the money was to come eventually from higher tolls on the ships using the waterway. There was some delay in settling the political and financial problems involved but eventually a three-man team headed by the 71-year-old American General Raymond A. ('Speck') Wheeler, a former United States Army Engineer who had been knighted for his war services, was appointed to supervise the salvage operations. Following the setting up of his headquarters in Ismailia, General Wheeler visited Port Said and, after praising the Anglo-French salvage command for what they had accomplished so far, announced that their work would be taken over by a United Nations salvage force which he reckoned would be assembled within the next ten days. His forecast soon proved incapable of substantiation and before many more days had passed it was apparent that not only was the Anglo-French team the only means to hand but that the salvage operations were considerably more complex than General Wheeler had foreseen. As none of the scuttled ships could be salvaged, the first task would be to clear a single shipping lane and this meant lifting, floating or simply dragging hulks aside so that they could be dismembered later. The El

[1] This could have made possible the release to the Mediterranean of the thirteen ships marooned north of El Ferdan but Colonel Nasser refused permission for them to move and they were only allowed to do so on 8th January, well after the evacuation. The other three vessels, trapped south of El Ferdan, left the Canal by the Suez exit on 28th January.

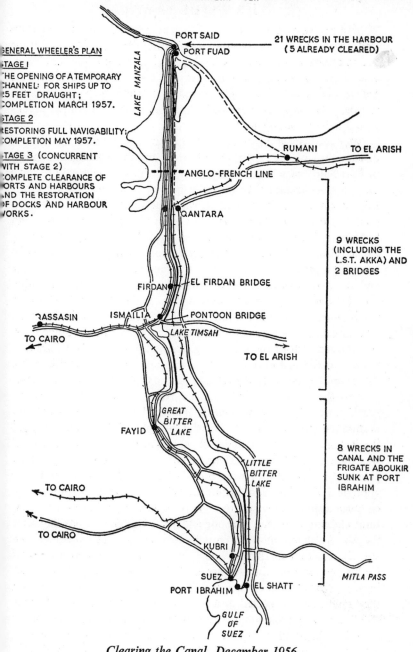

MEDITERRANEAN SEA

PORT SAID
PORT FUAD

21 WRECKS IN THE HARBOUR
(5 ALREADY CLEARED)

LAKE MANZALA

GENERAL WHEELER'S PLAN

STAGE I
THE OPENING OF A TEMPORARY
CHANNEL: FOR SHIPS UP TO
25 FEET DRAUGHT;
COMPLETION MARCH 1957.

STAGE 2
RESTORING FULL NAVIGABILITY;
COMPLETION MAY 1957.

STAGE 3 (CONCURRENT
WITH STAGE 2)
COMPLETE CLEARANCE OF
PORTS AND HARBOURS
AND THE RESTORATION
OF DOCKS AND HARBOUR
WORKS.

RUMANI   TO EL ARISH

ANGLO-FRENCH LINE

QANTARA

9 WRECKS
(INCLUDING THE
L.S.T. AKKA) AND
2 BRIDGES

FIRDAN   EL FIRDAN BRIDGE

RASSASIN   ISMAILIA   PONTOON BRIDGE

TO CAIRO   LAKE TIMSAH

TO EL ARISH

GREAT
BITTER
LAKE

FAYID

LITTLE
BITTER
LAKE

8 WRECKS IN
CANAL AND THE
FRIGATE ABOUKIR
SUNK AT PORT
IBRAHIM

TO CAIRO

TO CAIRO

KUBRI

MITLA PASS

SUEZ   EL SHATT
PORT IBRAHIM

GULF
OF
SUEZ

Clearing the Canal, December 1956

189

Ferdan bridge and one or two of the ships would have to be cut up under water by divers; blasting was inadvisable since it would leave pieces of wreckage which could clog suction dredges later on. Then, after a shipping lane had been cleared, it would still be some time before the Canal could be restored to normal working since the normal 'housekeeping' fleet which had formed the bulk of the wrecks would have to be replaced.

After an inspection of the Canal obstructions and a number of discussions with the Egyptian authorities and the Allied commanders in Port Said—at which some very straight talking was said to have been done—General Wheeler published a three-stage plan for clearing the waterway. The first stage, which he envisaged would be completed by early March, would be to extend beyond El Cap, through to Suez, the twenty-five-foot channel already cleared by the Anglo-French fleet. This would permit the passage of ships of up to 10,000 tons displacement and necessitate the removal of nine more wrecks and the two bridges. Stage two was the removal of the remaining obstructions in the Canal, together with the necessary dredging which would allow ships of maximum draught to negotiate the Canal: this, he estimated, would be completed early in May. Finally, stage three was the removal of the remaining obstructions from Port Said and Suez, and the restoration of the docks and harbour facilities; this work would proceed concurrently with the Canal clearance of course.

Even the assembly of the United Nations salvage force proved much more difficult than General Wheeler had ever anticipated and despite the reluctance of the British Government for salvage ships of the Royal Navy to work under the auspices of the United Nations it was soon obvious that the clearance of the Canal was going to be a protracted affair if they were not allowed to be used. There was a good deal of acrimonious argument but an agreement permitting the eighteen British ships and the one remaining French vessel to continue clearing Port Said harbour under the United Nations flag after the Allied evacuation was eventually reached. As Colonel Nasser was equally reluctant for British and French ships to be used, the terms for his agreement to the deal meant that the crews of the ships would have to wear civilian clothes and forgo many of the amenities which they might have expected in more normal circumstances. Not only would they be unable to go ashore but their security was a matter for considerable concern. For their safety and that of the ships, armed 'civilian' guards, provided by the Swedes and Finns of the U.N.E.F., were posted on the vessels whilst United Nations Patrols patrolled the banks of the Canal in the area where they were working. Fortunately no incidents occurred where force had to be used. The charter of the two German vessels was taken over by General Wheeler's organization which by mid December had only managed to assemble seventeen other salvage ships although Dr. Hammarskjold reported to the General Assembly on 11th January that the United Nations salvage fleet 'as of January' comprised thirty-two vessels with crews drawn from Belgium, Denmark, Germany, Italy and the Netherlands in addition to the British fleet and the solitary French ship.

With the departure of the Anglo-French forces from Port Said, General Wheeler's work began in earnest and by 1st February half the wrecks in the stretch of the Canal from El Cap to Suez—about two-thirds of its length—had been cleared; the removal of five more obstructions would mean the completion of the first stage of his plan. But now the key to the remainder of the operation was the old LST *Akka* which, it will be remembered, the Allied Air Forces had tried to prevent being towed from Lake Timsah into the main shipping channel. When she was sunk, loaded with reinforced concrete, the *Akka* had rolled over with her bow jammed into the side of the Canal and her stern buried in forty feet of water. And when the United Nations salvage experts first saw her, their conclusion was that the wreck could only be removed by cutting her up—a slow and messy procedure. However, in spite of considerable delays and inconvenience imposed by the Egyptians, the German teams in the *Ausdauer* and *Energie* managed to get steel cables underneath the wreck preparatory to hoisting her on to an even keel. It then took two more weeks to lift and shift her out of the Canal. Meantime the Egyptians were pursuing a 'go-slow' policy in order to blackmail the United Nations and delay the passage of tankers to the oil-hungry West.

After completing the clearance of Port Said harbour, the last ships of the original Anglo-French salvage fleet were withdrawn on 24th January. Their crews were more than glad to go and in a statement issued by the Admiralty at Valetta on the following day it was disclosed that they had cleared 17,000 tons of wrecks 'in the face of every conceivable form of obstruction and irritation'. Not that Egyptian obstructions and irritations were confined solely to the Anglo-British operations: when on 7th May General Wheeler announced that the Canal had been cleared a month ahead of schedule, he implied that the time could have been shortened by another month

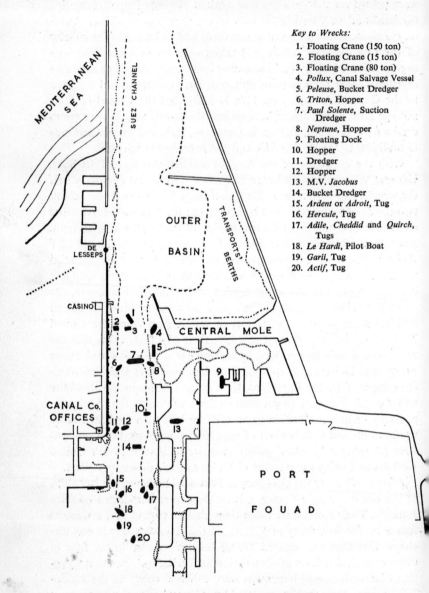

Chart of Wrecks in Port Said Harbour, November 1956

192

11*a*. The withdrawal from Port Said.

11*b*. General Burns, the UNEF commander with a Yugoslav soldier at El Ballah in December 1956.

12*a*. Port Said harbour, November 1956.
(Photograph taken from the High Light window.)

12*b*. Brigadier Rex Madoc, the Royal Marines Commander (now Major-General R. W. Madoc, C.B., D.S.O., O.B.E.)

if Egypt had been more co-operative. All that remained now was to pay for the operation[1] and for Egypt to say how she would permit the Canal to be used. One thing was certain, she was not going to permit its use at all until Israel evacuated Sinai. On 24th April Colonel Nasser submitted a plan to the United Nations which professed adherence to the 1888 Constantinople Convention in so far as it stipulated 'the unimpeded use of the Canal by ships of all nations, promised not to increase tolls unduly without negotiations with those who used the Canal and to submit disputes to arbitration'. Although there were some important omissions from the plan the United Nations decided to accept it on a trial basis and Britain and France, who were still sending their ships round the Cape, concluded that their continued boycott was pointless. The first British ship to pass through the Canal since October did so on 19th April—after paying tolls in Swiss francs.

Finally, when in July 1958 the Suez Canal Company recognized Egyptian ownership of the Canal, it seemed that the world had at last accepted Colonel Nasser's nationalization act. This, in spite of the fact that the Canal is not yet open to all nations without discrimination; Israeli ships are still debarred from using it and cargoes which pass through the Canal bound for Israel are still liable to confiscation.

Colonel Nasser is now trying to correct the military weaknesses revealed during Operation 'Kadesh'. With the assistance of the Soviet-bloc countries he is building a strong army and German technicians in Egypt are said to be working on rocket weapons. Since he has confessed that these are intended to be used against Israel the problems of peace in the Middle East and protection of an international waterway still await a solution that could have been settled in 1956—if the troops had been ready at the right time, if our politicians had been sufficiently resolute and if we had not had to face American hostility.

[1] In a House of Commons debate on 19th March 1963, the Parliamentary Secretary to the Ministry of Transport said that the British Government's final liability for clearing the Canal would possibly total £1,450,000. It is difficult to assess in terms of money the real cost of the military operation, although Lord Avon quotes a figure of £100 million. The loss of prestige cannot be costed in terms of money.

Epilogue

Field-Marshal Lord Montgomery has said that success in battle can only be achieved if the fighting machine is set in motion in such a manner that it can develop its maximum power very quickly. 'What may be called the stage-management of battle', he said, 'must be first class.' Operation 'Musketeer' must surely illustrate the converse of this maxim. As a classic example of a 'limited' warfare operation it is unique, as an example of how such an operation should not be planned and mounted, with political interference at every step, it is equally classic. The popular conception now seems to be that this was the last occasion that Britain and France—or any other country for that matter—could ever act on their own initiative in defence of strategic interests, and that the need for resources sufficient to mount an operation of this magnitude will never arise again. There are plenty of arguments, associated with the moral virtues of such independent action in the face of the United Nations Organization and the risk of escalation from limited to thermo-nuclear war, with which to support this concept. Politically also, it can seem a desirable as well as virtuous ideal since the provision of expensive equipment and ancillaries needed to keep such a force in being may be excused and—theoretically anyway—more resources allocated to the nuclear deterrent shield.

Without a sufficiently large or suitably equipped mobile reserve, capable of striking as soon as Colonel Nasser pulled his nationalization *coup*, we were compelled to spend weeks in scraping an inadequate barrel to gather the necessary resources. During this time, world opinion was mobilized against us and when the decision eventually was taken to invade Egypt the Government seems to have put almost every form of restriction on to the military machine which was to take the necessary action to implement their decision. There can surely have been only one real political objective: securing the Suez Canal. This was certainly General Keightley's declared military aim and as it was not achieved, 'Musketeer' must be regarded as having failed militarily. If the political objectives were attained by the capture of Port Said—as was claimed—then they must have been at variance with those of the military. 'War', said the French statesman, 'is too serious a business to be left to the generals.' Few generals in the Western world would disagree with this and in Britain they have found no difficulty in adopting the role of professional adviser, content to leave the vital decisions to a civilian Cabinet. When once the decisions have been taken, invariably they have loyally endeavoured to carry them out; over the years this system has engendered trust between politician and soldier so that the politician has left the technical management of any military action following his decisions to the soldier. In this instance the usual method seems to have been ignored and General Keightley's task was made doubly difficult by the constant political interference which was experienced during the period of launching the operation, after the decision to part Israel and Egypt had been made. It is not known whether the effect which the changes consequent on this interference would have on the complex programme, was impressed on the Government by General Keightley in sufficiently strong terms, however.

The Israeli attack is an excellent example of the use of surprise, mobility and superior tactics; in accordance with Field-Marshal Montgomery's precept, the Anglo-French assault needed speed as well as technical superiority even if it could not include an element of surprise. The five days of air operations which ponderously paved the way for the arrival of the assault force can hardly be said to be a quick development of the fighting machine. In retrospect a more realistic plan would appear to have been two days of air bombardment to eliminate the Egyptian Air Force, then a co-ordinated land assault by both airborne and seaborne forces, followed by a quick exploitation by an armoured group. This is what happened in the invasion of Sicily during World War II which was a quick and very successful operation. The claim that air forces using conventional armaments can win wars without land forces should have been disproved by the experience of Korea when the United States Air Forces were not allowed to use nuclear bombs to prevent the build-up of Chinese reserves. In Egypt, the Allied air forces were additionally limited by the restrictions which were placed on targets they were allowed to attack. However, their overwhelming superiority in numbers and types of aircraft, pilots and techniques does not detract from the fact that they put up an outstanding performance, not only in the annihilation of the Egyptian Air Force, but in the support they gave to the ground troops later.

Not having the right sort of assault force at hand to exploit the success of the first phase seems to be a justifiable criticism of the operation. From its earliest conception the plan for 'Musketeer' had envisaged an armoured force moving quickly down the Canal to secure the vital areas—General Keightley being a cavalryman, nothing less could have been expected. Yet when the time came, only the armoured regiment that had moved with the assault force was available, the rest of the armoured group being afloat in Southampton. It is not proposed to dwell on how this situation arose or the difficulties imposed by the last-minute changes in plan—these have already been stressed; sufficient to say that such changes are bound to complicate the operation and may produce hazards totally out of proportion to their apparent effect when the change is initiated.

The difficulties associated with getting the assault force to its objectives—lack of suitable aircraft for the parachutists and shortage of amphibious craft for the seaborne forces—have also been stressed. It is a regrettable fact that in spite of the technical means of achieving mobility which are available, the British Army's movement capability even now is not much greater than what it was in 1945. 'Short take off and landing' (STOL) and 'vertical take off' (VTOL) aircraft, as well as ground cushion aerial vehicles, all offer striking—albeit expensive—possibilities, yet there is still little sign of any of these developments being taken into service in sufficient quantities to meet our foreseeable needs. There is a special need for transport aircraft which can carry tanks and artillery quickly into an area where a brushfire operation threatens to develop into something more serious. Yet the British aircraft industry is reputedly in the doldrums.

In the days when Great Britain controlled a huge empire there was little quibbling over military expenditure and, although her land forces were kept small, at least they were equipped with first-class weapons. When Crook's parachutists landed at Gamil they were astounded to find that the Egyptians were armed with more modern weapons of superior design than their own. (The self-loading F.N. rifle, now in service, had not yet been issued.) Signals equipment on which an army largely depends for its organized and concerted actions, was obsolete and defective and even in 1958 reports of this poor equipment still being in service were heard.

Wireless links between General Stockwell in H.M.S. *Tyne* and General Beaufré in the *Georges Leygues* were bad, as they were between them and Cyprus, and the forward troops. Indeed, General Stockwell is reputed to have said that he made one big mistake during the course of the operation; this was in keeping a twenty-four-hour watch on the Cyprus radio link rather than on the B.B.C. If he had, it may be that he could have anticipated the 'cease-fire' and so, by accepting a risk urged a speedier movement down the road to Ismailia, although from the account which has been given, it is problematical how this could be attained.

Without question, the most outstanding feature of the operation was the use of the helicopters from *Theseus* and *Ocean*. The landing of 45 Commando marked a new advance in the sea mobility of the Royal Marines, from which the concept of 'Instant' troops—following the lines first developed by the United States Marine Corps for a vertical assault—has been expanded. It will be noticed that the term 'mobility' appears repetitively in this short epilogue. No excuse is made for this, it is the key requirement for troops, equipment and casualty evacuation when a situation arises from a localized trouble spot; at Port Said the helicopter showed that it was an ideal vehicle for such operations provided that the limitations associated with its maintenance, vulnerability and the prerequisite of air superiority are accepted. Working from a floating base, helicopters can provide the means whereby a task force can be surprise-landed in alien territory at short notice. This is one lesson which appears to have been accepted and H.M.S. *Albion* and H.M.S. *Bulwark* which were converted into Commando carriers have done sterling work in the Far East recently.

Operation 'Musketeer' showed up the inadequacy of our land bases; Libya and Jordan were closed to us; facilities at Cyprus were inadequate; Malta was too far away and too small. As Britain's internal security commitments overseas diminish with the independence of Commonwealth countries, our need for military bases should diminish with them—so also will our voice in the world. If, however, we are to exert some influence in the interests of the free world we shall still need some bases and for these we shall have to adapt our present strategy. The Canal base is no more; the facilities available to us in the independent African states and Cyprus may prove more of an embarrassment than a help; Malta now has little military significance except as a base for N.A.T.O.'s southern responsibilities; Aden is just about the only land base in the Middle East which now remains—and for how long is an enigma. In any case, if a possibility exists that nuclear weapons may be used, fixed bases, whose latitudes and longitudes are known exactly, are useless. An alternative would seem to be the development of floating bases, but these are expensive in both capital and running costs—Commando carriers functioning as floating barracks, particularly so. Nor are such bases able normally to function as stockpiles for the heavy equipment likely to be needed in any sizeable operation.

The alternative is to rely on our air portable strategic reserve, based in the United Kingdom; this is behind the planning for the R.A.F. to be re-equipped with Belfast freighters and VC-10 troop carriers, all of which can be refuelled in the air and so travel considerable distances without landing. There are two immediate problems attached to this solution: first there is the question of overflying sovereign territories—the Middle East countries are markedly touchy on this score—and there is also the problem of acclimatization of the troops involved. Troops suddenly transferred from a temperate zone to a tropical climate require some weeks in order to adjust their metabolism to their new surroundings. It is possible that a solution may be found to this problem—periodically cooking the troops of the strategic reserve in special hot chambers perhaps—but for the time being this remains a difficulty. But there are less obvious problems associated with the deployment of an air-transported reserve for which there is no easy solution. Such forces may well provide a quick reaction at a trouble spot but, unless the operation is very close to a suitable base, reinforcement will have to be by sea. And in a real emergency heavy equipment will be needed quickly and the huge aircraft capable of moving such equipment will consume considerable quantities of fuel. It seems that we cannot get away from our prime reliance on sea power even if we should wish to do so.

The Suez operation emphasized the role of the Royal Navy, which despite its apparent slick efficiency off Port Said, had its own set of problems; these also go back a long way and certainly have not yet been resolved. Sea power laid the foundations of Britain's imperial expansion and at the height of her greatness the Royal Navy was always strong enough to protect Britain's seaways, yet since 1945 the fleet has been ruthlessly shrunk and for eighteen years over 1,000 fighting ships have been disposed of. For the Navy to become really efficient it is once more primarily a matter of expense. Amphibious forces are expensive; it is not just a matter of providing modern LST's—and even of these we have only had one solitary new one in the last year or so. To back them there must be a well-balanced support that only the Royal Navy can provide if they are to be made capable of operating without a land base. The first requirement is carrier-borne air cover, and aircraft carriers cost about £100 million each with their aircraft embarked. (At present we have five carriers which will be worn out by the early 1970s.) To defend the carriers, guided-missile destroyers, escort ships and all the rest of the fleet train is needed, so as to make up a balanced unit. If we cannot, or will not, afford the expense which all this entails, then the Royal Navy might just as well dwindle to a coastal force and we can give up any idea of responsibilities in the Mediterranean, let alone east of Suez.

The thorny problem of manpower has not been discussed: if the requirement is for 'instant' troops then it is no use relying on the call-up of reserves—the men must be trained and ready at a moment's notice. Certain obvious gaps should be plugged at once. It may be difficult for a Government of any political view to authorize an adequate Movement and Port organization in time of peace, but there should at least be in existence an efficient regular nucleus which is capable of being expanded rapidly to cope with any emergency.

Existing manpower shortages are already a sufficient threat to efficiency in standing N.A.T.O. commitments, without any sudden demands for participation in even minor disturbances. Overcoming this problem does not necessarily mean a return to conscription; it has been suggested that the role of the Territorial Army could be revised in order to make it a really effective reserve capable of rapid reinforcement of the Rhine Army. If this were possible, then regulars stationed in Germany could presumably be released to strategic reserve roles and the sort of situation precipitated in July 1956 avoided. It is doubtful whether N.A.T.O. would approve of such a procedure however, unless British forces in Germany are first brought up to strength. There will also have to be a considerable inducement to get members of the Territorial Army to take on an 'ever-ready' role, since they will have to be prepared to accept uncertainties which are not very popular in civilian employment. If this is not possible, then some form of return to conscription seems to be the only answer.

EPILOGUE

In 1956, the attitude of the Americans[1] was difficult for most of us to understand; in many of our military dilemmas since then it is still difficult to understand. We are probably the best and most accommodating ally that the United States has ever had, yet the reproach at our concern for Anglo-French strategic interests in the Suez Canal is not the only instance of their disapproving attitude, and there have been other rebuffs in the military-economic fields which are equally difficult to understand. Even before the Suez venture the British EM2 rifle which, technically, was a far superior weapon to the F.N. with which we are now equipped, was killed by the Americans; so also was the adoption of the tactical missile Blue Water; lately the sale of the new British strike aircraft, the TSR-2, has been rejected by the Australians, seemingly at U.S. instigation, by an offer of their own rival TFX. But even if it is at our expense, it is to be hoped that 'Musketeer' and its aftermath have provided lessons for our American friends. Perhaps we are more sympathetic to American difficulties than they are to ours. When, shortly after the Suez débâcle, and again in 1963, there were political murmurings in the Republic of Panama against the United States claims to full sovereignty in the Panama Canal Zone, and they made it abundantly clear that they were not prepared to tolerate any change in the status of 'their' canal, people in Britain and France were not slow in sharing United States anxieties.

Finally, to turn to Egypt: in all fairness it must be said that the Egyptians have proved that they have the technical skill to operate the Suez Canal efficiently on their own. Somewhat naturally this is a great source of pride to Arab Nationalists and has greatly enhanced Colonel Nasser's personal prestige. We have no reason to doubt his abilities or his pre-eminence in the Arab world—yet he remains a man of whom we have every reason to be wary. The Middle East is as combustible as ever it was, and Israel is cautiously watching for any change in the internal situation of her Arab neighbours which would affect the security of her borders. If a flashpoint is reached, it

[1] Undoubtedly some Americans were sympathetic, and one or two U.S. officers who were on courses in the U.K. probably came to appreciate the British point of view. In discussions one such officer who tried to follow the line set by his Government was nicknamed 'John Foster ——'. Any ribbing he received in the British mess was marginal compared with the indignation expressed by his bride of a few months when he got home, however. She was a Frenchwoman!

is difficult to see how we can avoid being drawn into the conflagration, and if this should happen we should do well to remember the advice of Montaigne:

'Il faut être toujours botté et prêt à partir.'

The Army Reserve Organization

1. The Royal Army Reserve is divided into the categories shown:

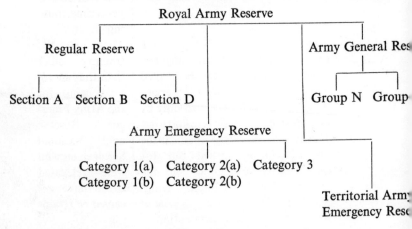

The Regular Reserve is made up of ex-regular soldiers.

Section A comprises volunteer (and some drafted) soldiers who may be called out for service overseas *without* Royal Proclamation.

Section B are liable to be recalled to the colours by Royal Proclamation.

Section D consists of volunteers with no normal reserve liability but can be recalled on a Royal Proclamation.

None of the regular reserve have any peacetime training liability.

The Army General Reserve took in all the ex-Class 'A', W(T), Z and Z(T) reservists. In peacetime the Army General Reservist has no liability; in an emergency he may be called out for service in the same way as a Section 'B' reservist, i.e. for Home Defence in the event of an attack in the U.K. Otherwise he can only be called up after a Royal Proclamation.

THE ARMY RESERVE ORGANIZATION

2. Categories and responsibilities of the Army Emergency Reserve are shown below:

Category	Composition	Liability for Service	Training
AER 1	Units to complete the mobilization order of battle of the active army.	All agree to be liable to call out for service *anywhere* in an emergency *without proclamations*.	Categories 1(a), 2(a) and 3 attend a 14-days annual camp. Categories 1(b) and 2(b) do NO peacetime training.
AER 2	Ex - National Service soldiers living where they could not be posted to Territorial Army units during their part-time training. This category serves to make up the strength of the Territorial Army.	These categories may be called out for service *overseas* only by proclamations but they can be called out for service in the United Kingdom *without* proclamation.	There is NO training other than that an annual camp for the Army Emergency Reserve and National Servicemen who were relegated to it have received NO training.
AER 3	A pool of highly skilled tradesmen and women. (There are NO officers in this category.)		

3. The *Territorial Army*, whose role is to provide a reserve deployed over the United Kingdom, has home defence as its main task but some parts of it are organized to reinforce the regular army at home

and overseas on mobilization. For this reason it includes a parachute brigade group, two armoured brigades, two Port task forces, etc.

4. The *Territorial Army Emergency Reserve* (The 'Ever-Readies') is a special volunteer category of the T.A. which did not exist in 1956; its planned target was for 20,000 men, but in 1963 only about a quarter of this target had been attained. Volunteers are liable to be called out, *without Royal Proclamation*, for service with the Regular Army either at home or overseas for a total period not exceeding six months. The 'Ever-Readies' each receive an annual bounty of £150 whether or not they are called out. If they are called out they also receive a tax-free gratuity of £50.

Their liability extends to a fifteen-day camp (or course) and they also carry out their normal T.A. training.

5. There are also categories of women's Army Emergency Reserve— the Q.A.R.A.N.C. (AER) and W.R.A.C. (AER) whose conditions of service are broadly the same as for the men.

The Cost of the Anglo-French Operations in Egypt in 1956

1. *Casualties*

(*a*) British and French casualties sustained in the Port Said landing appear[1] to have been 32 killed, 1 missing and 130 wounded, divided amongst the Allied services as follows:

British	Killed	Missing	Wounded
Royal Navy	1		
Royal Marines	9		60
Army	8		36
Royal Air Force	4		1
Totals	22		97

French	Killed	Missing	Wounded
Navy		1	
Army	10		33
Air Force			
Totals	10	1	33

Six aircraft of the Royal Navy were lost—four as a result of enemy action and two in accidents; the R.A.F. lost two aircraft: one by enemy action and one as the result of an accident.

The French lost two planes: one missing and one in an accident.

[1] There is a slight discrepancy with the 'final figures' announced on 14th November by General Keightley's headquarters. These were given as 32 killed and 129 wounded, 1 missing.

(*b*) Egyptian.

Egyptian casualties were the subject of a Government report by Sir Edwin Herbert. His finding was that the casualties in Port Said were 650 dead, 900 wounded and detained in hospital with a further 1,200 slightly wounded. To this must be added approximately 100 killed in Port Fuad.

This official estimate of Egyptian casualties has been criticized as being too low; even if this is true, it is certain that the reduction of the naval bombardment saved many Egyptian lives—probably at the cost of an increased British casualty list.

Egyptian equipment captured by the Anglo-French forces during the operations were listed by the Ministry of Defence on the 21st November. The list included the following:

Equipment of Soviet-bloc origin

3 SU-100 self-propelled artillery pieces.

A new type of Czech anti-tank gun.

5 32-barrelled rocket launchers.

10 'Praga' 10-ton vehicles.

52 light machine-guns, over 500 rifles and sub-machine-guns, large quantities of ammunition and anti-tank mines.

Equipment of British origin

4, 6-pdr anti-tank guns.

2, 3·7-inch guns.

40, Bedford and Fordson 3-ton vehicles.

420, rifles and considerable quantities of ammunition.

2. *Financial and Economic Costs*

Lord Avon quotes an all-up figure of £100 million pounds as the estimated cost of the military operation. A Labour Party estimate, which takes into account the loss of exports and increase in cost of imports directly attributable to the operation, is for £328 million. (This figure includes £57 million extra spent by the Services but does NOT include Britain's share of the Canal clearance bill which, the Parliamentary Secretary to the Ministry of Transport announced in a House of Commons debate on 19th March 1963, would possibly total £1·45 million.)

Chronicle of Events

JULY

26th Colonel Nasser announces the nationalization of the Suez Canal.

27th Britain and France lodge formal protests in Cairo.

30th Sir Anthony Eden tells the House of Commons that 'precautionary military measures' are being taken by Britain and France.

AUGUST

A Royal Proclamation on the 2nd signals the call-up of reservists.

On the 9th Operation 'Nursery' caters for the evacuation of British wives and children from Egypt.

Joint planning for an operation in Egypt by British and French military staffs.

(The appointment of General Sir Charles Keightley as Allied Supreme Commander is announced on the 11th.) The first tentative plan for an operation called 'Hamilcar' is ready by mid August; subsequently this is reshaped and renamed 'Musketeer'. The 1st and 3rd Battalions of the 16th Independent Parachute Brigade are flown from Cyprus to the U.K. for airborne training whilst the 2nd Battalion is moved to Cyprus.

Both 40 and 45 Commandos of the 3rd Commando Brigade move from Cyprus to Malta, where they are joined by 42 Commando from the U.K. In Malta they start in on an intensive training programme.

The 3rd Infantry Division, in the U.K., mobilizes and forms an armoured brigade of two armoured regiments.

In Egypt, Colonel Nasser forms a 'Home National Army of Liberation' on the 9th August and on the 12th refuses to join the London Conference on the future of the Canal. (The 16th, the day on which the Conference opens, is declared to be an Egyptian national day of mourning.) On the 28th British nationals are arrested on spy charges.

SEPTEMBER

French troops are stationed in Cyprus.

The 1st and 3rd Parachute Battalions return to Cyprus and the 16th Parachute Brigade Group concentrates in the Nicosia area.

On the 4th, the 6th Battalion Royal Tank Regiment sails for Malta.

OCTOBER

The yacht *Athos*, loaded with Egyptian arms, is captured by the French.

On the 26th, whilst the Israeli forces mobilize, Colonel Sharon's airborne brigade make a feint move towards the Jordanian border. The following day the Allied Command in Cyprus issue a warning order of the possibility of 'Musketeer' becoming necessary.

On the 28th the aircraft carriers H.M.S. *Bulwark*, *Eagle* and *Ocean*, together with the French aircraft carrier *Arromanches*, sail from Malta for the eastern Mediterranean.

ISRAELI Operations

The 29th is D day for Operation 'Kadesh'.

29th Sharon's brigade crosses the Israeli frontier into Sinai at 1600 hours and at 1700 hours one of his battalions is parachuted into the Mitla Pass area. After capturing Kuntilla his main column moves on to Thamed which is captured by 0600 hours on the 30th.

30th (The day of the Franco–British ultimatum to Israel and Egypt.) *Sharon's brigade* is attacked by Egyptian MIG's and his parachute column is shelled and strafed. By 1730 he has captured Nakhl and Mitla is occupied by 0800 hours; 31st *Ben Avi and Harpaz* with two other brigades capture Kuseima by 0630 and advance on Abu Aweigila where an intense tank battle develops, but by the early hours of the 31st Harpaz has managed to link up with Sharon at Nakhl and the whole of southern Sinai is cut off. The fighting continues at Abu Aweigila, which the Egyptians make an abortive attempt to reinforce.

31st The fight continues at Abu Aweigila and the Egyptians counterattack. The French are reported to have shelled Rafa with a naval force. Yoffe's brigade crosses into Sinai at 0530 hours and advances towards Sharm-El-Sheikh.

ALLIED Operations

The go-ahead for 'Musketeer' is given at 1500 hours Z on the 31st. Meanwhile 40 and 42 Commandos and the 6th Battalion Royal Tank

Regiment have embarked in the Amphibious Warfare Squadron and sailed from Malta. They are followed by 45 Commando in H.M.S. *Theseus* and H.M.S. *Ocean* which sail on the 3rd November.

The first air strikes against Egyptian targets are made by the R.A.F. during the night of 31st.

NOVEMBER

1st *ISRAELI Operations*
A fresh Israeli task force by-passes Abu Aweigila and strikes at Rafa. Abu Aweigila is captured and reconnaissance patrols exploit to within ten miles of the Canal.
ALLIED Operations
Air attacks on Egyptian targets, by land-based and naval aircraft, continue. H.M.S. *Newfoundland* sinks the Egyptian frigate *Domiat* in the Red Sea.

2nd *ISRAELI Operations*
Gaza surrenders at 1000 hours. Yoffe's brigade arrives at Ras Nasrani.
ALLIED Operations
Air strikes on Egypt continue. Tanks and soft-skinned military vehicles near Cairo are attacked. The radar station at Abu Sultan is destroyed by French aircraft.

3rd *ISRAELI Operations*
Yoffe's brigade captures Sharm-El-Sheikh.
ALLIED Operations
H.M.S. *Crane* is attacked by Israeli fighters. Troops in Cyprus embark. The airborne operation by the British 3rd Parachute Battalion and French Parachute Battalion is advanced by twenty-four hours.

4th *ISRAELI Operations*
The island of Tiran surrenders to Yoffe's brigade.
ALLIED Operations
The Allied tank force sails for Port Said from Cyprus. Allied aircraft endeavour to isolate Port Said.

5th The 3rd Parachute Battalion and French Parachute Regiment emplane at 0200 hours, take-off 0245 hours and drop on Gamil airfield at 0515 hours and the bridges across the Interior Basin at 0530 hours. Both objectives are captured by 0700 hours and the French report the west bridge to be intact. At 0930 hours the first casualties are evacuated by helicopter and an hour later a French Dakota lands on Gamil airfield. An Anglo-French reconnaissance party reports the road to Ismailia is clear as far as Kilo 10. A second French battalion drops on Port Fuad and captures it. At 1415 hours the Egyptian Commander asks to discuss surrender terms with the Anglo-French Commander and between 1500 hours and 2000 hours there is a temporary cease-fire. The French occupy Port Fuad during the night 5th/6th November.

6th The seaborne assault by the 3rd Commando Brigade starts about 0500 hours when 40 and 42 Commando land on the beaches astride Casino Pier. By 0530 hours 'C' Squadron of the 6th Royal Tank Regiment has married up with the Royal Marines and the first of the tanks reaches the golf-course, south of the town, by about 1000 hours. (At 1200 hours these tanks arrive at the Raswa bridge across the Interior Basin.)

At 0615 hours the first wave of 45 Commando—helicopter-borne—touches down near De Lesseps's statue and by 0740 the Commando has landed complete. By 0700 hours the Royal Navy are at work clearing the harbour for ships to be berthed near the Casino Palace Hotel. Fighting continues in Port Said throughout the day.

At 1600 hours the parachute brigade (less the 3rd Battalion who landed at Gamil and are battling near Arab town) disembark near the Casino Palace. At 1720 hours the 2nd Battalion Parachute Regiment advances south through the town arriving at the French bridgehead at Raswa about 1900 hours. There they marry up with tanks of the 6th Royal Tank Regiment and are ordered to press on to reach El Cap by 2359 hours. They arrive there by 2345 hours and at 2359 hours they are two miles beyond it.

7th Vehicles of the 6th Royal Tank Regiment at El Cap are fired on by an Egyptian patrol and one man is wounded. When the fire is returned the Egyptians flee, leaving two dead; 1st Battalion Parachute Regiment returns to Cyprus.

11th The 2nd Battalion Parachute Regiment hands over to the 1st Battalion Royal West Kents and embarks for Cyprus in H.M.T. *New Australia* on the following day. (The 29th and 19th Infantry Brigades (of the 3rd Infantry Division, ex-U.K.) disembark between the 11th and 12th and relieve the parachutists and the commandos of their duties in Port Said.)

21st The 1st Battalion Royal Fusiliers relieved the Royal West Kents at El Cap. The first contingent of United Nations troops flies in to Abu Sueir.

24th The United Nations accept responsibility for clearing the Canal after the Anglo-French withdrawal.

27th The 1st Battalion York and Lancaster Regiment relieves the Royal Fusiliers at El Cap. Shortly afterwards the El Cap positions are taken over by United Nations troops.

DECEMBER

3rd The Anglo-French intention to withdraw is formally announced. Troops start to evacuate Port Said.

10th Lieutenant Moorhouse is abducted and the number of incidents between Egyptian guerrillas and Allied troops increases sharply.

21st Operation 'Yo-Yo' is staged to repatriate prisoners.

22nd The final evacuation of Port Said.

JANUARY 1957

24th The last ships of the Anglo-French salvage fleet are withdrawn from the Canal clearance operations.

APRIL

19th The first British ship passes through the Canal since it was nationalized ten months before.

Note on the Israeli Withdrawal

The Israeli forces were withdrawn from Sinai in three stages. These were phased with the take-over by United Nations troops of the areas they were evacuating. The first stage—withdrawal to the Abu Aweigila–Kuseima, tip of the peninsula, line—was completed by the 8th January, the second stage, the evacuation of El Arish, was effected a week later; and the final stage, withdrawal from the whole of Sinai except for the west coast of the Gulf of Aqaba and the Gaza Strip was completed by the 22nd January. All Egyptian military installations were destroyed before the areas were evacuated and the Israelis took with them all the equipment which it was possible to move.

Works Consulted

1. OPERATION 'KADESH'

Edgar O'Ballance. *The Sinai Campaign 1956* (Faber & Faber).
Robert Henriques. *One hundred hours to Suez* (Collins).
S. L. A. Marshall. *Sinai Victory* (William Morrow, New York).
Erskine B. Childers. *The Road to Suez* (MacGibbon & Kee).
D. R. Elston. *No Alternative—Israel Observed* (Hutchinson).
Shlomo Barer. *The Weekend War* (Thomas Yoseloff, New York).

2. EGYPTIAN BACKGROUND

Robert St. John. *The Boss—The Story of Gamal Abdel Nasser* (Barker).
Joachim Joesten. *Nasser—The Rise to Power* (Birchall).
Jean and Simmone Lacouture. *Egypt in Transition* (Methuen).
Desmond Stewart. *Young Egypt* (Wingate).

3. OPERATION 'MUSKETEER' AND THE OCCUPATION OF PORT SAID

Eden. *The Memoirs of Sir Anthony Eden* (Cassell).
W. Byford Jones. *Oil on Troubled Waters* (Hale).
Paul E. Garbutt. *Naval Challenge 1945–1961* (Macdonald).
Bernard Fergusson. *The Watery Maze* (Collins).
Paul Johnson. *The Suez War* (MacGibbon & Kee).
Maurice Tugwell (Ed.). *The Unquiet Peace—Stories from the Post War Army* (Wingate).
Merry and Serge Bromberger. *Secrets of Suez* (Pan Books).
Augustus Muir. *The First of Foot* (The Royal Scots History Committee).
Lieut.-General E. L. M. Burns. *Between Arab and Israeli* (Hassop).

Despatch by General Sir Charles F. Keightley, G.C.B., G.B.E., D.S.O. *Operations in Egypt* (published as a supplement to *The London Gazette*, 10th September 1957).

Damage and Casualties in Port Said. Report by Sir Edwin Herbert on his investigation into the effects of the Military Actions in October and November 1956 (H.M.S.O., December 1956).

H.M.S. Newfoundland 1956 (privately printed in Hong Kong for members of the ship's crew).

4. GENERAL

Liddell Hart. *Determent or Defence* (Stevens).

Neville Brown. *Strategic Mobility* (Chatto and Windus for the Institute for Strategic Studies).

Raymond Fletcher. *£60 a second on Defence* (MacGibbon & Kee).

5. OTHER PUBLISHED SOURCES

(a) REGIMENTAL JOURNALS

The Globe and Laurel (Journal of the Royal Marines).

Ça Ira (The Journal of the West Yorkshire Regiment).

The Royal Fusiliers Chronicle.

The Tiger and Rose (Journal of the York and Lancaster Regiment).

The Queen's Own Gazette (Journal of the Royal West Kent Regiment).

(b) ARTICLES

Brigadier C. N. Barclay, C.B.E., D.S.O. 'Anglo-French Operations against Port Said' (*The Army Quarterly*, April 1957).

Lieut.-Colonel P. E. Crook, O.B.E. 'The Capture of Gamil Airfield by 3 PARA Bn Gp' (*British Army Review*).

Captain Cyril Falls. 'Operation "Musketeer" ' (*Brassey's Annual*, 1957).

Captain C. J. Smith, R.M. 'Suez and the Commando Carrier Concept' (*R.U.S.I. Journal*, February 1963).

Commander C. G. Forsberg, R.N. 'Naval Salvage Organization' (*Brassey's Annual*, 1957).

Major George Fielding Eliot. 'Lessons from Suez' (U.S. Magazine *Ordnance*).

Index

Abbas Hilmi basin, 149

Abu Aweigila area, fighting in, 74, 75 seqq., 105, 208–9; map of defences, 78

Abu Sueir, airfield and area, 32, 60, 98, 99, 100; U.N. troops at, 175, 181

Abu Sultan, destruction of radar station at, by French, 106, 209

Aden, importance of, as land base, 198

Air bombardment patterns, 100 seqq.

Air Contact Teams, 153 n.

Air cover, importance of, 25–6, 52–3; carrier-borne, for Royal Navy, 199, *and see* named carriers; airborne assault, *see* 'Musketeer', aftermath

Air intelligence, weakness of, 101, 102

Air-portable strategic reserves, future importance of, 198

Akka (blockship): bombed, 100; salvaged, 191

Akrotiri, Cyprus, R.A.F. base at, 37, 101, 103

Albion, H.M.S., 30 n., 51, 133; in record run to Malta, 51; in convoy, 86–7, 208; in early phase of 'Musketeer', 100 seqq.; recent role of, 197

Alexandria, as possible first objective, 31, 32, 33, 35

Al Fatteh (Egyptian destroyer), 60, 60 n.

Algeria crisis, relevance of, 19, 26

Al Maya artillery barracks, 106

Almaza, bombing of, 98, 99, 100

Al Qaher (Egyptian destroyer), 60, 60 n.

Amer, General, and 'Arab Entente Militaire' of October, 71

America, *see* U.S.A.

Amiralai, Brigadier, garrison commander at Port Said, 149, 151

Amphibious Warfare Squadron, 26, 88, 92, 208–9

AMX light tanks, 156, 184

Anglo-French Salvage Command, 188

Antic (tug), 157

Aqaba, Gulf of, in strategic planning, 73, 74, 75; Israeli shipping excluded from, 70

Argyll and Sutherland Highlanders, 176–7

Arms running, before crisis, 67–8

Army Emergency Reserve, 26, 26 n., 42, 45, App. A

Arromanches (French naval aircraft carrier), 30 n.; used as trainer, 51; in the convoy, 86–7; in early 'Musketeer' phase, 100 seqq.

Ascania, H.M.S. (troopship), 184

Asturias, H.M.S. (troopship), 21, 171

Aswan dam, 17

Athos (motor yacht), French seize, 67

Ausdauer (German heavy lifting vessel), 188, 191

Baghdad Pact, 70; Jordan declines to join, 19

Bahrein, sabotage in, 105

Barjot, *see* d'Escadre Barjot

Barlev, Colonel (Israeli forces), 81

Barnett, Air Marshal D., 28; task

INDEX

Haifa (Israeli navy), 80 n.
'Hamilcar', *see* Operation 'Hamilcar'
Hammarskjold, Dr., reports on U.N. salvage fleet, 191
Harpaz, Colonel, 77–8, 81, 208
Hatan, Colonel, head of Egyptian Information Office, 66
Helicopters in action, 52, 90; early in assault, 93; as reinforcements, 121; make history, 151, 152–3, 197; *see* J.E.H.U.
Heliopolis, bombing of, 100
Helwan, bombing of, 100
Herbert, Sir Edwin, reports on Port Suez casualties, etc., 151, 206
Hobbs, Major-General R. G. S., 37 n.
Holland-Martin, Rear-Admiral D.E., 88
Huckstep Barracks, 106, 108
Hussein, King, of Jordan, 71

Ibrahim el Awal (Egyptian destroyer), 80, 80 n.; timeliness of capture on, 102
Inchas, bombing of, 98, 99, 100
'Instant' troops, 197; and Reserves, 199
International Convention of 1888, 20
Iraq, Great Britain's commitment with, 70
Ismailia, 18, 82, 115, 210; as Egyptian headquarters, 74; at moments of crisis, 161, 162, 169, 178
Israeli: mobilization begins, 23, 71–2; shipping in Canal, 20; shipping excluded from Gulf of Aqaba, 70; attack in Sinai, 23, 75; Air Force of, 60; attacks Egypt, 68; wins 'War of Independence', 69; first raids against, 70; and entry of Iraqi troops into Jordan, 70–1; standing army of, 72; launches Operation 'Kadesh',

73; at height of success, 105; army described, 84; summary of operations, 208–9; three stages of withdrawal from Sinai, 193, 211; element of surprise in attack, 195

Jamaica, H.M.S., 17, 21; at Port Said, 144
Jasmine (French minesweeper), 104
Jean Bart at Port Said, 144
Jebel Libni area, 74
J.E.H.U. (Army and R.A.F. Joint Experimental Helicopter Unit), 90, 152 n.; embarking of, 52
Jordan: refuses to join Baghdad Pact, 19; airfields of, 30; early retaliatory raids into, 68; Britain committed to, 70–1; in union with Egypt, 71; bases in, impossible, 197; breaks with France, 105

Kabrit airfield, 60; bombing of, 98, 99, 100
'Kadesh', *see* Operation 'Kadesh'
Kafr Kassim incident, 73 n.
Kantara: as strategic point, 136; in Operation 'Yo-yo', 185
Kasfareet airfield, 60; bombarded, 99, 100, 103
Keightley, General Sir Charles, 23, 28, 37, 56, 97, 207; Episkopi headquarters of, 33; forces finally allocated to, 36; difficulties facing, 44, 56–7, 195, 196; proceeds on first phase of 'Musketeer', 97; planning after cease-fire, 175–6; planning evacuation procedures with General Burns, 183
Korea, the lesson of, 195
Kuntilla, 75, 76, 77, 208
Kuseima area, 74, 75, 208
Kyrenia, Cyprus, 30

Lafayette (French aircraft-carrier), 30 n.; in early 'Musketeer', 100 seqq.

INDEX